# Islam
# &
# Terrorism
## MYTH & REALITY

Mauri' Saalakhan

Second Edition
1428AH/2007AC
AWAKENING PUBLISHING GROUP
ISBN  978-0-9776400-1-0

Responses are welcome.
You may contact the author at the following:

THE PEACE AND JUSTICE FOUNDATION,
11006 Veirs Mill Rd., L-15, PMB 298
Silver Spring, MD 20902

Tel: (301) 762-9162
Email: peacethrujustice@aol.com
Website: www.peacethrujustice.org

# ACKNOWLEDGMENT

ur thanks go out, first and foremost, to The Creator and Sustainer of all life between heaven and earth.

Our prayers go out on behalf of all individuals, families, and communities impacted – both here and abroad—by man's *inhumanity to man.*

Our deepest appreciation for those whose support of this project made it possible, of special note are: Abukar Arman, Said El-Marzouki, Magdy Haggag, Rubina Tareen and Imam Siraj Wahhaj.

A special note of thanks also goes out to the masjid administrations that permitted me to come in and talk about the importance of this project, and to solicit support from their respective communities with the full endorsement of said administrations. These are: The Islamic Association of Raleigh (IAR), Islamic Society of Baltimore (ISB), Islamic Center of Maryland (ICM), Islamic Society of Central Jersey (ISCJ), and Masjid At-Taqwa of Brooklyn, NY.

A very special note of thanks to all those (far too many to list, but *you* know who you are) whose trust and confidence truly made this project possible—those who donated to this project in a variety of ways. Your trust touched my heart and deepened my sense of obligation. Thank you!

Last, but certainly not least, we thank the friends who contributed to this project in other ways: Heather Gray, Rev. Graylan Hagler, John Sugg, Hussam Ayloush, Dr. Hina Azzam and *The Muslim Link* newspaper. May The Creator's blessings be upon you all.

# A Note from a Reader
# of the First Edition

I thought I knew all that I needed to know about Islam and Muslims...that is until I read "Islam & Terrorism, Myth vs. Reality." Like many African Americans I have Muslims in my family. I also went to college with a number of Muslims who I valued as friends. This book, however, gave me a whole new perspective on the religion and what it means to be a Muslim in present day America.

The approach Mr. Saalakhan takes to such a hot button issue is enlightening and unique. He begins and ends the book by addressing himself to the non-Muslim reader, and he's not shy about telling the truth, even when it doesn't reflect well on his own co-religionists. This too is refreshing.

From the war in Iraq to the war on terrorism, the author covers his subject with the penetrating mind of a meticulous researcher. For a book of this genre the style is both fluid and evocative. I thank you for publishing this book and enlightening the public on one of the most challenging, yet misunderstood issues of the day.

Omari Obama
New York

# TABLE OF CONTENTS

# INTRODUCTION

In a very unfortunate book of malicious propaganda targeting Islam and Muslims, titled <u>Infiltration</u>, Paul Sperry takes aim at some of the most active and "moderate" Muslims in America. Sperry and publisher, Nelson Current, describe their book as follows:

"This is the untold story about the silent, yet extremely dangerous threat from the Muslim establishment in America—an alarming expose of how Muslims have for years been secretly infiltrating American society, government, and culture, pretending to be peace-loving and patriotic, while supporting violent jihad and working to turn America into an Islamic state."

As if this were not sufficient as a poisonous introduction, they continue with the following. *In this powder keg of a book, you'll learn:*

- How radical Muslims have penetrated the U.S. Military, the FBI, the Homeland Security Department, and even the White House—where subversive Muslims and Arabs have received top-secret clearance.

- How they've infiltrated the chaplains program in the federal and state prison systems—a top recruiting ground for al-Qaida.

- How they've successfully run influence operations against our political system with the help of both Democrats and Republicans, badgering corporate boards into Islamizing the workplace.

- How we've been utterly duped about what the Quran does and doesn't teach. Sadly, much of anti-Western terrorism is simply Islam in practice, the text of the Quran in action.

The author and publisher then conclude their description of this venal piece of hate-filled propaganda with the following words: "In a time when religious and political leaders are scrambling to smooth over differences in faith and beliefs, this book gives the terrifying truth about the very real, very deadly agenda of Islam and how it has already infiltrated key American institutions with agents, spies, and subversives."

**Islam & Terrorism: Myth vs. Reality** contains our response to the allegations made by Paul Sperry, Nelson Current, and the long list of other Islamophobes who have taken aim at Islam and committed Muslims, both here and abroad. These attacks are nothing new. Even before the tragic attacks of September 11, 2001, Islam, the Prophet Mohammed (peace be upon him), and committed Muslims in practically every corner of the world were already under attack. September 11th merely legitimized and deepened the Islamophobia that had already reared its ugly head. In this humble offering we simply attempt to lay out a few facts and then challenge the reader to conduct his or her own independent investigation to discover the truth.

This is the second edition of Islam & Terrorism: Myth vs. Reality; the first edition was a blessing in many respects. Not only were we able to positively impact the discussion and debate around Islam and terrorism in different parts of the American landscape, out of proceeds from the book we also provided a modest but consistent amount of financial support to one of the families affected by the Post 9/11 madness. We did this for well over a year (praise be to God).

We have expanded the content of this second edition. Of particular note are updates for a number of the cases profiled in the second section of the book (*Faces Behind the Masks*). We've also added an index. That being said, we now resume the discourse that began with the first edition of the book with an examination of the divinely ordained system of life and living called Islam.

**What is Islam?**

One of the most oft-repeated oral traditions of Islam is the report of an encounter between the Prophet Mohammed (may ALLAH's peace and blessings be upon him) and a stranger who appeared one day out of nowhere. This tradition was related by one of the companions of the Prophet (pbuh), and reads (in translation) as follows:

> One day while we were sitting with the Messenger of ALLAH (pbuh), there appeared before us a man who clothes were exceedingly white, and whose hair was exceedingly black. No signs of journeying could be seen on him, but none of us knew him. He walked up and sat down beside the Prophet (pbuh). Resting his knees against the Prophet's knees, and placing the palms of his hands on his thighs, the stranger said: *"O Mohammed, tell me about Islam."*
>
> The Prophet replied: **"Islam is to testify that there is no god but ALLAH, and that Mohammed is the Messenger of ALLAH; to perform the prayers; to pay the charity; to fast in Ramadan; and to make the pilgrimage to the House, if you are able to do so."** He [the stranger] said, *"You have spoken rightly."*
>
> We were amazed that this stranger would ask a question, and upon hearing the answer, inform the Prophet that he had answered rightly.
>
> The stranger then inquired, *"Tell me about iman (faith)."* The Prophet responded: **'It is to believe in ALLAH, His Angels, His Books, His Messengers, and the Last Day; and to believe**

in divine destiny, both the good and evil thereof." Again the stranger responded, *"You have spoken rightly."*

The stranger then inquired, *"Tell me about ihsan"* (right action, goodness, sincerity, and the like). The Prophet responded: "It is to worship ALLAH as though you are seeing him, with the knowledge that while you see Him not, truly He sees you."

The stranger then inquired, *"Tell me about the Hour"* (The Day of Judgment). The Prophet responded: ***"The one being questioned, knows no more than the questioner."*** The stranger then said, *"Tell me about its signs."* The Prophet responded: "One of its signs is this, that the slave girl will give birth to her master (or mistress—Arabic: rabb or rabba), and you will see the barefooted, naked, destitute herdsmen competing in constructing lofty buildings."

The stranger then got up and walked away, and I (the narrator) remained with the Prophet for while; whereupon the Prophet turned to me and said: *"O Umar, do you know who the questioner was?"* I responded, "ALLAH and His Messenger know best." The Prophet then stated: *"It was Jibril, who came to teach you your religion."* (Jibril is the angel of revelation, known by the name Gabriel in the Judeo-Christian tradition.)

This oral tradition captures the essence of Islam. It reflects the five principles (or pillars) of the faith, which are the following: (1) **Belief** in One God (Muslims and other Middle Easterners have historically referred to this One God as ALLAH), and belief in the divinely sent Messengers or Prophets—beginning with Adam and ending with Mohammed (may Allah's peace and blessings be upon them all); (2) to engage in the regular performance of **Salat** (prayer), at least five prescribed times a day; (3) to engage in the giving of **Zakat** (charity); (4) to engage in **Saum** (fasting) especially in the sacred month of Ramadan; (5) and the performance of the **Hajj** (pilgrimage to Mecca), at least once in your lifetime, if able to do so.

The first pillar, the most important of all, is the pillar of belief; and the following pillars are pillars of action (the living manifestation of that belief).

It doesn't end there, however. Properly understood, the five principles of Islam are nothing more than *conditional requirements for higher spiritual development.* Such development is predicated upon a much maligned and misunderstood sixth principle —**Jihad fi sabililah**—the internal and external struggle in the way of ALLAH. We will have more to say on this principle in one of the later chapters of the book.

## Who is ALLAH?

*In the heavens and earth and all in between*
*Your Greatness, Your Omnipotence*
*Can be easily seen*

*In ignorance, we are asked if we worship another*
*And we smile, for we know beside You*
*There is no other*

*In a universe of darkness You gave to it light*
*In a womb where there was nothing*
*You gave to it life*

*The Alpha, The Omega —The beginning, The End*
*Without You—time, even time*
*Could not begin*

*O Allah, You are known by so many names*
*But whatever You're called*
*You're still ONE and the same*

*By whatever the name, You created us all*
*Allah simply means*
*You encompass them all!*

Muslims believe that ALLAH is The One Sovereign Creator of all that exists, and that there is nothing comparable to Allah. Muslims believe that this Omnipotent, Omniscient Supreme Being is known by many names, in many cultures—but He is One and the same. It is written in the Noble Qur'an (the last divinely sent revelation to all humanity):

> *"The most beautiful names belong to Allah, so call on Him by them. But shun such men as use profanity in His names; for what they do, they will soon be requited."* (7:180)

## Who is Mohammed (pbuh)?

*O Prophets, O Messengers, from Adam to Mohammed*
*What a magnificent brotherhood are you*
*You all came from One God*
*With one mission in mind*
*You all came with the*
*Very same truth*

Mohammed ibn Abdullah was born in the city of Mecca, on the Arabian peninsula, in the year 571 AD. Before receiving the gift and divinely commissioned responsibility of prophethood, at the age of 40, he was widely known for a pious character, generosity of spirit, and compassion toward all living things.

Muslims the world over believe that this man is the last divinely sent Messenger from Almighty Allah, and the seal of the prophethood (meaning after him there will be no more). Muslims also believe that Mohammed (pbuh) is but one among a highly distinguished prophetic brotherhood that began with Adam (pbuh), the father of all humanity. Muslims do not believe that Mohammed (pbuh) or any other living creature, past or present, is God.

Muslims believe that The Almighty sent Prophets and Messengers to different peoples at different times in history, and that many of them (such as Moses and Jesus, peace be upon them) brought books of divine revelation. As a part of their faith, Muslims believe in all of the divinely sent messengers and prophets (may peace and blessings be upon them all); but Muslims also believe that Prophet Mohammed (pbuh) was distinguished by two things: (a) he was the last in a series of divinely sent prophetic messengers; (b) and he was sent to *all humanity* with a message that will be binding until the end of time.

# Part 1

# AMERICA
# THE BEAUTIFUL

# FIVE MISTAKES OF U.S. POLICYMAKERS IN THE MUSLIM WORLD

*The following commentary was written by the author several years ago (BEFORE 9/11). It was initially offered to the Washington Post newspaper for publication, but The Washington Post was not interested. It later came to the attention of Mr. Richard Curtis of American Education Trust, who then offered to publish the commentary in its entirety (without edit). It appeared in the March 1999 issue of **The Washington Report On Middle East Affairs**.*

The First Amendment to the Constitution of the United States provides in part: *"Congress shall make no law respecting an establishment of religion, or prohibiting the free exercise thereof..."* There are few constitutional provisions which have generated more discussion and heated debate in America than the religious clauses of the First Amendment. In the words of Professor P. Kurland, the proper line between church and state remains an issue destined "to generate heat rather than light." {Religion and the Law, 1962}

Prof. Kurland's observation, notwithstanding, there is a certain fundamental principle clearly expressed from the earliest, most formative years of this nation's life. This principle is reflected in the religious liberty standard included in the *Northwest Ordinance of 1787* (reenacted by the First Congress in 1789). It provided that "no person, demeaning himself in a peaceful and orderly manner, shall ever be molested on account of his mode of worship, or religious sentiments..."

In 1986, the Office of Legal Policy issued a U.S. Department of Justice report to the U.S. Attorney General; among its summary conclusions was the following: "...We believe that the Free Exercise

Clause, as evident from its text and supported by its history, prohibits the government from enacting any law that either forbids or prevents an individual or institution from expressing or acting upon its sincerely-held 'religious' beliefs... The Free Exercise Clause demands not only state neutrality toward religion, and state abstention from regulation of religious belief, but also special protections for religion.

> According to the original understanding of the Framers and the states that ratified the First Amendment, the only exception to the general rule that the government has no right to interfere with the free exercise of religion is when government action is necessary to prevent manifest danger to the existence of the state; to protect peace, safety, and order; or to secure the religious liberty of others. Under these limited and compelling circumstances the government may interfere with religious liberty, but it may do *so only by the least restrictive means necessary to protect these interests.* (emphasis mine)

It is truly ironic that this report was issued four months after the U.S. bombing of Libya; during a time when the opinion shaping apparatus had shifted into high gear in portraying political Islam as the new bogeyman on the block, and at the stage of the Iran-Iraq war when all pretensions of American neutrality had been completely abandoned. This brings us to America's first mistake.

### Mistake #1

On Thursday, October 8, 1998, a hearing was held in the Dirksen Senate Office Building, under the auspices of the Senate Judiciary Committee's Subcommittee on Technology, Terrorism, and Government Information. The issue on the table: The use of *classified evidence* in immigration and deportation proceedings. This hearing, which dealt with a group of pro-American asylum seekers known as the **Iraqi Six**, was remarkable for a number of reasons. In the words of committee chairman Sen. Jon Kyl (R-Az), "The Committee seldom holds a hearing about a pending matter." However, he concluded, "I believe that the seriousness of the policy concerns at issue warrant a hearing at this time."

One of the witnesses arguing for the Iraqis, as their legal counsel, was Mr. James Woolsey, former Director of Central Intelligence. Despite him still having "the highest possible security clearance," he was consistently denied access to the secret evidence presented by the government to the immigration judge. Evidence used to deny his clients' entry into the United States. While the presence and argumentation of Mr. Woolsey commanded attention, it was an observation made by the government's attorney that this writer found most striking.

Paul W. Virtue, general counsel for the Department of Justice and the Immigration and Naturalization Service, stated during the course of his testimony: "It is important to note that while the use of classified information has garnered much recent media attention, it is, in fact, quite rare. Classified evidence is introduced and considered in less than 20 out of nearly 300,000 cases adjudicated by the immigration courts each year." This statement is all the more telling when juxtaposed with an observation made by David Cole, a constitutional law professor at Georgetown University Law Center.

Writing in the May 18, 1998, edition of Legal Times, Professor Cole begins with his analysis of the case of **Nasser Ahmed,** a 37 year old Egyptian who on April 23 marked two years of solitary confinement in a New York City detention center, justified solely on the basis of *secret evidence.* He writes: "But the most troubling aspect of Ahmed's case is that there are a dozen more like it, and they all involve Arab immigrants. In a deeply disturbing pattern, the INS has over the last few years selectively subjected Arab citizens, and only Arab citizens, to the same Star Chamber treatment—using secret evidence of their political associations to deprive them of their liberty, deny them immigration status to which they are otherwise entitled, and expel them."

Professor Cole then proceeded to highlight the following additional cases: **Mazen Al-Najjar** (Florida), **Anwar Haddam** (Virginia), **Imad Hamad** (Michigan), **Hany Kiureldeen** (New Jersey), **Yahia Meddah** (Florida), **Ali Termos** (Michigan), and a group of eight aliens in California whom the government admits it targeted for deportation based solely on their associations with the *Popular Front for the Liberation of Palestine*. "In each case," Professor Cole observes, "the charges boil down to guilt by association. And most troubling, all of the individuals involved are Arabs, and most are Muslims."

Professor Cole's observation underscores America's first mistake: *the violation of the First Amendment of the U.S. Constitution.*

## Mistake #2

While this nation came to birth via a revolution predicated on the foundational principle of the "inalienable rights" of mankind, to "life, liberty, and the pursuit of happiness," America's behavior, from its very inception, has often been quite the opposite. The late Rev. Dr. Martin Luther King, Jr., once referred to the Declaration of Independence as a "huge promissory note," that required "dramatic non-violent action to call attention to the gulf between promise and fulfillment." The gulf to which he refers, while clearly visible in America's domestic policy, is even more pronounced on the foreign policy front.

The late Senator J. William Fulbright (a man who chaired the Senate Foreign Relations Committee longer than any other congressional leader in history), made the following observation in his book entitled, **The Arrogance of Power**:

> There are two Americas. One is the America of Lincoln and Adlai Stevenson, the other is the America of Teddy Roosevelt and the modern superpatriots. One is generous and humane, the other narrowly egotistical; one is self-critical, the other is self-righteous; one is sensible, the other romantic; one is good-humored, the other solemn; one is inquiring, the other pontificating; one is moderate, the other filled with passionate intensity; one is judicious, and the other arrogant in the use of great power.

If we examine Senator Fulbright's observation as it relates to the Muslim world, a disturbing pattern emerges. America's actions in nation after nation (i.e., Bosnia, Iran, Iraq, Kosovo, Libya, Palestine, Sudan, etc.) reveal a corrosive double standard, and, at times, an outright suspension of the whole idea of *liberty and justice for all*. In fact, one of the most egregious cases of U.S. duplicity, in this regard, involves Algeria.

In Algeria, a democratically-elected pro-Islamic government was forcibly removed by a military coup d'etat on January 11, 1992. The result has been a barbaric civil war, where incontrovertible evidence suggests government forces have been responsible for the lion's share of atrocities; and a democratically elected leader—and president of the

Islamic Salvation Front's Parlimentary Delegation Abroad—**Anwar Haddam,** has been jailed in Virginia for almost two years without criminal charges. He's been denied asylum simply because "classified evidence" suggests he is a "national security threat." And this, despite Mr. Haddam's consistent and well documented efforts to pursue a peaceful resolution to the Algerian crisis!

It would behoove America and the West to ponder the advice of Edward Mortimer, foreign affairs editor of the London-based *Financial Times*, who wrote the following: "If Islamic parties do come to power, European governments should not adopt an attitude of a priori hostility towards them. The fact that these parties wish to reduce or even eradicate what they see as corrupting Western moral or cultural influences within their own societies does not mean there will be an inevitable conflict of interest between them and Europe..." [*Foreign Affairs*, Summer 1993, pg.38]

Unfortunately, *selective democracy* has been the rule in America's dealings with much of the world; and it constitutes the second major mistake in the Muslim world.

### Mistake #3

America's third tragic mistake is in advancing the notion of a *global Islamic conspiracy against the West*, along with the presumption that the values, ethics, and civilizational  mores of an Islamic society are not universal, and are in direct contravention to the requisites of modernity, and to the overall welfare of a healthy, stable, well-ordered society.

On this note, U.S. policymakers would greatly benefit from a perusal of the presentations made by a number of well-informed non-Muslim guests, to the roundtable discussions of the Virginia-based United *Association for Studies and Research* (UASR).

One such speaker, Robert G. Neumann, a senior advisor at the Center for Strategic and International Studies, and a former ambassador to Afghanistan, Morocco, and Saudi Arabia, noted: "I accept that Islamism is not uniform, not a 'world conspiracy' directed by some sort of international Islamic leadership... I further accept that 'Islamism' is not a new phenomenon suddenly thrust upon the world. We have seen it develop since the twenties as a debate on how to organize the Ummah, the Islamic World, following disputes over the consequences of the dissolution of the Caliphate." (*Islam And The West: A Dialog*, edited by Imad Ad-Dean Ahmad & Ahmed Yousef, pg.39)

Another presenter was Michael Collins Dunn, a senior analyst and co-founder of International Estimate Inc, who stated: "*I, and many other observers of these [Islamic] movements, have tried for years to convince policymakers and the media in the West that we must not stereotype these movements, by seeing them as a unified global movement or monolithic structure.* Just as the countries in which they have emerged are quite different from each other, and the societies differ profoundly at times, so too these movements differ from one another in precise goals, in tactics, and in their own view of their role in the existing system." (ibid., pg.116)

And then there is Joyce Davis, a journalist with National Public Radio (and former fellow with the United States Institute of Peace): "There's really a great prejudice many Americans have toward Islam. I realized, frankly, that I am partially responsible for that prejudice. I being a journalist in this country share the guilt, because we are helping to continue to propagate the erroneous stereotypes about Muslims." And further, "*My message to American policymakers is that they should be aware that there is a great sympathy in many parts of the world for Islamists. Why? They are some of the smartest, most charismatic, most dedicated people in the Muslim world - people with a platform of opening and cleaning government, and of caring for the poor.*" (ibid., pgs. 154 & 156)

Taking these observations into consideration, one must give credence to an assessment made by Stephen C. Pelletiere, a professor at the *Strategic Studies Institute* co-located with the *U.S. Army War College:* "The advice that experts have been giving to policymakers on the rise of political Islamic movements must be seen as suspect."(ibid., pg. 67) *This constitutes America's third mistake: listening to the wrong "experts."*

**Mistake #4**

One of the most needless, costly, and heart-rendering mistakes that America has made to date, has been in the area of Mideast policy. There is, perhaps, no other area of foreign policy wherein America has consistently demonstrated a pattern of bias, and a total lack of resolve for being a truly "honest broker," than in this [now] 50 year ongoing tragedy known as the "Arab-Israeli conflict." When one examines the facts, and the historical record, it has all been so unnecessary.

The first President of the United States, General George Washington, warned against the pitfalls of a policy which succeeding presidents, and a host of other high level politicians and policymakers, have unfortunately chosen to follow. President Washington cautioned in his farewell address to the Union:

A passionate attachment of one nation for another produces a variety of evils, because it leads to concessions to the favorite nation of privileges denied to others; which is apt doubly to injure the nation making the concession, both by unnecessarily parting with what ought to have been retained, and by exciting jealousy, ill-will and a disposition to retaliate, in the parties from whom equal privileges are withheld. It gives to ambitious, corrupted, or deluded citizens [who devote themselves to the favorite nation] the facility to betray or sacrifice the interest of their own country without odium, sometimes even with popularity. Real patriots who may resist the intrigues of the favorite are liable to become suspected and odious, while its tools and dupes usurp the applause and confidence of the people to surrender their interests.

What a prophetic observation, particularly when viewed within the context of present day American realities.  An objective appraisal of American Mideast policy would lead to the following conclusions: (a) the actions of our leaders have violated the most fundamental principles that we as a nation are supposed to represent; (b) our nation's Mideast policy has not been in our national interest! One way to better understand the immorality of America's failed policy in the "Holy Land," is by revisiting a profound and moving observation made decades ago by one of America's premier peacemakers, the Rev. Dr. Martin Luther King, Jr:

Being a Negro in America is not a comfortable experience. It means being part of the company of the bruised, the battered, the scarred, and the defeated. Being a Negro in America means trying to smile when you want to cry. It means trying to hold on to physical life amid psychological death. It means the pain of watching your children grow up with clouds of inferiority in their mental skies. It means having your legs cut off, and then being condemned for being a cripple. It means seeing your mother and father spiritually murdered by the slings and arrows of daily exploitation, and then being hated for being an orphan. Being a Negro in America means listening to suburban politicians talk eloquently against public housing, while arguing in the same breath that they are not racists. It means being harried by day and haunted by night by a nagging sense of nobodiness, and constantly fighting to be saved from the poison of bitterness. It means the ache and anguish of living in so many situations where hopes unborn have died.

How easy it would be to transpose being Negro in America with being *Palestinian in Israel and the territories*. For the daily lot of Palestinians in Occupied Palestine is one of misery with no end. This is why the so-called "Peace Process" will continue to fail; without the presence of justice, there can never be peace!

Since 1967, Israel has been the single largest recipient of U.S. foreign aid; while U.S. Foreign Aid Law prohibits military and economic aid to any country that engages in a *"consistent pattern of gross violations of internationally recognized human rights."* —Sections 502[b], 116[a] of the U.S. **Foreign Assistance Act.** To date (1999), American aid to Israel is over $78 billion. In 1996, cuts to America's poor totaled $5.7 billion, while aid to Israel was $5.5 billion. And how is this money used?

In the aftermath of the 1967 War, Israel immediately annexed East Jerusalem and declared the whole of Jerusalem its "eternal capitol;" while annexing territory taken by force is illegal under international law. **United Nations General Assembly Resolution** 2253, of July 1967, declared the annexation of East Jerusalem invalid.

**The Geneva Convention of 1949, Article 49** (paragraph 6) states: "The occupying power shall not deport or transfer parts of its own civilian population into the territories it occupies." To date, Israel has transferred well over 140,000 Jews into settlements throughout the "occupied territories." These are 100 percent segregated communities, for Jews only, built with taxes from a country where housing discrimination is illegal.

As settlements are being built, Palestinian homes are being demolished - while **Article 53 of the Geneva Accords** states: "Any destruction by the occupying power of the real or personal property is prohibited." Israel has consistently refused to halt land expropriation and home demolitions. Settlement expansion is justified on the basis of Jewish population growth, while little consideration is given the Palestinians who are being displaced. Its been reported that during the tenure of the present Israeli Defense Minister alone (Yitzhak Mordechai), the Israeli Civil Administration has demolished more than 400 Palestinian homes, and dozens of Bedouin dwellings in the West Bank.

The systematic and unrelenting brutality visited upon the Palestinian people should also be a cause for heightened concern within the international community, for this too represents a gross violation of international law. **Article 27 of the Geneva Accords** states: "Persons under control of an occupying power shall at all times be humanely treated, and shall be protected, especially against all acts of violence or threats thereof." *The UN Human Rights Commission* declared that, "Israel's grave breach of the Geneva Convention, relative to the protection of civilian persons in time of war, are war crimes and an affront against humanity."

For the past 50 years, the Palestinian experience (for Muslims *and Christians*) has been collective punishment; economic strangulation and acute poverty; school closures; home demolitions; torture (both physical and psychological); mass arrests and detentions without trial; and indiscriminant killings at the hands of the military and settlers.

Unfortunately, America has been a major partner in these crimes against humanity, as a result of the unswerving material and diplomatic support we've consistently given to a nation that our policymakers insist on calling the only democracy in the region; a nation that many others consider the apartheid South Africa of the Middle East.

## Mistake #5

Too often America, and nations like America, have mis-read the pulse of the people by listening to leaders of the establishment telling them all is well. Don't continue to make this mistake in the Muslim community. Our rapidly growing community in America is maturing socially and politically. It would behoove American politicians and policymakers to keep their ears to the ground in order to get the most accurate read on how the grass-roots are feeling, as it pertains to U.S. domestic and foreign policy and its impact on our extended community.

Our major organizations and mainstream leaders serve an important function, and are appreciated for what they do. However, they are not always the ones that you should be listening to; for they will sometimes tell you what you want to hear, and not what you need to hear. Don't make the mistake of thinking that by inviting representatives of our community to the White House or Congress; or by acknowledging a Muslim holiday or even celebrating that holiday with us, that you've adequately served this constituency. We (collectively) don't come that cheap!

## Summary

As I near my conclusion, I'd like to offer some words of advice to the policymakers of America. I am an American. My family's roots run generations deep in the soil of this land. While I am not always proud of what my nation does, I am, generally speaking, proud to be an American. I am, however, a Muslim first; and this keeps the nationalistic tendencies I might otherwise exude in check. To be Muslim first, is to be always aware of my membership in a global tribe called humanity, accountable first and foremost to the Omnipotent and Omniscient Creator of all life. And I am not alone in feeling this way. For too many years, America and the former Soviet Union engaged in a so-called *Cold War* that really wasn't cold at all. It was a hot war with fires raging (via each nation's respective proxies) in different parts of the globe. In its wake were consumed untold numbers of innocent and defenseless men, women and children; most of whom could not even begin to render an intelligent definition of capitalism or communism, socialism or democracy—mere pawns in the bi-polarity struggle of two very selfish "superpowers."

The Soviet Union is no more; and now it appears that the victor, the only remaining superpower on the block (the good ol' USA), is itching for another fight. What are its motives? To justify itself and its unparalleled war-making capacity? To solidify its place in history, perhaps, as the only true empire of its era? Or to divert attention from its never ending and deepening domestic problems? Whatever the reasons, it really doesn't matter. It sees another formidable contender on the horizon - militant, fundamentalist, political Islam (whichever nomenclature fits your fancy), and has decided to launch a preemptive strike. A note of caution is in order.

*Unlike the Soviet Union, sincere Muslims in every corner of the globe are threaded together by an ideology which is consciously or unconsciously imbedded within the very fiber of their being.* No matter how uneducated, unsophisticated, or illiterate, the Muslim you happen to meet—and conversely, no matter how educated, sophisticated or westernized, the Muslim you happen to meet—there is always this instinctual awareness of being Muslim; this instinctual awareness of being part of a global community with an accountability to God. And this is something that the U.S., and its respective allies, would do well to consider.

**No nation can indiscriminately bomb, maim and kill innocent Muslims without the pain, grief, and anguish, being felt on some level by Muslims the world over.** No matter how many official disclaimers are issued—such as, "This is not to be taken as an attack on Islam, or all Muslims"—the actions are going to be seen for what they are, and the impact is going to be felt.

U.S. policymakers should listen to the voices of reason among us, such as [former U.S. Attorney General] Ramsey Clark, who remarked in a speech in the Washington, DC, area not too long ago: "I hope that the Muslims of this country will help this country, and the best way you possibly can is by standing up for Islam... *Islam is the best chance the poor of the planet have for any hope of decency in their lives. It is the one revolutionary force that cares about humanity.*"

In my conclusion, I do hope that the policymakers of my country will learn from our Cold War experience, and understand that the time has come to "study war no more." We should use our enormous gifts— our material substance, our knowledge, our science and technology—to carve out an oasis in this life for all of humanity. We must take **The Golden Rule** off of the theoretical shelves of our day-today existence; dust it off, internalize it, and make it a living, breathing part of our lives. We've achieved the capacity to walk in space, isn't it time we learn how to walk on the earth in dignity and tranquility with one another?

Let us not repeat the mistakes of the past. Let our nation's posture toward resurgent Islam and the Muslim world be something along these lines: *I sincerely believe that we [non-Muslims] have a better system than yours, but if you can prove that yours is better, and improve the lot of your people, than God bless you. I will not behave in a violent way toward you, if you don't behave in a violent way toward us.* I pray that this commentary will be accepted in the spirit in which it is being conveyed. I am an American. But I am a Muslim first!

# THE SPEECH OF PRESIDENT GEORGE W. BUSH (OCTOBER 6, 2005)

The following is the transcript of President Bush's speech to the National Endowment for Democracy, on 10/6/05. The author's analysis follows.

PRESIDENT BUSH: Thank you for the warm welcome. I'm honored once again to be with the supporters of the National Endowment for Democracy.

Since the day President Ronald Reagan set out the vision for this endowment, the world has seen the swiftest advance of democratic institutions in history. And Americans are proud to have played our role in this great story.

Our nation stood guard on tense borders. We spoke for the rights of dissidents and the hopes of exiles. We aided the rise of new democracies on the ruins of tyranny. And all the costs and sacrifice of that struggle has been worth it because from Latin America to Europe to Asia we've gained the peace that freedom brings.

In this new century, freedom is once again assaulted by enemies, determined to roll back generations of democratic progress. Once again, we're responding to a global campaign of fear with a global campaign of freedom. And once again, we will see freedom's victory.

Again, I want to thank you for inviting me back. Thank you for the short introduction.

I appreciate Carl Gershman. I want to welcome former Congressman Dick Gephardt, who is a board member of the National Endowment for Democracy. It's good to see you, Dick. And I appreciate Chris Cox, who's the chairman of the U.S. Security and Exchange Commission and a board member for the National Endowment of Democracy, for being here as well. And I want to thank all the other board members.

I appreciate the Secretary of State, Condi Rice, who has joined us. Alongside her, our Secretary of Defense, Donald Rumsfeld. Thank you all for being here.

I'm proud as well that the newly sworn-in chairman of the Joint Chiefs, the first Marine ever to hold that position, is with us today, General Peter Pace.

And I thank members of the diplomatic corps who are here, as well. Recently, our country observed the fourth anniversary of a great evil and looked back on a great turning point in our history.

We still remember a proud city covered in smoke and ashes, a fire across the Potomac, and passengers who spent their final moments on earth fighting the enemy. We still remember the men who rejoice in every death, and Americans in uniform rising to duty. And we remember the calling that came to us on that day and continues to this hour. We will confront this mortal danger to all humanity. We will not tire or rest until the war on terror is won.

The images and experience of September the 11th are unique for Americans. Yet the evil of that morning has reappeared on other days in other places—in Mombasa and Casablanca and Riyadh and Jakarta and Istanbul, in Madrid, in Beslan, in Taba and Natanya and Baghdad and elsewhere.

In the past few months, we've seen a new terror offensive with attacks in London, Sharm el-Sheikh and a deadly bombing in Bali once again. All these separate images of destruction and suffering that we see on the news can seem like random and isolated acts of madness. Innocent men and women and children have died simply because they boarded the wrong train or worked in the wrong building or checked into the wrong hotel.

And while the killers choose their victims indiscriminately, their attacks serve a clear and focused ideology, a set of beliefs and goals that are evil but not insane. Some call this evil Islamic radicalism. Others militant jihadism. Still, others Islamo-fascism.

Whatever it's called, this ideology is very different from the religion of Islam. This form of radicalism exploits Islam to serve a violent political vision: the establishment, by terrorism and subversion and insurgency, of a totalitarian empire that denies all political and religious freedom.

These extremists distort the idea of jihad into a call for terrorist murder against Christians and Jews and Hindus and also against Muslims from other traditions that they regard as heretics. Many militants are part of global borderless terrorist organizations like Al Qaida, which spreads propaganda and provides financing and technical assistance to local extremists and conducts dramatic and brutal operations like September 11th.

Other militants are found in regional groups often associated with Al Qaida; paramilitary insurgencies and separatist movements in places like Somalia and the Philippines and Pakistan and Chechnya and Kashmir and Algeria.

Still others spring up in local cells inspired by Islamic radicalism but not centrally directed. Islamic radicalism is more like a loose network with many branches, than an army under a single command. Yet these operatives fighting on scattered battlefields share a similar ideology and vision for our world.

We know the vision of the radicals because they've openly stated it in videos and audiotapes and letters and declarations and Web sites. First, these extremists want to end American and Western influence in the broader Middle East, because we stand for democracy and peace and stand in the way of their ambitions.

Al Qaida's leader, Osama bin Laden, has called on Muslims to dedicate, quote, their resources sons and money to driving infidels out of their lands. Their tactic to meet this goal has been consistent for a quarter century: They hit us and expect us to run. They want us to repeat the sad history of Beirut in 1983 and Mogadishu in 1993, only this time on a larger scale with greater consequences.

Second, the militant network wants to use the vacuum created by an American retreat to gain control of a country, a base from which to launch attacks and conduct their war against non-radical Muslim governments.

Over the past few decades, radicals have specifically targeted Egypt and Saudi Arabia and Pakistan and Jordan for potential takeover. They achieved their goal for a time in Afghanistan. Now they've set their sights on Iraq. Bin Laden has stated the whole world is watching this war and the two adversaries: It's either victory and glory or misery and humiliation.

The terrorists regard Iraq as the central front in their war against humanity, and we must recognize Iraq as the central front in our war on terror.

Third, the militants believe that controlling one country will rally the Muslim masses, enabling them to overthrow all moderate governments in the region and establish a radical Islamic empire that spans from Spain to Indonesia. With greater economic and military and political power, the terrorists would be able to advance their stated agenda: to develop weapons of mass destruction, to destroy Israel, to intimidate Europe, to assault the American people and to blackmail our government into isolation.

Some might be tempted to dismiss these goals as fanatical or extreme. Well, they are fanatical and extreme and they should not be dismissed. Our enemy is utterly committed. As Zarqawi has vowed, We will either achieve victory over the human race or we will pass to the eternal life.

And the civilized world knows very well that other fanatics in history, from Hitler to Stalin to Pol Pot, consumed whole nations in war and genocide before leaving the stage of history. Evil men obsessed with ambition and unburdened by conscience must be taken very seriously, and we must stop them before their crimes can multiply.

Defeating a militant network is difficult because it thrives like a parasite on the suffering and frustration of others. The radicals exploit local conflicts to build a culture of victimization in which someone else is always to blame and violence is always the solution. They exploit resentful and disillusioned young men and women, recruiting them through radical mosques as the pawns of terror.

And they exploit modern technology to multiply their destructive power. Instead of attending faraway training camps, recruits can now access online training libraries to learn how to build a roadside bomb or fire a rocket-propelled grenade.

And this further spreads the threat of violence, even within peaceful democratic societies. The influence of Islamic radicalism is also magnified by helpers and enablers. They have been sheltered by authoritarian regimes: allies of convenience like Syria and Iran that share the goal of hurting America and moderate Muslim governments and use terrorist propaganda to blame their own failures on the West and America and on the Jews.

The radicals depend on front operations such as corrupted charities which direct money to terrorist activity. They are strengthened by those who aggressively fund the spread of radical, intolerant versions of Islam in unstable parts of the world.

The militants are aided as well by elements of the Arab news media that incite hatred and anti-Semitism, that feed conspiracy theories and speak of so-called American war on Islam with seldom a word about American actions to protect Muslims in Afghanistan, Bosnia, Somalia, Kosovo, Kuwait and Iraq.

Some have also argued that extremism has been strengthened by the actions of our coalition in Iraq, claiming that our presence in that country has somehow caused or triggered the rage of radicals. I would remind them that we were not in Iraq on September the 11th, 2001, and Al Qaida attacked us anyway. The hatred of the radicals existed before Iraq was an issue and it will exist after Iraq is no longer an excuse.

The government of Russia did not support Operation Iraqi Freedom, and yet militants killed more than 180 Russian school children in Beslan. Over the years, these extremists have used a litany of excuses for violence: Israeli presence on the West Bank or the U.S. military presence in Saudi Arabia or the defeat of the Taliban or the crusades of a thousand years ago.

In fact, we're not facing a set of grievances that can be soothed and addressed. We're facing a radical ideology with unalterable objectives: to enslave whole nations and intimidate the world. No act of ours invited the rage of the killers, and no concession, bribe or act of appeasement would change or limit their plans for murder. On the contrary, they target nations whose behavior they believe they can change through violence.

Against such an enemy there is only one effective response: We will never back down, never give in and never accept anything less than complete victory.

The murderous ideology of the Islamic radicals is the great challenge of our new century. Yet in many ways, this fight resembles the struggle against communism in the last century. Like the ideology of communism, Islamic radicalism is elitist, led by a self-appointed vanguard that presumes to speak for the Muslim masses.

Osama bin Laden says his own role is to tell Muslims, quote, What is good for them and what is not. And what this man who grew up in wealth and privilege considers good for poor Muslims is that they become killers and suicide bombers. He assures them that this is the road to paradise, though he never offers to go along for the ride.

Like the ideology of communism, our new enemy teaches that innocent individuals can be sacrificed to serve a political vision. And this explains their cold-blooded contempt for human life. We've seen it in the murders of Daniel Pearl, Nicholas Berg and Margaret Hassan and many others.

In a courtroom in the Netherlands, the killer of Theo Van Gogh turned to the victim's grieving mother and said, I do not feel your pain because I believe you are an infidel.

And in spite of this veneer of religious rhetoric, most of the victims claimed by the militants are fellow Muslims. When 25 Iraqi children are killed in a bombing or Iraqi teachers are executed at their school or hospital workers are killed caring for the wounded, this is murder, pure and simple; the total rejection of justice and honor and moral and religion.

These militants are not just the enemies of America or the enemies of Iraq, they are the enemies of Islam and the enemies of humanity. We have seen this kind of shameless cruelty before, in the heartless zealotry that led to the gulags and the Cultural Revolution and the killing fields.

Like the ideology of communism, our new enemy pursues totalitarian aims. Its leaders pretend to be in an aggrieved party, representing the powerless against imperial enemies. In truth, they have endless ambitions of imperial domination and they wish to make everyone powerless except themselves.

Under their rule, they have banned books and desecrated historical monuments and brutalized women. They seek to end dissent in every form and to control every aspect of life and to rule the soul itself. While promising a future of justice and holiness, the terrorists are preparing for a future of oppression and misery.

Like the ideology of communism, our new enemy is dismissive of free peoples, claiming that men and women who live in liberty are weak and decadent.

Zarqawi has said that Americans are, quote, the most cowardly of God's creatures, but let's be clear: It is cowardice that seeks to kill children and the elderly with car bombs and cuts the throat of a bound captive and targets worshipers leaving a mosque. It is courage that liberated more than 50 million people. It is courage that keeps an untiring vigil against the enemies of a rising democracy. And it is courage and the cause of freedom that once again will destroy the enemies of freedom.

And Islamic radicalism, like the ideology of communism, contains inherent contradictions that doom it to failure. By fearing freedom, by distrusting human creativity and punishing change and limiting the contributions of half the population, this ideology undermines the very qualities that make human progress possible and human society successful.

The only thing modern about the militants' vision is the weapons they want to use against us. The rest of their grim vision is defined by a warped image of the past, a declaration of war on the idea of progress itself. And whatever lies ahead in the war against this ideology, the outcome is not in doubt: Those who despise freedom and progress have condemned themselves to isolation decline and collapse. Because free peoples believe in the future, free peoples will own the future.

We didn't ask for this global struggle, but we're answering history's call with confidence and a comprehensive strategy.

Defeating a broad and adaptive network requires patience, constant pressure, and strong partners in Europe, the Middle East, North Africa, Asia and beyond. Working with these partners, we're disrupting militant conspiracies, destroying their ability to make war, and working to give millions in a troubled region of the world a hopeful alternative to resentment and violence.

First, we're determined to prevent the attacks of terrorist network before they occur. We're reorganizing our government to give this nation a broad and coordinated homeland defense. We're reforming our intelligence agency for the incredibly difficult task of tracking enemy activity, based on information that often comes in small fragments from widely scattered sources here and abroad. We're acting, along with the governments from many countries, to destroy the terrorist networks and incapacitate their leaders.

Together, we've killed or captured nearly all of those directly responsible for the September the 11th attacks, as well as some of bin Laden's most senior deputies, Al Qaida managers and operatives in more than

24 countries: the mastermind of the USS Cole bombing who was chief of Al Qaida operations in the Persian Gulf, the mastermind of the Jakarta and the first Bali bombings, a senior Zarqawi terrorist planner who was planning attacks in Turkey, and many of Al Qaida's senior leaders in Saudi Arabia.

Overall, the United States and our partners have disrupted at least 10 serious Al Qaida terrorist plots since September the 11th, including three Al Qaida plots to attack inside the United States. We've stopped at least five more Al Qaida efforts to case targets in the United States or infiltrate operatives into our country.

Because of the steady progress, the enemy is wounded. But the enemy is still capable of global operations. Our commitment is clear: We will not relent until the organized, international terror networks are exposed and broken and their leaders held to account for their acts of murder.

Second, we're determined to deny weapons of mass destruction to outlaw regimes and to their terrorist allies who would use them without hesitation. The United States, working with Great Britain, Pakistan and other nations, has exposed and disrupted a major black market operation in nuclear technology led by A.Q. Khan. Libya has abandoned its chemical and nuclear programs as well as long-range ballistic missiles.

In this last year, America and our partners in the Proliferation Security Initiative have stopped more than a dozen shipments of suspected weapons technology, including equipment for Iran's ballistic missile program.

This progress has reduced the danger to free nations, but it has not removed it. Evil men who want to use horrendous weapons against us are working in deadly earnest to gain them. And we're working urgently to keep weapons of mass destruction out of their hands.

Third, we're determined to deny radical groups the support and sanctuary of outlaw regimes. State sponsors like Syria and Iran have a long history of collaboration with terrorists, and they deserve no patience from the victims of terror.

The United States makes no distinction between those who commit acts of terror and those who support and harbor them, because they're equally as guilty of murder. Any government that chooses to be an ally of terror has also chosen to be an enemy of civilization. And the civilized world must hold those regimes to account.

Fourth, we're determined to deny the militant's control of any nation which they would use as a home base and a launching pad for terror. For this reason, we're fighting beside our Afghan partners against remnants of the Taliban and their Al Qaida allies. For this reason, we're working with President Musharraf to oppose and isolate the militants in Pakistan. And for this reason, we're fighting the regime remnants and terrorists in Iraq.

The terrorists' goal is to overthrow a rising democracy, claim a strategic country as a haven for terror, destabilize the Middle East and strike America and other free nations with ever-increasing violence. Our goal is to defeat the terrorists and their allies at the heart of their power. And so we will defeat the enemy in Iraq.

Our coalition, along with our Iraqi allies, is moving forward with a comprehensive, specific military plan. Area by area, city by city, we're conducting offensive operations to clear out enemy forces and leaving behind Iraqi units to prevent the enemy from returning.

Within these areas, we're working for tangible improvements in the lives of Iraqi citizens. And we're aiding the rise of an elected government that unites the Iraqi people against extremism and violence.

This work involves great risk for Iraqis and for Americans and coalition forces. Wars are not won without sacrifice and this war will require more sacrifice, more time and more resolve. The terrorists are as brutal an enemy as we've ever faced. They're unconstrained by any notion of our common humanity or by the rules of warfare. No one should underestimate the difficulties ahead, nor should they overlook the advantages we bring to this fight.

Some observers look at the job ahead and adopt a self-defeating pessimism. It is not justified. With every random bombing and with every funeral of a child it becomes more clear that the extremists are not patriots or resistance fighters. They are murderers at war with the Iraqi people themselves.

In contrast, the elected leaders of Iraq are proving to be strong and steadfast. By any standard or precedent of history, Iraq has made incredible political progress: from tyranny, to liberation, to national elections, to the writing of a constitution in the space of two and a half years. With our help, the Iraqi military is gaining new capabilities and new confidence with every passing month.

At the time of our Fallujah operations 11 months ago there were only a few Iraqi army battalions in combat. Today there are more than 80 Iraqi army battalions fighting the insurgency alongside our forces. Progress isn't easy, but it is steady. And no fair-minded person should ignore, deny or dismiss the achievements of the Iraqi people.

Some observers question the durability of democracy in Iraq. They underestimate the power and appeal of freedom. We've heard it suggested that Iraq's democracy must be on shaky ground because Iraqis are arguing with each other. But that's the essence of democracy: making your case, debating with those who disagree, building consensus by persuasion and answering to the will of the people.

We've heard it said that the Shias, Sunnis and Kurds of Iraq are too divided to form a lasting democracy. In fact, democratic federalism is the best hope for unifying a diverse population, because a federal constitutional system respects the rights and religious traditions of all citizens while giving all minorities, including the Sunnis, a stake and a voice in the future of their country.

It is true that the seeds of freedom have only recently been planted in Iraq but democracy, when it grows, is not a fragile flower. It is a healthy, sturdy tree.

As Americans, we believe that people everywhere —everywhere prefer freedom to slavery and that liberty, once chosen, improves the lives of all. And so we're confident, as our coalition and the Iraqi people each do their part, Iraqi democracy will succeed.

Some observers also claim that America would be better off by cutting our losses and leaving Iraq now. It's a dangerous illusion refuted with a simple question: Would the United States and other free nations be more safe or less safe with Zarqawi and bin Laden in control of Iraq, its people and its resources?

Having removed a dictator and aided free peoples, we will not stand by as a new set of killers dedicated to the destruction of our own country seizes control of Iraq by violence. There's always a temptation in the middle of a long struggle to seek the quiet life, to escape the duties and problems of the world, and to hope the enemy grows weary of fanaticism and tired of murder.

This would be a pleasant world, but it's not the world we live in. The enemy is never tired, never sated, never content with yesterday's brutality. The enemy considers every retreat of the civilized world as an invitation to greater violence. In Iraq, there is no peace without victory. We will keep our nerve and we will win that victory.

The fifth element of our strategy in the war on terror is to deny the militants future recruits by replacing hatred and resentment with democracy and hope across the broader Middle East. This is a difficult, long-term project, yet there's no alternative to it. Our future and the future of that region are linked.

If the broader Middle East is left to grow in bitterness, if countries remain in misery, while radicals stir the resentments of millions, then that part of the world will be a source of endless conflict and mounting danger for our generation and the next. If the peoples in that region are permitted to chose their own destiny and advance by their own energy and by their participation as free men and women, then the extremists will be marginalized and the flow of violent radicalism to the rest of the world will slow and eventually end.

By standing for the hope and freedom of others we make our own freedom more secure.

America is making this stand in practical ways. We're encouraging our friends in the Middle East, including Egypt and Saudi Arabia, to take the path of reform, to strengthen their own societies in the fight against terror by respecting the rights and choices of their own people. We're standing with dissidents and exiles against oppressive regimes, because we know that the dissidents of today will be the democratic leaders of tomorrow.

We're making our case through public diplomacy, stating clearly and confidently our belief in self-determination and the rule of law and religious freedom and equal rights for women; beliefs that are right and true in every land and in every culture.

As we do our part to confront radicalism, we know that the most vital work will be done within the Islamic world itself. And this work has begun.

Many Muslim scholars have already publicly condemned terrorism, often citing Chapter 5, Verse 32 of the Koran, which states that killing an innocent human being is like killing all humanity, and saving the life of one person is like saving all of humanity. After the attacks in London on July the 7th, an imam in the United Arab Emirates declared, Whoever does such a thing is not a Muslim, nor a religious person.

The time has come for all responsible Islamic leaders to join in denouncing an ideology that exploits Islam for political ends and defiles a noble faith.

Many people of the Muslim faith are proving their commitment at great personal risk. Everywhere we have engaged the fight against extremism, Muslim allies have stood up and joined the fight, becoming partners in a vital cause.

Afghan troops are in combat against Taliban remnants. Iraqi soldiers are sacrificing to defeat Al Qaida in their own country. These brave citizens know the stakes: the survival of their own liberty, the future of their own region, the justice and humanity of their own tradition. And the United States of America is proud to stand beside them.

With the rise of a deadly enemy and the unfolding of a global ideological struggle, our time in history will be remembered for new challenges and unprecedented dangers. And yet the fight we have joined is also the current expression of an ancient struggle between those who put their faith in dictators and those who put their faith in the people.

Throughout history, tyrants and would-be tyrants have always claimed that murder is justified to serve their grand vision. And they end up alienating decent people across the globe. Tyrants and would-be tyrants have always claimed that regimented societies are strong and pure until those societies collapse in corruption and decay. Tyrants and would-be tyrants have always claimed that free men and women are weak and decadent until the day that free men and women defeat them.

We don't know the course of our own struggle, the course our own struggle will take, or the sacrifices that might lie ahead. We do know, however, that the defense of freedom is worth our sacrifice. We do know the love of freedom is the mightiest force of history. And we do know the cause of freedom will once again prevail.

May God bless you.

## OUR RESPONSE TO THE PRESIDENT'S SPEECH

Our response to key issues raised in the president's speech at the National Endowment for Democracy is as follows:

1). It is indeed ironic that President Bush should invoke President Reagan in his opening statement, for the record will show that the "democracy" championed by the Reagan Administration—especially in Latin America—was the democracy of the wolf and the fox. Proof of this can be a found in a book authored by Washington Post executive Bob Woodward. The title of the book, "Veil: The Secret Wars of the CIA."

2). What are the "generations of democratic progress" of which the president speaks? When one reflects upon the support that America has consistently given to some of the most brutal and repressive regimes in modern history, a reasonable man or woman is compelled to wonder about our government's definition of freedom and democracy. For all too often "the global campaign of fear" and intimidation has been led by the United States and its "allies."

3). While the images and experience of September the 11th are indeed unique for Americans, they are not unique for many peoples around the world who have been the victims of **Americanism**. How many 9/11s have misplaced U.S. foreign policy caused in different parts of the world?

4). It appears that "Al Qaida" has become a catch-all phrase of convenience for repressive [post 9/11] U.S. domestic and foreign policy. It has also provided many of America's allies with a green light to increase their repression against legitimate calls for genuine democratization in their respective countries; and all of this is done in the name of another catch-all phrase, "the war on terrorism." *It does nothing but reinforce a belief among Muslims around the globe that Islam has replaced communism as the new boogeyman on the block.*

5). When the president stated, "These extremists want to end American and Western influence in the broader Middle East, because we stand for democracy and peace, and stand in the way of their ambitions," I was reminded of the words of the French philosopher Voltaire who said, *"Those who can make us believe absurdities can also cause us to commit atrocities."* The people of Muslim lands (like peoples everywhere else) want to enjoy peace, freedom, and self-determination. And thus, *"They hate us for our freedom"* is a ridiculous absurdity!

6). The repeated references to Osama bin Laden (and a growing number of other "al-Qaeda leaders") reminds this writer of an observation made by a western diplomat following America's wrongful attacks on Afghanistan and Sudan in 1998: *"If Osama bin Laden did not exist, America would have to create him."* I believe that I can safely say, given the ideological investment that America and its allies have made in the manufacture of adversarial images, Osama bin Laden (dead or alive), Abu Mus'ah al-Zarqawi (dead or alive), and al-Qaeda carry far more weight in the West than they do in Muslim societies anywhere in the world.

7). If Iraq has become the "central front" of the so-called "war on terrorism," it is because America, Britain, corrupt and dependent regimes throughout the region, and an ill-spirited campaign of lies and deceits made it that way.

8). America's definition of a "moderate government" has too often translated into weak, repressive government for other peoples of the world (both Muslim and non-Muslim). And this must change!

9). Where the president said, "Evil men obsessed with ambition and unburdened by conscience must be taken very seriously, and we must stop them before their crimes can multiply"—we would wholeheartedly agree, both here and abroad! America and other "western democracies," however, must stop contributing (through wrong-headed policies) to a "culture of victimization."

10). On the issue of "corrupted charities," it is indeed interesting how America can recognize distinctions when it comes to organizations like the *Irish Republican Army* (IRA) and its political wing Sein Fein; or recognize distinctions among the anti-Castro Cuban-American organizations; or look the other way when it comes to some of the more violence-prone *Zionist organizations* operating in America and other parts of the West, but are quick to investigate, shut down and seize the assets of ANY Muslim-run humanitarian organization providing much needed material support to the suffering people of Occupied Palestine.  Herein lay a glaring double-standard that does not go unnoticed on the Muslim street.

11). As for the president's concern about certain "elements" within the "Arab news media," I too share some of his concern. I am more concerned, however, about the hate-mongering that routinely takes place within our own establishment media; often in support of nihilistic U.S. Government policies.

12). *"Some have also argued that extremism has been strengthened by the actions of our coalition in Iraq, claiming that our presence in that country has somehow caused or triggered the rage of radicals. I would remind them that we were not in Iraq on September the 11th, 2001, and Al Qaida attacked us anyway."*

Wrong again, Mr. President. The United States has been waging war against the people of Iraq since *the first Gulf War*, over a decade ago, and the accompanying regime of sanctions – the real weapon of mass destruction! We should now revisit a memorable question raised years ago (during the previous administration): **Was it worth the price?**

13). What happened at the school in Beslan (Russia) was a shock to the conscience of the entire world! It was a shameful and barbaric act that in no way represented Islam or Muslim peoples of the world. That being said, it is this writer's sincerely held view that Russia (because of its own profoundly oppressive policies) bears as much responsibility for what happened at that school as do the crazed persons who carried out that terrible act.

14). *"In fact, we're not facing a set of grievances that can be soothed and addressed. We're facing a radical ideology with unalterable objectives: to enslave whole nations and intimidate the world."*

This writer knows of no "ideology" that fits this description more accurately than the *by any means necessary*, no holds barred, *survival of the fittest*, capitalism of the West—along with the cultural and political machinery that advances it.

15). *"In many ways, this fight resembles the struggle against communism in the last century."*

Indeed it does; and for this our "leaders" should be ashamed. A wise man once said, "Those who cannot remember the past are condemned to repeat it." Ours is not an issue of remembrance; ours is more an issue of arrogance. (The arrogance of power!)

16). On the issue of "innocents" who have been sacrificed by Osama and crew—this is indeed blameworthy. When the "insurgents" deliberately attack and kill innocent people (including Muslims), they demonstrate how far removed from Islam they are. But how many "innocents" have been cold-bloodedly sacrificed (labeled *"collateral damage"*) by western forces, Mr. President?

17). *"We're determined to prevent the attacks of terrorist network before they occur. We're reorganizing our government to give this nation a broad and coordinated homeland defense."*

Homeland Defense should never become a Homeland Offense against the U.S. Constitution.

18). *"The United States makes no distinction between those who commit acts of terror and those who support and harbor them, because they're equally as guilty of murder."*

This is precisely why there is so much anger in the Muslim (and non-Muslim) world against the United States; because of this very principle. It's about time that our leaders internalize the maxim: **Those who would protest against a thing should be the last to practice it!**

19). *"With every random bombing and with every funeral of a child it becomes more clear that the extremists are not patriots or resistance fighters. They are murderers at war with the Iraqi people themselves."*

We couldn't agree more! But we must never forget that America (and its allies) set this destructive cycle in motion.

20). *"The fifth element of our strategy in the war on terror is to deny the militants future recruits by replacing hatred and resentment with democracy and hope across the broader Middle East. This is a difficult, long-term project, yet there's no alternative to it. Our future and the future of that region are linked."*

From what we have seen thus far coming from the United States along these lines, there isn't much reason for optimism. (But I wish there was.)

21). *"If the broader Middle East is left to grow in bitterness, if countries remain in misery, while radicals stir the resentments of millions, then that part of the world will be a source of endless conflict and mounting danger for our generation and the next. If the peoples in that region are permitted to choose their own destiny and advance by their own energy and by their participation as free men and women, then the extremists will be marginalized and the flow of violent radicalism to the rest of the world will slow and eventually end. By standing for the hope and freedom of others we make our own freedom more secure."*

Once again, I couldn't agree more.

22). *"America is making this stand in practical ways. We're encouraging our friends in the Middle East, including Egypt and Saudi Arabia, to take the path of reform, to strengthen their own societies in the fight against terror by respecting the rights and choices of their own people... We're standing with dissidents and exiles against oppressive regimes..."*

If only this were true.

23). *"We're making our case through public diplomacy..."*
As the saying goes, **"Talk is cheap."**

24). *"The time has come for all responsible Islamic leaders to join in denouncing an ideology that exploits Islam for political ends and defiles a noble faith."*

Indeed. And "responsible Islamic leaders" must find the courage and integrity to do this on all sides of the equation. As our Prophet (pbuh) has said: **"One of the greatest jihads is to speak truth to a caliph (governing authority) who has deviated from the right way."**

May ALLAH (God) fortify us toward this end.

# Part 2

# FACES
# BEHIND
# THE MASKS

# A NATION'S SHAME IN TULIA TEXAS

*"That Justice is a blind goddess is a thing to which we blacks are wise; her bandage hides to festering sores, which once, perhaps, were eyes."* – Langston Hughes

The celebrated Harlem Renaissance writer and poet, Langston Hughes, hit the nail on the head with his poem titled "Justice." Blacks are indeed well acquainted with the realities of American jurisprudence. I will not burden the reader with a long litany of injustices from times past, I will simply share one relevant example from the more recent past.

The place is a small town in the southwestern part of the United States —called Tulia, Texas. The population of Tulia was estimated in 1999 to be about 5,000 persons, with less than 500 being African American. On July 23rd of that year more than 10% of the black population was arrested on the word of one white police officer, Tom Coleman. Of the 46 persons arrested on that fateful day, 40 were black, three were Mexican, and the remaining three had bi-racial children, or had other social or marital ties to the black community.

The arrests were the result of a so-called sting operation by a lone white officer with a checkered past. All but one of the indictments alleged the sale of small amounts of cocaine. The first ones to go to trial did so to prove their innocence, but as "guilty verdicts" began to mount—with sentences ranging from 20 to 341 years!—other defendants began to enter into coerced plea agreements with the District Attorneys office.

Joe Moore, a 57 year old hog farmer, was labeled a "kingpin" and drew a sentence of 90 years! Those who entered into "plea bargains" received sentences ranging from one year probation to 18 years in prison. In the words of the NAACP–Legal Defense Fund (who became involved in the case):

> All of the trials or pleas emerging from Coleman's sting were marred by serious due process violations. One recurring theme that runs through the Tulia undercover operation and the subsequent prosecutions is an indifference on the part of law enforcement to ensuring that (1) their undercover agent was credible and trustworthy; (2) the undercover operation protocols were observed to guarantee the validity of the agent's version of his encounters with Tulia residents; and (3) full disclosure was made to the defense prior to trial of evidence that raised significant questions about the agent's credibility.

Agent Coleman reportedly spent 18 months buying drugs in Tulia, Texas –but he never wore a wire during any of the alleged transactions; no video surveillance was ever done; and no second officer was ever present to corroborate any reports. During testimony in the first few trials Coleman claimed to have recorded names, dates, and other pertinent facts by WRITING ON HIS LEG! Yet most of the convictions were based almost exclusively on this man's questionable testimony

Agent Coleman had minimal training; prior to this assignment he had never been an undercover agent before. What he did have was a well documented checkered history as a law enforcement officer in other counties. However, the *Panhandle Regional Narcotics Task Force,* which was funded by the federal government, failed to perform an adequate background check. (Coleman was known in other areas to be dishonest, corrupt, and racist.)

In March 2003, defense attorneys argued during an evidentiary hearing that none of the Tulia drug convictions should stand. A parade of witnesses testified over a five day period—many of whom were law enforcement officers—to Tom Coleman's bad character and lack of credibility. Coleman himself was cross-examined over a six hour period, during which he committed perjury at least five times, and testified to the pervasive use of the N-word on and off the job!

Habeas defense counsel broke off the testimony and approached the state for settlement talks; and on April 1, 2003, presiding Judge Ron Chapman stated that he would recommend that the Texas Court of Criminal Appeals overturn the convictions of everyone convicted in the tainted sting operation because, "it is established by all parties and approved by the court that Tom Coleman is simply not a credible witness under oath."

I wanted to relate this story because of the significant connection it has to what will follow. The wrongfully imprisoned men and women of Tulia, Texas—most of whom had never had any trouble with law enforcement before this case—were the victims of "**racial profiling.**" Black, poor, and deemed socially insignificant by a state apparatus more concerned with impressive looking statistics  (in the "Drug War") than in the dictates of justice!

Ours is a country that likes to declare "war." And in the present "War on Terrorism" a new type of profiling has emerged–one that may prove to be even more sinister than the profiling that I, a black man in America, have come to know all too well.

## THE CASE OF IMAM JAMIL ABDULLAH AL-AMIN

When this writer posed a question to former US Attorney General Ramsey Clark, at a 2002 press conference at the National Press Club in Washington, DC, to ask his opinion on the case of Imam Jamil Al-Amin, the 'war in Afghanistan,' and mounting civil liberties concerns in the US—Clark's response was immediate and straight to the point:

> Let me say first, I remember Rap Brown well from the 60s, and I thought that he was a splendid human being and leader of the civil rights movement, with a strong touch of nobility and commitment. I remember when Congress passed the H. Rap Brown law, just to try to get people like him; and finally he was indicted under the law that he honored with his name... **There can be no question that the United States government, through its intelligence agencies and most of its appointed leadership, and a great deal of its elected leadership, considers Islam—not just militant Islam, but Islam—to be the greatest threat to the domestic and international security of the United States.**

Imam Jamil Abdullah Al-Amin (born Hubert Gerold Brown) is no stranger to controversy. The man formerly known as H. Rap Brown has been an active public figure for all of his adult life, and his activism has taken many twists and turns. During the 60s he was known as a courageous firebrand for his *by any means necessary*, in your face approach to long overdue societal change. After his embrace of Islam in 1971, he gradually became committed to the principle of *revolution by the book* (Qur'an and sunnah).

In *Revolution By The Book* (published by Writer's Inc., 1994), he writes:

> It is criminal that, in the 1990s, we still approach struggle [by] sloganeering, saying, 'by any means necessary,' as if that's a program... or, 'we shall overcome,' as if that's a program. Slogans are not programs. We must define the means which will bring about change. This can be found in what Allah has brought for us in the Qur'an and in the example of the Prophet. Our revolution must be according to what Almighty God revealed...

> The mission of a believer in Islam is totally different from coexisting or being a part of the system. the prevailing morals are wrong. Their ethics are wrong. Western philosophy...has reduced man to food, clothing, shelter, and the sex drive, which means he doesn't have a spirit... Successful struggle requires a divine program. Allah has provided that program.

This revolutionary perspective resulted in Imam Jamil Abdullah Al-Amin being among a short list of American-born Muslims singled out by one of America's most prominent anti-Islam demagogues, Daniel Pipes, in an article that appeared in the Feb 21, 2000 edition of *The National Review.*

### The Night of March 16

We may never know what really happened the night of March 16, 2000. What is known is that a shootout occurred on the West End of Atlanta; two Fulton County sheriff's deputies exchanged gunfire with an assailant; and one deputy (Ricky Kinchen) died the next day while the other (Aldranon English) sustained serious injuries and remained hospitalized in the intensive care unit of the hospital. We know that between surgeries, and heavily sedated, the surviving deputy identified

Imam Jamil Al-Amin (by photograph) as the lone assailant, and that he claimed to have shot that lone assailant in the stomach area.

We now know that police radio transmissions within minutes of the tragedy recorded the following: "*[911] Caller advises perp in a vacant building on Westview bleeding begging for a ride.*" Police reportedly surrounded this abandoned house five blocks from the shooting scene where fresh blood was found, but found no assailant. Finally, while media reports nationwide (including the *Washington Times*) reported a wounded "former Black Panther" on the run, when the Imam was apprehended four days later in White Hall, Alabama, he had no injuries.

Georgia prosecutors based their case on three things: Deputy Aldranon English's identification of the Imam; a .223-caliber rifle and 9mm handgun allegedly found in a wooded area of White Hall, Alabama, a day after his capture; and the Imam's black Mercedes which was also allegedly recovered in White Hall.

The case against Imam Jamil has raised many persistent questions and concerns, for it is now a known fact that he was a high profile target of law enforcement for many years before his arrest. In 1995 an attempt was made by law enforcement authorities to frame Imam Jamil for a shooting that occurred on the West End of Atlanta. The effort backfired when the victim publicly stated that he had maintained from the beginning, that he didn't know who shot him in his leg; but authorities had pressured him into saying it was Jamil Al-Amin.

The Imam was arrested on suspicion of aggravated assault and paraded before the court on August 7, 1995, but then released on bail the following day. The charges were never pursued.

Since that time we've learned of the official five year undercover investigation mounted by the FBI and a special task force set up within the local Atlanta Police Department. This went on from 1992-1997, and included paid informants planted within the Community Mosque. With the exception of the August 1995 incident, however, the Imam was never charged with any crimes.

On May 31, 1999, Imam Jamil was the subject of a traffic stop in Cobb County, Georgia. (Was it a case of *racial profiling*, or was he stopped because they knew who he was?) He was subsequently placed under arrest for receiving stolen goods (the vehicle he was driving); impersonating a police officer (for the badge he had in his wallet); and driving without insurance. He was booked, and then released a few hours later on a $10,000 bond. By September, he was indicted on all three charges.

After his futile attempt to resolve the matter outside the courts—he provided a bill of sale for the used vehicle; the mayor of White Hall, Alabama, sent a letter to authorities supporting Imam Jamil's claim of being an auxiliary member of the town's police force—he failed to appear in court on January 24, 2000, and a bench warrant was issued for his arrest four days later (Jan 28th). Deputies Ricky Kinchen and Aldranon English served the warrant on the night before the celebration of Eid-ul-Adha, a major Muslim holiday, (March 16, 2000), and tragedy struck.

Before his trial began two years later, Imam Jamil had already been tried and convicted in the court of public opinion by the media and law enforcement community. The atmosphere was so poisonous, in fact, that when Mrs. Coretta Scott King issued a statement calling for a fair and impartial proceeding, so that the tragedy would not be "compounded by a flawed trial or a rushed verdict," she was severely criticized in a number of editorials.

At the end of the day it was *not* a fair proceeding, and as can be expected, Imam Jamil Abdullah Al-Amin was convicted on all counts. Fulton County District Attorney, Paul Howard, Jr., wanted the death penalty. However, in the penalty phase of the trial, the jury's decision was Life without the possibility of parole. Imam Jamil Abdullah Al-Amin now resides in 23 hour lockdown at the maximum security prison in Reidsville, Georgia.

What follows is a legal update provided by Sr. Karima Al-Amin, the wife of Imam Jamil (herself a practicing civil attorney)

Imam Jamil's convictions were affirmed by the Georgia Supreme Court on May 24, 2004. A timely Motion for Reconsideration was filed on June 3, 2004. It was denied by the Georgia Supreme Court on June 28, 2004. The Georgia Supreme Court agreed that the prosecution committed a grave constitutional error in its closing argument, when the assistant district attorney directed jurors to consider questions pertaining to the failure of Imam Jamil to present testimony or evidence. Nevertheless, the Georgia Supreme Court would not reverse the convictions.

By September 27, 2004, Imam Jamil filed a petition for a *writ of certiorari* to the United States Supreme Court; however during its October 2004 calendar, the U.S. Supreme Court denied the petition for *writ of certiorari*. The appeals process is not over because post- conviction remedies are available.

On November 14, 2005, counsel for Imam Jamil filed a Habeas Corpus (Jamil Abdullah Al-Amin v. Hugh Smith) in the Superior Court of Tattnall County, State of Georgia, citing 14 grounds for reversal of his conviction and sentence of life without parole. Grounds presented included ineffective assistance of counsel based on the failure of trial counsel to do the following:
• investigate the confession of Otis Jackson;
• request a change of venue due to negative publicity;
• permit Imam Jamil to testify in his own defense;
• challenge the issue of the prosecution striking all persons from the jury who indicated an affiliation to Muslims.

Other grounds included error on the part of the judge by denying Imam Jamil the following:
• the right to counsel of his choice by eliminating all but one of his four trial lawyers from participating in *voir dire* of the jury;
• the opportunity to present favorable evidence, including two 911 tapes, which directly contradicted the State's position;
• the right to introduce evidence relating to his work to improve the West End community;
• the presentation of favorable testimony;
• the opportunity to confront an FBI agent in the case with prior misconduct against a Muslim, his misleading and false testimony, and questionable activity in the case, including tampering of evidence.

Counsel also raised errors committed by the State, including:
• failure to provide discovery to the defense;

• inappropriate statements regarding the failure of Imam Jamil to testify, and his courtroom conduct by not standing for the jury as members entered the courtroom.

The habeas also challenges the government sponsored oath taken by the grand and petit jurors and witnesses, which resulted in a conflict between religious practices and state function in violation of the Establishment Clause and the First Amendment to the United States Constitution. Counsel also addressed the issue of violation of the 6th and 14th Amendments based on jury selection procedures.

At the time of this writing, Imam Jamil is preparing for a scheduled June 2006 hearing on the habeas corpus grounds.

Additionally, Imam Jamil has filed two lawsuits challenging his confinement in involuntary protective custody, resulting in his ongoing 23-hour lockdown status. Counsel filed a brief on September 6, 2005, in the United States Court of Appeals for the 11th Circuit, appealing the decision of the U. S. District Court of the Northern District of Georgia. Imam Jamil will continue to challenge the inhumane conditions of his incarceration.

The second lawsuit involves the opening of his legal mail outside of his presence, which is a violation of standard operating procedures and a violation of the attorney-client privilege. This challenge also will continue.

Imam Jamil remains in the Georgia State Prison, in Reidsville, Georgia. He is being held under orders of a 23-hour lockdown, with a one-hour period daily for "exercise" alone in a small walking yard. Although his record does not indicate institutional behavioral problems, the Georgia Department of Corrections has isolated Imam Jamil by labeling him a "threat" to the institution.

On March 11, 2002, two days after the jury announced the guilty verdict, the National Support Committee for Imam Jamil Al-Amin, consisting of major Muslim organizations, issued a statement:

We do not believe the facts presented in court warranted a guilty verdict against Imam Jamil. His defense team offered credible evidence indicating that he was not the person who shot the deputies. We believe Imam Jamil will be exonerated on appeal...The American Muslim community and its leadership will continue to support the cause of justice in this case and will work to ensure that Imam Jamil is able to exercise all the rights he is entitled to under the law...

## THE VIRGINIA JIHAD NETWORK CASE (AKA, "THE PAINTBALL CASE")

This case began with the indictment of eleven young Muslim men by a federal grand jury in June 2003. They were indicted on an assortment of weapons counts, and for an alleged conspiracy to wage war (in concert with a South Asian jihadi organization known as *Lashkar-e-Taiba*) against a nation with whom America is at peace —a violation of a rarely used statute known as "The Neutrality Act."

In short, they stood accused of conspiring to wage war against India over its brutal and contested occupation of Kashmir. What was the proof of this alleged conspiracy? Their semi-secretive indulgence in a rapidly growing American pastime known as *Paintball Games*, coupled with their interest in following conflicts (via the internet) involving Muslims overseas!

Mainstream media's reporting on this case was predictable. On the day the trial began (Monday, February 9, 2004) *National Public Radio* filed a report basically outlining the government's case against the accused; while the Tuesday, February 10th edition of the *Washington Times* concluded a front page report titled "Islamic extremists invade US, join sleeper cells," with the following: *"Eleven men, including nine US citizens, were arrested last year in Virginia in what authorities called the 'Virginia jihad.' The men were accused in a 41 count grand jury indictment of engaging in 'holy jihad' to drive India out of the disputed Kashmir territory. Six have since pleaded guilty."*

For its part, the *Washington Post* had an article in its Thursday, Feb. 12th edition under the headline, *"Jihad Trial Witness Says Paintball Was Training Drill."* A representative excerpt reads, "But while defense lawyers said in opening statements this week that the paintball games were harmless fun intended only as exercise, prosecutors have charged that they were used to simulate combat in preparation for violent jihad." (Leading your average reader to conclude, 'Ok, we got 'em. Case closed.)

It did appear that the guardians of democracy (the media) basically accepted the government's indictment of the accused on face value – without taking the time to investigate, research, or ask hard questions in an effort to uncover the truth. What they saw was that six plead guilty, and three of the six admitted to going overseas to visit "training camps." Consequently, the five holdouts must be guilty by association.

### The Charges and "Superseding Indictment"
In September 2003, after the government failed in its attempt to

frighten all of the "defendants" into accepting plea agreements, the holdouts were charged in a superseding indictment with additional offenses. The government sent the message loud and clear that it was time to play hardball; that if the holdouts decided to go to trial and lose, they would pay a heavy price—the remainder of their productive lives in prison.

It should be noted for the record that these are all young men—most of whom with young families! My intent here is to provide some in-depth and comprehensive background information on the case, so that the reader will be able to better understand what the issues were, and thus be in a better position to make an informed and independent judgment on this precedent-setting case.

The indictment in the case known as: UNITED STATES OF AMERICA v. RANDALL TODD ROYER, et. al. (Criminal No. 03-296-A) read as follows:
Count 1: 18 USC-371 Conspiracy
Count 2: 18 USC-2384 Conspiracy to Levy War Against the US
Count 3: 18 USC 2339B Conspiracy to Provide Material Support to Al-Qaeda
Count 4: 50 USC 1705 Conspiracy to Contribute Services to the Taliban
Count 5: 18 USC 2339A Conspiracy to Contribute Material Support to Lashkar-e-Taiba
Count 6: 50 USC 1705 Supplying Services to the Taliban
Counts 7-10: 18 USC 960 Commencing an Expedition Against a Friendly Nation
Count 11: 18 USC 924(o) Conspiracy to Possess and Use Firearms in Connection with a Crime of Violence

Counts 12-14: 18 USC 924(b) Receipt of Firearm or Ammunition with Cause to Believe a Felony will be Committed Therewith
Counts 15-16: 18 USC 1001(a) False Official Statements
Counts 17-32: 18 USC 924( c) Using Firearm in Connection with a Crime of Violence
The men who went to trial faced the following charges:
Masoud Ahmed Khan (Counts 1-5, 8, 10-11, 24-27, 32)
Seifullah Chapman (Counts 1, 5, 8-9, 11, 15, 19-22, 24-28)
Hammad Abdur-Raheem (Counts 1, 5, 8, 10-14, 19, 24-27, 31)
Caliph Basha Ibn Abdur-Raheem (Counts 1, 11, 13-14, 21, 30)
Sabri Benkhala (who is scheduled to go on trial in March, insha'Allah), faces Counts 6 and 16-17, according to the federal indictment dated September 25, 2003.

**How it fit in with the "War on Terrorism"**

On June 25, 2002, an article appeared in the Village Voice newspaper of New York City titled, *"Court Jousters: A Small Cartel of Conservative Lawyers Rewrites the American Rule."* In the course of this revealing article, [then] Deputy US Attorney General Viet Dinh became the first government official (to this writer's knowledge) to openly admit that the US government was engaged in racial (and religious) profiling in its "War on Terrorism." Mr. Dinh reportedly said, *"The US does use racial profiling—not for identification, but for investigation."*

When questioned on the criteria employed for such profiling, he responded, *"The criteria Al Qaeda itself uses. Eighteen to 35 year old males who entered the country after the start of 2000 using passports from countries where Al Qaeda has a strong presence."* (By the US government's theory and practice, this could be any predominantly Muslim populated nation.) But that isn't all. In his mid-January 2002 address to the *American Bar Association* conference in Naples (FL), Mr. Dinh arrogantly stated:

> We are reticent to provide a road map to Al Qaeda as to the progress and direction of our investigative activity. We don't want to taint people as being of interest to the investigation simply because of our attention. We will let them go if there is not enough of a predicate to hold them. But we will follow them closely, AND IF THEY SO MUCH AS SPIT ON THE SIDEWALK WE'LL ARREST THEM. The message is that if you are a *suspected* terrorist you better be squeaky clean. IF WE CAN, WE WILL KEEP YOU IN JAIL. (Emphasis mine)

This, in a nutshell, is what the so-called "Virginia Jihad" or "Paintball Case" was all about. It was about a group of young Muslim males between the ages of "18 to 35" playing PAINTBALL (equivalent to "spitting on the sidewalk") with, according to the government, a con-spiratorial agenda! Can we back such an assertion up with proof? Absolutely!

In addressing the court on the day of opening arguments, the lead prose-cutor, Gordon Kromberg, admitted, "Most of the evidence in this case will be provided by cooperators" - compromised co-defendants in the case who, under pressure from the government and their respective defense attorneys, accepted plea agreements for significantly less time than they would have received had they gone to trial and been found guilty. (Six of the accused had accepted such plea agreements.)

### The Uncontested Facts

The uncontested "facts" of the case were as follows:

(1) A group of young Muslim men began sometime in the summer

of 2000 to indulge in one of the fastest growing American pastimes, paintball. The group of paintball playing Muslims (whose numbers would fluctuate) indulged in the games on average twice a month—that is, until the attacks of September 11, 2001. (Their thoughts after the attacks were that Muslim men, dressed in fatigues and playing paintball in the Virginia countryside, might draw too much unwarranted suspicion.)

(2) Some of the men came from military backgrounds, and used their prior military training to instruct other players in a way that made the paintball games more competitive.

(3) Some of the men listened to lectures (which sometimes focused upon the doctrine of jihad), and discussed the assaults being committed against Muslim peoples in other parts of the world (i.e., Chechnya, Kashmir, Palestine, etc.); and some of the men saw videos of actual combat from the battle fields of Chechnya.

(4) A few of the men had been overseas and visited a Lashkar-e-Taiba training camp, BEFORE it was officially designated a "Terrorist organization" by the US government. It is important to emphasize that when they visited it was NOT against the law! (Lashkar-e-Taiba is an armed Muslim resistance organization struggling against India's brutal occupation of Kashmir.)

Beyond these uncontested and circumstantial "facts," however, there was little hard evidence to support any part of the aforementioned indictment.

### Paintball in America

*The Christian Paintball Players Association* (CPPA) was started in 1996 and reportedly has members in every state and more than half a dozen countries including Canada, Brazil, Korea, and Australia. Its Ohio chapter—the Ohio Christian Paintball Players Association (www.ohiocppa.org)—in 2003 was looking to start church leagues statewide to compete in Saturday tournaments. You heard it right, an activity that many still consider an *extreme sport* has made it well into the American mainstream, and is regularly enjoyed by millions of people from varied racial, religious and socio-economic backgrounds around the US.

During testimony in the case, the court heard from a paintball expert who testified, among other things, that all types of groups and people of all ages play paintball—involving an assortment of creative, expensive, and time consuming games and scenarios. The expert cited one such example known as D-Day Oklahoma—which features a military theme (German team vs. Allied team)—that went on day and night with about 3,000 players the previous year.

This "expert" also noted on the witness stand that the wearing of camouflage and military gear is common place in the sport, as is instruction in maneuvers and defensive techniques which make the games more competitive.

**Overseas Training Camps**

Of the four young men who went on trial, Masoud Ahmed Khan faced the most serious charges, which included "Conspiracy to contribute services to the Taliban," and "Conspiracy to levy war against the US." The basis for these charges was the visit that Masoud made to Pakistan for the primary purpose of resolving some rather onerous family business, following the death of his father. The government contends that his primary purpose was to visit a *Lashkar-e-Taiba* (LET) training camp in Kashmir, in order to train for jihad against US forces in Afghanistan. Since Masoud never made it to Afghanistan, the government's emphasis was on his visit to the LET camp, and on what Masoud's alleged intent was according to government "cooperators."

Masoud admits to having visited a *Lashkar-e-Taiba* training camp; but he insisted that the training camp experience was primarily about getting into shape and reducing stress. It is also important to note that this visit occurred BEFORE *Lashkar-e-Taiba* (on the advice of foreign intelligence) was listed as a "terrorist organization" by the US government; and therefore, Masoud's visit, whatever his "intent," was not illegal!

No doubt, there are some who will read this and conclude Masoud's visit to the LET camp is the "smoking gun" pointing to his guilt. However, for those of you who can still be reached by reasoned argument, I offer the following. How many of you have heard of the *Marva Army Experience Program*? Not many? I didn't think so.

Marva is part of the *Young Judea Year* Course in Israel, sponsored by the Israeli Army and the *Jewish Agency*. Marva reportedly consists of two months of a simulated basic training program involving hikes, marches, navigation, weapons training, simulated combat, military ceremonies and a study of the *Israeli Defense Forces* (IDF) history. Its stated purpose is to expose foreign students to the problems and challenges facing the Israeli Army and the role of the Israeli Defense Force within the country.

When one considers the FACT that: (a) a large part of "Greater Israel" is internationally recognized "Occupied Territory" (established in gross violation of international law); (b) the FACT that the IDF has been an indispensable instrument in this illegal occupation; (c) the FACT that young American Jewish citizens are among those who participate in the Marva program; and (d) the FACT that, of these American-born participants, a significant number will go on to become an official part of this internationally recognized illegal occupation (in one of the most *explosive* parts of the world). With this in mind, condemnation of any young Muslim for attending a training camp in the disputed territory of Kashmir reveals a double standard of the highest order.

To read more about Marva please visit:
www.funtour.co.il/other_opportunities-marva_daniel.html
and www.fzy.org.uk/yearcourse/security/nili/

**Selective Prosecutions and Plea-bargains**

There is another issue that should be considered of deep significance; the selective use of the rarely enforced "Neutrality Act"—making war (or in this case, *conspiring to make war*) against a nation with whom America is at peace.

That this particular case reflects the selectively applied use of this rarely applied "law" is without question. Case(s) in point:

– *American Zionists* (both Jewish and Christian Fundamentalist) who openly support, through a variety of means, the brutal occupation and subjugation of Palestine and its people.

– *Cuban Americans* who covertly (and sometimes openly) support the overthrow of the democratically elected government of Fidel Castro.

– *Irish Americans* (and others) who for years have openly given material support to the political wing (Sein Fein) of the Irish Republican Army (IRA); another political entity officially designated by the US Department of State as a "terrorist organization."

While I could go on and on, I do believe the point has been sufficiently made. As for the plea agreements that some Muslim defendants accepted from government prosecutors, I cite the following excerpt from page 86 of our book entitled, <u>The State of the Union 2003: Don't Say You Didn't Know!</u>

> In concluding this chapter I feel that I should caution the reader against giving too much weight to any reports of accused Muslims plea bargaining to alleged acts of terrorism (as in the case of the so-called "American Taliban," John Walker Lindh). While we as a nation pay lip service to the principle of *due process* and a *presumption of innocence,* and the right of the accused to a trial before a jury of his or her peers—the reality is that accused persons who come from socially and/or politically marginalized communities or groups, are severely punished at the end of the day (if found guilty) for even attempting to avail themselves of such constitutional guarantees!

This is a fact. And this, I believe, is what the "plea agreements" in this troubling case were really all about; the fearful capitulation by several young men to the possibility of life in prison. When the trial ended and the verdicts came in, three of the five who went to trial were found guilty as charged. One received a sentence of eight years; a second, 85 years; and the third, Life without the possibility of parole.

It is the belief of many (including this writer) that these men were guilty of nothing more than being conscientious Muslims at a time when Islam and Muslims have been demonized and find themselves at the center of a carefully constructed climate of fear. Even if they were guilty of the type of conspiracy that the government has alleged—and it was a conspiracy which (even according to the government) never achieved fruition—is it justice to give young men a sentence of 85 years and life (both forms of capitol punishment) for something that never ever went beyond *intention*. Sentences like these constitute *judicial barbarism* in the name of justice! I now conclude with what this case as a whole, in our humble view, was really all about.

### The Bill of Rights and America's Soul

At the conclusion of the Constitutional Convention in 1789, Benjamin Franklin was asked, *"What have you wrought?"* He responded, *"A republic, if you can keep it."*

In a collective effort to better safeguard and advance the ideals of the newly established American republic, the Founding Fathers drafted what is widely considered to be the heart and soul of the US Constitution—*The Bill of Rights*. The First Amendment, in particular, goes right to the heart of this case (i.e., freedom of *religion and speech*), as well as the right to freedom of *conscience* and *association*.

The Paintball Case was really about the *"Two Americas"* that the late Sen. J. William Fulbright so ably described in his thought-provoking book entitled, <u>The Arrogance of Power.</u> The question arises, which of these two Americas will emerge triumphant from the struggle that is currently being waged for America's soul? Indeed, The Paintball Case, properly understood, is but one of the many metaphors of this ongoing struggle. And the struggle must continue...

## THE CASE OF DR. ALI AL-TAMIMI

Ali Al Timimi is an American of Iraqi heritage, born and raised in Washington, DC. On December 1, 2004, he successfully defended his dissertation on "Chaos and Complexity in Cancer," and was awarded a Doctorate of Philosophy in Computational Biology. He also holds undergraduate degrees in both Biology and Computer Science.

In addition to his scientific prowess, Ali Al-Timimi possesses an impressive background in Islamic studies. In 1987, he was the recipient of a scholarship to study theology at the Islamic University of Medina, Saudi Arabia. While living in Medina, he also furthered his studies with some of the most prominent scholars of the Prophet's mosque. He is a recognized expert in the field of Islamic Theology and Philosophy. He has taught both Theology and Quranic studies at the University level, and has lectured around the world.

According to the U.S. Government, he was also the driving force, "the spiritual and intellectual leader," of the young men who comprised the so-called "Virginia Jihad Network" (or Paintball Case). During the trial, lead prosecutor Gordon Kromberg called Timimi "a purveyor of hate and war."

Dr. Al-Timimi was arraigned on Friday, February 3, 2005, in the U.S. District Court for the Eastern District of Virginia, and was indicted on the following ten counts:

Count 1: Inducing others to conspire to use firearms.
Count 2: Soliciting others to levy war against the United States.
Count 3: Inducing others to conspire to levy war on the United States.
Count 4: Attempting to contribute services to the Taliban.
Count 5: Inducing others to give aid to the Taliban.
Count 6: Inducing others to conspire to violate the neutrality act
Count 7: Inducing others to use firearms.
Count 8: Inducing others to use firearms.
Count 9: Inducing others to carry explosives.
Count 10: Inducing others to carry explosives.
(Note the overlapping, repetitive counts, as in the Paintball case.)
At the conclusion of the trial in July 2005, Ali al-Tamimi was found guilty on all counts and given a sentence of Life plus 70 years.

In urging a sentence of life imprisonment, Kromberg stated, *"Al-Timimi hates the United States and calls for its destruction. He's allowed to do that in this country. He's not allowed to solicit treason. That's what he did. He deserves every day of the time he will serve."*

That statement, which in the view of many did not comport with the facts of the case, accurately reflects the tone and tenor of Tamimi's trial, as well as the trial of the young men that preceded his. The thing that made his trial truly significant, however, is the fact that he was tried and convicted for "speech."

While Judge Leonie M. Brinkema—the same judge who presided over The Paintball Case—opined that there was sufficient evidence that Tamimi had "incited his followers" toward violence, she nevertheless considered the prison terms mandated by the guidelines (under four counts of the conviction) to be "very draconian." She said she had no choice but to impose the life sentence after refusing a defense request to set aside the guilty verdicts. (Judge Brinkema had a choice. However, rubber-stamping the "guidelines" was the easier way to go.)

On July 13, 2005, The Peace And Justice Foundation released the following statement after the sentencing of Dr. Ali al-Tamimi.

> One man is a non-Muslim business leader convicted of a tangible crime. He [former Worldcom CEO, Bernard Ebbers] presided over "the largest corporate fraud in U.S. History." His administration's actions wiped out billions of investor dollars and personal savings, resulting in untold human suffering. He received a sentence of 25 years, but doesn't have to begin his sentence until October of this year. Not only that, the federal judge in the case [Barbara Jones] has stated that she would accept written arguments from the lawyers involved, on whether Ebbers 'should be allowed to remain free while he appeals the verdict.

Another man, a Muslim religious leader [Dr. Ali Tamimi] is convicted of *thought crimes* in an alleged "terrorist conspiracy" —a conspiracy which, even according to the government, never achieved fruition. His was the crime of speech; and for his speech he received a sentence of Life, without the possibility of parole. This "criminal" was immediately taken into custody, and will no doubt begin serving his sentence in a federal prison far removed from his family. These are disgusting examples of "the rule of law," of justice *American style*."

Today a decision was made in the U.S. District Court for the Eastern District of Virginia that brings the United States of America no closer to the realization of "national security." If anything, it takes the nation further away from its illusory pursuit. Judge Leonie Brinkema sentenced Dr. Ali al-Tamimi to LIFE for essentially saying things that the court found offensive.

The Government's decision to prosecute this case; the jury's verdict after hearing this case; and Judge Brinkema's official stamp at the conclusion of this case, are all reflective of the pro-prosecutorial bias that surrounds any Muslim accused of a serious criminal offense. The tragic events in London just a few days ago helped to ensure that Ali Tamimi—and any other Muslim so situated—would not have a snowball's chance in hell of receiving a fair and impartial disposition in a "court of law."

We fully agree with the observation made by Dr. Tamimi at the conclusion of his statement to the court:

**Imprisonment of any term, as this Court well knows, is a crisis for the incarcerated and his or her loved ones. I am no**

exception. But the real crisis brought on by my imprison-ment, I sincerely believe, is America's. For if my conviction is to stand, it would mean that two hundred and thirty years of America's tradition of protecting the individual from the tyrannies and whims of the sovereign will have come to an end. And that which is exploited today to persecute a single member of a minority, will most assuredly come back to haunt the majority tomorrow.

Dr. Ali al-Tamimi's astute observation brings to mind the words of one of America's most distinguished "Founding Fathers." At the conclusion of the Constitutional Convention in 1789, *Benjamin Franklin* was asked, "What have you wrought?" His response: "A Republic, if you can keep it!"

## THE CASE OF AHMED OMAR ABU-ALI (THE SHAME OF THE U.S. GOVERNMENT)

*We begin this commentary on the Ahmed Abu-Ali case with a very personal commentary written by his sister, Tasneem. It was written at a time when Ahmed was still being detained and tortured in a Saudi Arabian prison. Tasneem's synopsis is followed by information on the unfortunate events that have transpired in this young man's case since that time.*

Ahmed Abu Ali is a U.S. citizen who has been detained in Saudi Arabia for over seven months without charge. Ahmed went to Medinah University in August 2002 on a scholarship to study Islamic Sciences. He was arrested June 11, 2003 while taking a final exam.

It was not until after a month of pressuring the State Department, that they arranged for a consul from the U.S. Embassy in Riyadh to check on Ahmed's conditions, and it was only after two months that Ahmed made his first phone call to us. The FBI, State Department, and American Embassy in Riyadh have all insisted that this is solely a Saudi case. Yet officials from the *American Embassy's Legal Attaché Office*—the name for FBI stations Overseas—had access to Ahmed from the very first moment of his arrest, interrogating him and witnessing his interrogation by Saudi Mubahith officers.

In addition, the FBI visited Ahmed in September, threatening to send him to *Guantanamo Bay*, or have him declared an "enemy combatant," which would allow U.S. authorities to jail him indefinitely without access to lawyers. They also threatened him with a trial in Saudi Arabia that would exclude the presence of a defense attorney. Their three day interrogation pertained to the **US. vs. Royer case in VA**. Their visit prompted his placement in solitary confinement for over three months.

Ahmed is a U.S. citizen who has been left in a country without any rights or protections. Ahmed has neither been charged nor found guilty of a crime. In fact, Caryl Murphy in *The Washington Post reported in a November 22nd article, "Saudi officials initially said that Abu Ali was suspected in connection with the May 12 bombings in Riyadh, but several U.S. law enforcement sources said the FBI has concluded that Abu Ali probably did not play a role in them." She also reported that a U.S. law enforcement officer told her, "I'm not aware of any information that he broke any U.S. laws."*

She also reported, "In a written statement issued in response to a reporter's inquiries, the foreign affairs adviser to Saudi Arabia's Crown Prince Abdullah described the case as "an ongoing investigation by *both governments*."

Ahmed has lost weight. He has been subject to *psychological and physical torture*. His human rights have been violated, and his family has been left out in the dark. He should be brought to his own country where he can be afforded full rights and protections as a U.S. citizen.—The Family of Ahmed Omar Abu-Ali

Since the aforementioned report much has happened. After many months of pressure by his family and supporters—which also involved a lawsuit being filed against his own government—Ahmed was finally returned to the United States, but under very disturbing conditions. Instead of a joyous return to the warm embrace of a family that missed him dearly, he was accompanied by agents of the government and placed in a U.S. detention facility upon his arrival. Ahmed was then formally charged with an alarming list of alleged offenses, including *conspiracy to assassinate the president of the United States.*

The trial of **"The United States of America vs. Ahmed Omar Abu Ali"** established a new precedent of sorts, as it is reportedly "the first case in an American criminal courtroom to rely so heavily on evidence gathered by a foreign intelligence service." Abu-Ali was imprisoned in Saudi Arabia for almost two years without charge. It was the torture induced confession at the hands of Saudi security officers that provided the bulk of "evidence" against the defendant; this along with an assurance from Saudi officials (speaking in Arabic by video from the "kingdom") that the prisoner was *well treated.*

Abu Ali's name had been linked by U.S. authorities to the so-called *"Virginia Jihad"* (aka "Paintball Case"); but he was never formally charged. He was initially arrested in June 2003, while taking final exams in a Saudi university, for a suspected connection to the May 12, 2003, bombing of three residential compounds in Riyadh.

After being held without charge - with the United States and Saudi governments passing the buck on whose responsibility his detention was (and both governments claiming that they had nothing against him) - his family sued the United Sates government in U.S. District Court for condoning his torture, and demanded that he be returned to his country of birth. It was under these circumstances that formal terrorism charges were leveled against him, just before his *rendition* from Saudi Arabia to America.

On day three of deliberations, November 22, 2005, jurors at the U.S. District Court for the Eastern District of Virginia convicted 24 year old Ahmed Abu-Ali on all nine counts—which included *conspiracy to assassinate President Bush*, conspiracy to commit aircraft piracy, and [the perennial favorite] providing material support to al Qaeda. He faces 20 years to LIFE when he is sentenced February 17, 2006.

U.S. District Judge Gerald Bruce Lee had the power to abort this miscarriage of justice. He could have thrown out the indictment, based upon all known factors surrounding this case (before it ever went to trial). However, like his fellow jurist in the same federal courthouse, Judge Leonie M. Brinkema, at the end of the day he failed miserably in the struggle between fear-induced expediency and *conscience*!

## Update

On March 29, 2006, Ahmed Omar Abu Ali was sentenced to 30 YEARS in prison—considered a light sentence in view of what government prosecutors were arguing for (LIFE without parole). Judge Lee noted that **Ali's actions "did not result in one single actual victim.** That fact must be taken into account."

The Peace And Justice Foundation, Amnesty International, and a number of other civil and human rights organizations expressed serious concerns about the trial of Ahmed Omar Abu-Ali; of special note was the court's decision to allow the coerced confession (extracted by a foreign government known for its practice of torture) into the "terrorism" trial of an American citizen.

## THE CASE OF LYNNE STEWART
## AHMED ABDEL SATTAR & MOHAMED YOUSRY

There is no way that you can talk about the case of Lynne Stewart, Ahmed Abdel Sattar, and Mohamed Yousry, without talking about **Sheikh Omar Abdur Rahman**—the blind and highly respected religious leader who was a perpetual thorn in the side of the corrupt Egyptian government; that is until the U.S. government did the Mubarak regime a favor, by sending the troublesome cleric into the *American gulag* under a barbaric sentence of 240 years.

One can sometimes come across erroneous news reports which suggest Sheikh Omar Abdur Rahman was sentenced to life in prison by a federal court in 1996, *"over his role in the 1993 World Trade Center bombing."* That attack in the middle of a busy work day—on what had formerly been the tallest building in New York City (110 stories)—took the lives of six people and injured more than 1,000 others. The blind cleric was never charged with having any connection to that crime, although his name has often been mentioned in connection with it.

Sheikh Omar was arrested on bogus immigration charges on July 2, 1993. A short time later, he and eleven other co-defendants were indicted on a laundry list of criminal offenses, which included "seditious conspiracy against the United States." (What the late William "Bill" Kunstler called, *"the conspiracy to blow up everybody and everything."*)

In his book titled, *My Life As A Radical Lawyer*, Kunstler writes (page 334):

> The sheikh's fiery preachings, in which he denounced the secular Egyptian government and allegedly urged jihad, or holy war, were regarded by the United States and Egypt as the ideological basis of terrorist acts committed by Islamic revolutionaries in both countries. When he was arraigned, the sheikh denied that he inspired terrorism, led a conspiracy in this country, or directed the WTC bombing.
>
> I believe that [El-Sayyid] Nosair was indicted because Atty. Gen. Janet Reno capitulated to enormous pressure from the Jewish community to remedy the jury's acquittal in his state trial. I think Reno also gave in to political pressure when she indicted the sheikh, since there is absolutely no hard evidence of his involvement in any conspiracy or plot.

In short, Sheikh Omar Abdur Rahman (an Egyptian/Muslim/ immigrant) was tried, convicted, and given a life sentence in the mid-90s, for essentially the same "crime" that Dr. Ali al-Tamimi (an American/Muslim/citizen) was tried, convicted, and given a life sentence for in 2005—the crime of speech!

Bill Kunstler made another observation in his illuminating book (published in the mid-90s), that is still worthy of note more than a decade later. On page 317 of a chapter entitled *The Despised Muslim*, he writes: *"Today Muslims are the most hated group in the country; the moment a Muslim is accused of a crime, the specter of terrorism is raised, and everyone panics."* Kunstler's observation affirms an argument that we often make. Both the official and unofficial anti-Muslim bigotry that we are experiencing in America today is really nothing new. The tragic attacks of September 11th only legitimized and deepened the Islamophobia that had already reared its ugly head.

As for the case of Lynne Stewart, Ahmed Abdel Sattar, and Mohamed Yousry, I attended some of the trial (it went on for months) in December-January (2004-2005). It was held at the US District Court located at 40 Foley Square in New York City. During one of those visits I accompanied Lynne back to her office, a few blocks away from the courthouse, and conducted a short interview that sheds considerable light on the case. The date of the interview was January 6, 2005.

**Q. How much time do you and your codefendants potentially face?**
A. Mr. Sattar faces life in prison. Mr. Yousry faces, I believe, 25 years; and I face 45 years. The government did come back and they wanted to get enhancements. There is part of the sentencing law that says if it's tied to terrorism the judge can jack up the time even further...

**Q. What is your impression of this judge? Did you know him before this case?**
A. I didn't know him at all. I was impressed with him at the very beginning ... at the beginning we felt that he was really being fair, not just trying to be fair. He didn't let the government go through all of the materials that they had taken from the office; and he dismissed the first indictment. We really had high hopes that he would dismiss the second indictment for the same reasons—it was too vague, there was no way anyone could really understand what was prohibited by this law. But sometime between dismissal in July, and re-indictment in December, he either had a change of heart, or else someone spoke to him. We don't know what happened, but he was a very different judge

in December than he had been in June—and that very different judge has persisted. It's almost as if he was told, *'This is a very important case to the government and we don't expect you to be monkeying around with it, we expect you to go with the program.'*

Most of the rulings in the case, and certainly all of the rulings that would help the government—for example the Bin Laden references—he has gone along with. It's as if he doesn't want to make any mistake that they will reverse the case on; but as far as being fair, or giving us a fair trial, he no longer seems to really care very much about that.

**Q.It sounds as if you have divided this whole proceeding into two parts.**
A. We were arrested in April 2002, but then we needed time to review all of the materials, and everything else; so we made motions. In July 2002 he dismissed the first indictment, but he didn't dismiss all of the charges – just the one charge that had to do with *materially aiding*. He determined that no one could know what was and what wasn't materially aiding as long as it was written up the way that the government did it. So then they came back the following December with a new indictment; but basically it was just the old one in a new glass. It was nothing new, it was just putting it in a different way.

They did say that they had a higher burden, they now had to prove knowledge and intent—that we not only knew that we were aiding a terrorist conspiracy, but that we *intended* to aid it. And what was the terrorist conspiracy? It was this fictitious conspiracy that Ahmed Sattar was accused of being a member of; the conspiracy that says, 'The guy in Staten Island is going to conspire with the guy in Afghanistan to do something in Egypt—or maybe not Egypt! We don't know where this was supposed to be; they have never clarified where this conspiracy was supposed to occur. So we're not enamored with the judge. His instructions to the jury are good, but we don't see him cutting us much slack at all.

**Q. The trial began when?**
A. The trial began in May of 2004 with jury selection; jury selection took most of May and June to complete. Opening statements were given at the end of June.

**Q. The next question moves somewhat away from your trial, but it's definitely connected. Have the appeals for Sheikh Omar Abdel Rahman ended?**
A. Yes.

**Q. His case for all intents and purposes is now over?**
A. Well, as I explained on the witness stand, on a purely legal basis, the indictment that was brought and tried, and of which he was convicted, and the appeals of that trial have ended. But you know for criminal defendants it never ends, because there can always be newly discovered evidence. There can be a change in the law; something that reopens the case, so it's never really over. We always had that in the back of our minds. So was clemency, which the prosecution made fun of. But actually, the Puerto Rican nationalists attacked Blair House, they were all [subsequently] given clemency—so you can laugh at that in 2000, but in 2010 it could be a reality.

Also for me... for a person who is a *political prisoner*, the case is never over, because they always need the protection of a lawyer; they always need to have that buffer between them and the State—with the State knowing that they (that prisoner) can call a lawyer and that lawyer will come in. If there were lawyers at **Abu-Graib** there would have been no torture.

Right now the State has moved all of the Muslim prisoners that had any political connections to a separate prison. It's located in Florence, Colorado, it's part of the supermax [prison system] out there. The lawyers in this case did travel out there to meet with the Sheikh, and interview him for the purpose of this case. Ramsey Clark went with them. But it was such a ridiculous setup. First of all, they had to bring a government interpreter; they had to be accompanied by a US Attorney during the interview; they were all herded into this one little sound proof booth (about six lawyers), and the Sheikh on the other side of the glass so that there could be no contact of any kind. It was really a farce.

They had to get certain answers from him about what was supposed to happen, and whether he would agree to certain things or not agree to them – because a lot of the material in this case was privileged. And his answer, as I would have expected it to be was, *'If it helps Yousry, Sattar and Lynne I agree to it being used, if it helps the government I don't agree to it being used.'* (Lynne chuckles as she recounts this.) But it was determined that as a witness there was not really much that he could add.

**Q. So in light of what has happened to you, Mohamed Yoursy, and Ahmed Satter, I get the impression that Sheikh Omar is now completely cutoff from the outside world. Is that the case?**
A. I believe Ramsey Clark is still representing him, is still his contact person; but because of the restrictions they [the government] have

now put on him—every conversation must be monitored—Ramsey has said, we can't agree to that, but he also hasn't been able to get the issue in court either...

I think he still gets his [once per month] call to his family, those are always monitored. And when they visited him he seemed, I think the word Ramsey used is *remote*. It took a while for him to really get into the flow of things. We're talking about someone who is completely alone – who never has any human contact at all. Florence is completely inhuman. I think that the diabetes takes a tremendous toll on your body; and the blindness of course, the fact that he has this impairment.

He does have a television set, but the television is in English. I believe there is one channel where the Qur'an is recited, which he likes very much. On the other hand he can recite the Qur'an himself, he knows the whole book by memory, so while that's pleasant for him I don't think that it substitutes for being able to stimulate him [under those conditions]. We tried once to get him some books on tape, [but] I don't think there are Arabic books on tape... and charity organizations are not that charitable.

**Q. Well you've answered why you continue to be involved despite the fact that the door to any legal redress appears to be closed...**
A. Well like [Attorney] Michael Tigar said, people are locked up for years and years and years—and we all know about the African American political prisoners that came out of the BLA (*Black Liberation Movement*) and the Black Panther Party, and we still continue to visit them, despite there being nothing on their legal horizons that give us much hope. There are parole hearings every once and awhile, things of

that nature; but mainly it's because we believe in these people as people—that they are entitled to hear from the outside world and be kept in contact with it. As Michael said, and it was very moving for me, the lawyers who serve *pro-bono* and then go into the prisons to keep hope alive deserve a badge of honor in this profession—especially when they represent people that most people think are not deserving.

I think for us... even though we did have hopes of moving him, because he was a mover and a shaker—I mean Sheikh Omar was someone very important—the thought that we might be able to get him back to Egypt, and that things could change there... I understand that just a few days ago one of the leading human rights organizations in Egypt called for his return, and basically said, *'This is going to be an Islamic state sooner or later, so why don't we just stop acting like this is never going to happen and do what's right, and what's right would be to repatriate Sheikh Omar.'* But the United States right now is embedded in the notion that this is how you fight terrorism; lock people up, as they say, and throw away the key.

**Q. How has the legal community responded to your case? And is its response to it different now than it was at the beginning?**
A. At the beginning I think there were more people who said I want to see what it's all about. I think the word that the government has put out, that this case is about carrying messages of violence, this portrayal has of course turned a lot of people off. We also can't forget that a large part of the New York bar is very *Zionist*, very oriented to that—and sort of feels like this marvelous, liberal community that for years supported so much that was human rights, and the movement, and labor, has really sort of withdrawn at this point to some degree, because they've found a different interest, and that interest is, *I want*

*to have a country where I know I can always go* [Israel]. So that has had
an affect on the amount of support from lawyers.

But I can also say that some of my biggest supporters, some of the
people who represent me are from that very community —so it's hard
to draw any total conclusions. People are very afraid of terrorism; people are very afraid—and this includes lawyers—of being associated
with, and being accused of the same kind of thing. Do you know what
I mean? They don't want to be too close to me. They're afraid they'll
be tarred with the same brush or something.

But by and large the part of the bar that you'd expect—the *National
Lawyers Guild*, the criminal defense lawyers, the people that I've
worked personally with on cases that know me—none of them have
deserted, none of them have changed, all of them are coming to court.
My old comrades, Michael Warren, Roger Warrum, these are black
lawyers who have fought the fight for a long time, they're there. So
while it's not as broad based as we had hoped it would be, we had
hoped the entire bar would be up in arms about the infringement on
the attorney-client privilege—but as my husband Ralph pointed out,
those lawyers from the fancy law firms are privileged. They don't have
to worry about that privilege. It's only when you represent people
who are over on *Rikers Island* (a well known and notorious prison
in New York) who are powerless and voiceless—then they are not
automatically given the privilege. So we didn't garner that kind of
support, but we've done very well without it.

**Q. Lynne, I expected two things: I expected that this case would
galvanize and sustain the attention of the legal community, because
of the very important potential precedent here; but on the other**

hand, given my years of activism, given my reading of <u>My Life As A Radical Lawyer</u>, by Bill Kunstler, and knowing how he received cautionary messages from many of his colleagues in the legal community when he began representing Muslims, I expected that...you know...

A. The people who support me—who come to court, and contribute to the defense committee—they support me absolutely. Are people paying attention to it? Oh yes. I think that there's a lot of attention being paid to it, maybe not as a supporter, but because people want to know, *'Am I going to have to give another three feet to the government,'* because they're always encroaching on the defense function. There is no question that *if this case is lost,* we will lose a lot of the autonomy that lawyers have in defending people. *It then will become very obvious that by setting up a series of prison regulations they can control how you represent someone.*

Would I like a lot of people out there signing petitions, and being very outspoken, and going to bar association meetings, sure; but I also understand that the case has focussed the media attention as it has because it wants to undercut that fear and say, 'It's all going to be okay, because we're watching out for you. You don't have to worry about this.'

Q. New experiences provide new insights. You are someone who has been in the struggle for many years, but this is a new experience for you . As I said during our walk from the courthouse to your office, never would I have expected, years ago when we first met, that I would be coming to a courthouse with you in the dock as a defendant. This is a new experience (for both of us), and no doubt you are gleaning new insights from this experience. How would you advise the community—especially the Muslim community, which is bearing the brunt of this Post 911 madness, this so-called "War on Terrorism" - what would you say to the community in light of this case, and other similar cases around the country?

A. I think the first lesson I learned in this case was to step outside the usual parameters that constrain us; by that I mean, most defendants are told, 'Don't speak to the press.' But from the very first day I've been speaking out; **because in cases like this the government counts on people not talking about the case, not making a public statement** out of the case. Even though I know from many, many immigrants, and people who are not familiar with this system of justice, and who come from a place where to step out and say 'I'm fighting the government,' means to end up in a torture chamber—still in all, to me, if the person has the right lawyer, that is the thing to do. If the person can't do it himself then empower the lawyer to do it for him; to speak out, to go public, to make sure that people understand that you're not isolated; that this case isn't one of a kind, that there are others happening—that people need to focus on what the government is doing as a whole.

*I think the scariest thing about what is happening is the isolation we all sense;* that I'm alone in all of this. Am I the only one thinking like this? I hope that to some degree I've been an example of the goodness that comes with speaking out – that people come to support you, that this empowers other people, like jurors, hopefully, to do the right thing. That's one lesson.

The other lesson I've learned—and of course I'm in a little different position being a lawyer—is not to be constrained, as a defendant, from speaking to your lawyer and saying, *'Look, this is how I want to do the case.*

*I don't want to plea bargain and go talk to the government, I want to fight the case. I want to do it in a way that's principled, I don't want to point at my codefendants and say they did it,* I don't even speak Arabic.' My lawyer has said that more times than I would have liked, perhaps (that Lynne doesn't speak Arabic), but he also has a duty to defend me.

I had to learn to be more passive in the courtroom, that I'm not conducting this trial; I have counsel who is very able, but it provides a different perspective. I understand better how clients feel when they're sitting there and they've put all of their trust and hope into the lawyer. It really is an *awsome responsibility* to be a lawyer.

I was asked on the witness stand, if you may remember, would I do it again? Would I take a press release from Sheikh Omar and make it public? And you know, I had a moment there - because I thought about what terrible destruction this case has brought to my practice as a lawyer, to my wonderful family who love me so much, to my friends – and I thought, could I visit this upon them knowing that the government might do what it's doing; and I ended up saying, 'I'd like to think I would. Because it was the right thing to do, it still is the right thing to do.

**Q. This final question segweys from the observation you just made about attorneys and clients. Unfortunately these days, Lynne, I come into contact with too many cases around the country involving Muslims who for the first time in their lives are finding themselves at the mercy of a process they don't really understand. I'm also seeing far too many practicing attorneys who have become involved in these cases who are just like *sharks in bloody water.* I wish that we had attorneys like you in every city that we could refer**

people to, when calls come in from time-to-time for assistance or advice. But there aren't. What would you advise the Muslim community to do in order to better safeguard themselves from being exploited by these sharks?

And secondly, how would you advise young Muslim (and non-Muslim) law students who approach me for advise when I speak at some of the nation's colleges and universities? Young people who want to become involved, and who are looking for direction.

A. I do believe, and I know that it's asking much of the mosques, as well as people who attend the *mosque*, but it is possible to *set up educational classes*. For example, the local lawyers guild could send some lawyers to talk about what people's rights are if there's a knock at the door from immigration, or the FBI, the local police, whoever it's from – so that there's some point of reference for people, they know what their rights are. I have to also say that another great safe-guard, and what I did when I was first arrested is, to get in touch with the *National Lawyers Guild*. I can't speak for every legal organization in the country, I can speak for the Lawyers Guild, and I know they are there. They were there when the government vamped on the Communists. I know that they are there today for people, they still remain there; and they are a tremendous resource of course. I think that there is a chapter in just about every city.

Along with that is the *Arab American Anti-Defamation Committee* (ADC), that was founded by Abdeen Jabara, whose name has been mentioned so often, I think that they also have literature or something to direct people on how to defend their rights. Some of it is **education**, because some people have no idea. They think a knock at the door is synonymous with being taken away, and I think with the government we have right now it may become that way, but it's not quite there yet.

The thing that I say to most people when I speak to groups is, understand that you don't have to speak to them; you don't have to be nasty, you don't have to slam the door in peoples face, but you can say I'm not speaking to you. If you want a lawyer to call, give me your card and I'll have a lawyer call you. That of course invites the next question, which you just made—*where do we find a lawyer* to call back? That is a very, very, hard question. I don't know if I can answer that question, I just have to hope that there are people of good will, and that some how or other we'll get them all together.

But I go back again to the [National Lawyers] Guild. I do know the Guild; I know that most of their members are people who are *dedicated to people*, not to money, not to things, not to the institutions. But I think its got to be *a combination of educating the community and developing power*; getting together and making elected representatives accountable... I think our elected representatives are out there running without any thought of who put them in power, who keeps them in power, they're just not responsive at all—they vote whatever way the man upstairs tells them to vote. But that's a bigger question for a bigger day.

The question regarding the young people, all I can say is go to law school, get the best marks you can get, get good training in a *public defenders* office, or even a *prosecutors* office; and then when you get out try to apprentice yourself, in whatever way, to lawyers who are dedicated to this work—people like Michael Tigar, like [the late] Bill Kunstler was, like myself—people who can point you in the right direction. It isn't easy, because they have tremendous debt coming out of law school that they have to pay back. It isn't easy because jobs are not all that easy to come by. It takes a lot of guts these days to hang out a shingle, unless you're going to *steal* from people—which of course is what *lawyering* is, someone said, a *license to steal*—while people need to be able to trust lawyers. Still in all there's room for everybody, and if you have that fire in your belly to do it, you'll find a place to accommodate that kind of fire.

For more information on the case: www.lynnestewart.org

**My Knowledge of the Defendants**

This writer has known Lynne Stewart and Ahmed Abdel Sattar for a number of years. I first met them, along with former U.S. Attorney General Ramsey Clark through Sheikh Omar's case. (We all consider Sheik Omar to be a political prisoner in America.) Our initial ties were deepened when a Muslim brother by the name of Nasser Ahmed—also connected with Sheikh Omar as a paralegal—became a victim of America's growing anti-Muslim bias after Omar's imprisonment.

I've always known Lynne and Ahmed to be two deeply committed and courageous individuals, for whom I've had an abiding respect. And thus, when I first learned of Ahmed's arrest, with the climate being what it is, I couldn't really say I was surprised.

I don't recall ever meeting Mohamed Yousry until their trial; but he is probably a good man as well. (*Birds of a feather tend to flock together.*)

As Lynne indicated in our interview, Ahmed faced the most serious charges of the three. Tragically, he and his co-defendants were found guilty on all counts. Do I believe he is guilty of "plotting to murder and kidnap" people overseas? No. The government did not prove its case in my opinion. Is he committed to doing whatever he can to help bring about much needed social and political reform in his native country of Egypt? Yes, I do believe that he is deeply committed to such endeavors—but until I see the clear evidence to suggest otherwise, *within the limits of Islam*!

Ahmed grew up in Cairo and joined the Egyptian Army in 1979. After a two-year stint he was honorably discharged. During his testimony in the trial he described the Egyptian government as oppressive and intolerant of political expression, and noted the fact that violence is a two way street. ("*Some people in Egypt react to the violence of the government.*") He also testified that he met Sheikh Omar at a Brooklyn masjid in 1990, but did not get to know him well until he began driving him regularly to the mosque about two years later.

Ahmed testified to having moved to the United States in 1982, he married Lisa, a Chicago native (who later embraced Islam) in 1985, and joined the U.S. Postal Service in 1988. Some of the most moving and emotional testimony during the trial came from *non-Muslim postal workers*, friends of Ahmed and his family, who came into the court in a *terrorism* case, to testify on Ahmed's behalf (as character witnesses).

Ahmed testified that he showed up in early 1993 at an immigration hearing for the Sheik, and tried to explain to the U.S. media that the Sheik was "not a religious fanatic." He did not fear speaking out on Sheik Omar's behalf, even after being questioned by the FBI on three separate occasions—twice before the February 1993 bombing of the World Trade Center, and once soon afterward when he permitted the FBI to swab his hand for any traces of chemical residues. There were none.

Not long after the February 10, 2005, guilty verdicts for all three defendants, a controversy erupted. A juror revealed that she had been unduly pressured to vote guilty with the other jurors, and allegations arose that another juror had lied about his past. U.S. District Judge John G. Koeltl, however, in a 54 page ruling, rejected defense arguments for a new trial and upheld the verdict.

## Legal Update

Lynne Stewart, Mohamed Yousry, and Ahmed Abdel Sattar were sentenced on October 16, 2006. Lynne was sentenced to 28 months imprisonment, though she (thankfully) remains free on bond pending the outcome of her appeal. Mohamed Yousry, I believe, was sentenced to one year and eight months. While his case attracted the least amount of interest out of the three, in some respects it was far more significant. Mohamed was a court-appointed interpreter and translator, following the lead of court appointed counsel. It appears that his only "crime" was to translate a letter as part of his court appointed duties!

Ahmed Abdel Sattar was sentenced to 24 years and is currently being held at the supermax prison in Florence, Colorado. In addition to his wife, Ahmed's family consists of three sons and a daughter. The two oldest sons are now in college and the youngest son and daughter have entered high school. Ahmed has 15 minutes each month to visit with his family by telephone.

What follows is the text of two important statements. The first is a written appeal to U.S. District John G. Koeltl, by Ahmed Sattar's daughter (Amina), for merciful consideration before the sentencing of her father. Amina's passionate appeal underscores the very personal toll that cases like this are having on Muslim families across the nation.

Amina's letter to Judge Koeltl is followed by Lynne Stewart's triumphant statement (all things considered) to her jubilant supporters on the day of sentencing. (The text of Lynn's statement comes courtesy of Democracy Now.)

Dear Judge Koeltl,

Having my father gone is like having a part of my body gone I can't live without it. My father is more then you think he is. He is not just a man who is in jail and he is not a dangerous man. He is a father and a husband in a family who misses him very much. Not only is he in jail, he is isolated when he shouldn't be. It hurts to know that my father won't be there when we graduate or when it is our birthday, he is not there because you and the rest of the people think he is a "dangerous man". If you look at him and I mean really look at him you will see what I mean. You will see that he is hurting because there is a wall blocking him from the only thing he ever cared for, his family. He always would help a person in need. If you keep him in jail not only will be hurting him but you will be hurting his children and his wife. When I heard he was in jail my heart sank tears came streaming down my face and my mothers face. When I leave from the visit it hurts that he won't be walking though those doors with us.

Every day I look at my mother and see her pain even underneath her smile I see what she is feeling. I see that she is hurt just like the rest of my family. I see that she wants someone to talk to when we are at school and she is left alone. When my father would come home from work I remember jumping up and down and hugging him and kissing him and him hugging me. And since he was taken away I will never feel that feeling again. When I would come home he would always want to know how my day was and what happened that day.

If you have kids, I don't know, but if you do, God forbid one of them had to be sent to Europe or Egypt. And you can only see them once a month or once a year wouldn't you feel isolated would you feel like that there is hole in side of you that can't be filled? Well that's how my family and I feel. I just can't stand the fact that only my mom will be there to make me feel better or help me with homework, or most of all to pick me up when I'm down. Yes he may be in jail and yes you may think he is dangerous but he is kind and he is a wonderful man. Just please if my father was home I would be the happiest girl in the world. So please I beg you to listen to what we are saying and let him come home sooner rather than never.

Thank you very much.

## The Statement of Lynne Stewart

This is a moment that I share with every supporter that came, that called, that sent me a card, that stopped me in the street. It's the cab drivers who gave me the thumbs up this morning. It's everybody who had some role to play in this. I am very grateful to the judge that he gave me time off for good behavior, and he gave it to me in advance of the sentence, when he said that *my extraordinary work meant that I could not get a sentence that the government wanted.* They were disappointed, but I tell you, he did a fair and right thing, and I am grateful to him, but I am more grateful to the peo-ple—the people who showed up today, the people who have showed up, the people who had the meetings, the people who had dinners in their apartments, the people who raised funds, whatever it was. The support and love of the people is what has sustained me.

I am standing here with three of my 14 grandchildren. My lawyers pointed out to the judge that under new regulations, the government could have forbade me to ever see them again. This is how we have become in this country. And I hope the government realizes their error, because I am back out and I am staying out until after an appeal that I hope will vindicate me, that I hope will make me back into the lawyer I was.

Any regrets? I don't think anybody would say that going to jail for two years is something you look forward to, but as my clients have said to me, I can do that standing on my head. No, the circle continues. We are going to go on. We have more struggle there. *This is a time that cries out for renewed resistance* to a government that is not only overreaching in a case like mine—I am the point person—but to a government that overreaches into all our lives.

I see the people before me today. We are not torturers. They are torturers, and we have to stop the torture. I do hope that we will be vindicated on appeal. We are surely going to take a militant and timely appeal, and there are plenty of issues, and we hope that that will be the result.

But I tell you, it is such a feeling of relief. I had my medications, my book. I had a pair of sweatpants to change into, because I was prepared for the worst. But like all Irish people, you prepare for the worst, something good happens. And something good did happen.

## THE TRIALS OF DR. SAMI AL-ARIAN

The case of Dr. Sami al-Arian is one of the most important cases in the country. It's about academic freedom; it's about the vitality of the first amendment; and it's about how much influence a foreign government (in this case, Israel) should have in the domestic and foreign policy of the United States of America.

At the time of this writing the case has gone to the jury, after many months of a trial that consisted primarily (on the government's side) of the reading of pages and pages of significantly redacted transcripts, and a handful of Israeli citizens brought in to provide highly emotional and prejudicial impact statements on how they have been affected by acts of terrorism; this despite the fact that none of the defendants—Sami al-Arian, Ghassan Ballut, Sameeh Hammoudeh, and Hatim Fariz, have been charged with committing acts of terrorism!

We have written much about this tragic saga over the years, beginning with the political imprisonment of Dr. Sami al-Arian's brother-in-law, **Dr. Mazen al-Najjar**. It became our belief during Mazen's ordeal, that the real target all along was Sami al-Arian! (As we believe Dr. Ali al-Tamimi was always the main target during the Paintball Case.)

The government took its time in building a web of legal entanglement for Dr. al-Arian, because he was a respected academic, a legal resident of the U.S., and an influential leader in the Muslim community on a first name basis with people in high places. That said, we feel the reader would be best served by reading an excellent post-trial interview of Dr. Sami al-Arian, conducted by the award winning investigative journalist John Sugg.

## Al-Arian Speaks

*In his first interview since the trial began, Sami Al-Arian talks about what the jury didn't hear.*

The Hillsborough County jail on Orient Road, a monument of austere institutional concrete, is the home of sorrows. I was there last week to see Sami Al-Arian, arguably the most famous man in Tampa nowadays and one who should be among the most sorrowful, facing what could be life imprisonment for daring to be an advocate for his people.

As I waited in the lobby, watching the often tearful parents and wives and children of prisoners, I was thinking of an article I'd just read—trying to get my mind off of the Al-Arian case, a subject I've written about, and been sued over (winning the case), for a decade. The article was about famed scientist Carl Sagan, and he was quoted as saying: "If you want to make an apple pie from scratch, you must first create the universe."

That's a good metaphor, I thought, for the Al-Arian case. At what point do we have the beginning, the creation of the peculiar legal universe in which Al-Arian is now an unhappy denizen? The answer is the difference between Al-Arian being a passionate advocate or being a terrorist.

Was it when the government began wiretapping the academic in the early 1990s? When pseudo-journalist Steven Emerson captured Al-Arian on tape in the 1994 agit-prop film Jihad in America? Perhaps it was on April 21, 1995, when Tampa Tribune reporter Michael Fechter first began targeting the Palestinian professor—by trying to hang the Oklahoma City bombing on Muslims, specifically Al-Arian?

My exclusive interview with Al-Arian—the first media op he has agreed to since the trial began—produced several nuggets of information, including what can only be called reckless endangerment of Al-Arian's life by federal marshals.

Throughout the interview, Al-Arian - dressed in blue jail garb, thinner and paler than when I last saw him four years ago—remained upbeat and animated. "I'm optimistic," he predicted about the trial's outcome.

Al-Arian also raised issues of why the government is prosecuting him now. Officials have claimed that it wasn't until intelligence agencies were able to share material—resulting from the so-called PATRIOT Act - that wiretaps were made available to the prosecution.

"The case would not have been brought except for three things," Al-Arian said. "First there was 9/11 and then [Attorney General John] Ashcroft.

"Despite what the government says, we know they were sharing the information," Al-Arian said. "We found an original indictment, from August of 2000 [when Al-Arian's brother in law, Mazen Al-Najjar, was fighting deportation at a hearing that amounted to a prequel of the current trial]. It had almost all of the same overt acts as the current indictment, and that came from wiretaps. It wasn't the PATRIOT Act.

"But [then-Attorney General] Janet Reno wouldn't go for it," Al-Arian said.

The third factor was lead FBI agent Kerry Myers. "He's a zealot," Al-

Arian said. *"When he arrested me, he came up behind me and whispered in my ear, 'You're charged with terrrrr-orrrrrr-issssmmmmm.'"*

Al-Arian's thoughts on the cause of his prosecution—or persecution—were tops on my agenda. And, had he lied to me and others about his involvement with the Palestinian Islamic Jihad?

"I didn't tell you and others everything," he said. "I said I was part of a movement. Some parts of the movement went one way, some another. That was true. But I didn't tell you other things, but I promise you someday I will."

[My notes from several interviews show that when I asked Al-Arian if he was a member of the PIJ, he responded, "No." However, he always expanded that answer by saying he was part of a broad intellectual movement, in which some of the people became violent and others didn't.]

During closing arguments, federal prosecutor Terry Zitek proclaimed his version of the big bang that began the crusade against Al-Arian.

The PIJ, Zitek told jurors, "wanted Israelis to give up their land from the river to the sea." And if the Israelis balked, Zitek contended, the PIJ "would kill them."

The government whistled Dixie and neglected to show the involvement of Al-Arian or his co-defendants, **Ghassan Ballut, Hatim Fariz** and **Sameeh Hammoudeh**, in violence—and, in fact, conceded that the men weren't engaged in actual acts of terrorism.

The federales have had help with their strategy. *U.S. District Judge James Moody has allowed only testimony backing Zitek's view of what precipitated the trial,* the spin from one side in the tragic events in the Middle East. Even a United Nations resolution mentioned in the government's own exhibits was not allowed to be explained in the closing arguments—because the document might provoke sympathy for Palestinians.

As I sat down on an uncomfortable plastic chair, facing Al-Arian through what looked like four inches of glass, I'd brought a piece of information. I was curious whether Al-Arian thought the jurors in his case had been privileged to see the same data: **The Israeli human rights organization B'Tselem reports that more than 3,300 Palestinians, almost 700 of them children, have been slain by Israelis in the last five years. Fewer than 1,000 Israelis, including about 120 kids, have been killed by Palestinians.**

Al-Arian: "That's the context. That's what Americans never hear. Who is getting killed, who is killing. That's what people [in America] never hear. All they hear is that Palestinians bomb civilians, but almost never that Israelis kill our children. You tell me, why will no one in America ever talk about the terrorism we have lived with" since 1948? Good question.

More context the jurors never heard: Israel has been caught repeatedly spying on the United States. In 1967, **Israel intentionally attacked the USS Liberty, killing 34 American servicemen** (and claims by Israel that it was a mistake were labeled as "ridiculous" by the former chairman of the Joint Chiefs of Staff, Adm. Thomas Moorer). In 1954, Israel set up a spy ring to attack American and British targets—and blame the terrorism on Arabs; old history, maybe, but Israel recently honored the terrorists involved in what is called the

"Lavon Affair."

By comparison, Palestinians have never targeted America—although Moody let the jurors hear unproven and highly prejudicial innuendo from FBI agent Kerry Myers that such an attack was planned. Here are excerpts from the interview with Al-Arian. Some parts have been withheld at his and his attorneys' request pending the jury verdict. My questions aren't verbatim, but include context from the conversation.

.

Q: How do you feel?
A: Well, yesterday, when they [marshals] were bringing me back [to the jail] they hit a car. They were speeding, going fast and had to stop. I didn't have a seatbelt on. They only cared about handcuffing me, not about safety. [Al-Arian's wife, Nahla, was at the interview, and added that he had been thrown around in the car, hitting his head.]

Q: What do you think about the progress of the trial, the likely verdict?
A: From day one, this has been a political case. There's no way the so-called evidence proves what the government claims.

Q: The jury?
A: It depends on [juror] 325. [Other jurors have reported that one of their colleagues, No. 325, has tried to prejudice them against Al-Arian. Judge Moody, for inexplicable reasons, has allowed this tainting influence to remain on the jury.]

Q: If you're acquitted?
A: My family. What is really hard is the suffering of my family. That is my first priority. Then [Al-Arian gave a big smile and put both palms on the glass barrier] I want to get a law degree.

**Q: Do you think the Tribune's Michael Fechter has been vindicated?**
A: No. The mistakes he made then are still mistakes. He wasn't working alone. He was on a first-name basis [with the federal agents]. Who gave him the Al-Shatti letter? [Fechter obtained a letter from agents—a letter Al-Arian claimed was never sent, and which prosecutors couldn't prove otherwise—that solicited funds from a Kuwaiti official. More on the Tribune's faulty reporting can be found here.

**Q: Did you want to testify?**
A: Yes. I have an answer to every single thing, every single transaction. For every penny, I have an explanation.

**Q: What do you think of the legal process?**
A: The system is absolutely not fair. There were 400 [wiretapped] conversations I wanted the jury to hear. Where I say this is not a religious war. My own words about Jews. My involvement with American politicians. In one conversation, June 19, 2002, I condemned [a terrorist attack]. But I can't bring that into court. Moody wouldn't allow that. Only the government could introduce conversations. If we wanted to introduce tapes of my own words, Moody said I would have to testify, which is what the government wanted.

And, the judge introduced agent Myers as an expert witness. He testified for six weeks on everything as an expert. But when it came our turn to ask questions, Moody says he was a "summary" witness [just summarizing evidence], and we couldn't go deep into his investigation. Again, how fair is that?

**Q: Your attorneys have depicted you as splitting from the PIJ as it became violent in the mid-1990s. Is that accurate?**
A: Yes, of course. April 28, 1994. There are no calls dealing with the PIJ after April 28. None.

**Q: The government claims the conspiracy was going on until just a few years ago. Did you realize you were under surveillance?**
A: I've listened to you on the tapes. When you would call me, you'd say, 'Hello Sami, hello Barry.'" [Barry Carmody was the original FBI agent on the case.] Yes, I knew they were watching.

## Update

Since the government's stunning defeat in this multi-million dollar, high profile case, Sami Al-Arian's situation has worsened. What follows is a very personal, well written, chronological recap of this troubling case, which brings the reader all the way up to the present. The author is Laila Al-Arian, the daughter of Dr. Sami Al-Arian. For additional information on the case, please visit: www.freesamialarian.com

## My father, 9/11 Scapegoat

> *"If they can kill each other during Ramadan, they can appear before the grand jury. I am not going to put off Dr. Al-Arian's grand jury appearance just to assist in what is becoming the Islamization of America."*—federal prosecutor Gordon Kromberg

> *"The conditions under which Dr. Al-Arian has been detained both during his pre-trial detention, and since his sentencing appear to be unacceptably harsh and punitive."*—Amnesty International

My father, a Palestinian professor named Sami Al-Arian, was arrested over four years ago on trumped up terrorism charges and submitted to a prosecution over the course of six months that bordered on the farcical. Though he was ultimately acquitted by a jury of the most serious charges against him, the Bush administration has prolonged his imprisonment indefinitely. My father now languishes in a Virginia jail, another victim of the demagogic politics of the so-called *war on terror.*

Many have wondered why my father would be targeted so vigorously, especially after the government lost a case that cost $50 million. But as with its firing of the eight federal prosecutors who "chafed" against its radical agenda, the administration of President George W. Bush has injected its politics into the system, prolonging my father's imprisonment to punish him for the humiliation his acquittal caused them.

Last month, my father completed a 60-day hunger strike to protest his continued imprisonment that left him in such a weakened state he was confined to a wheelchair. Soon after receiving medical treatment, he was transferred to a Federal Correctional Institute in Petersburg, Virginia. Upon my father's arrival, a prison guard remarked while strip-searching him: "Where are you from? Afghanistan?" Though my father refused to answer the demeaning question, the guard repeated it several times. He went on:

> "It doesn't matter where you're from. If I had my way, you wouldn't be in prison. I'd put a bullet in your head and get it done with. You're nothing but a piece of s***."

This is not the first time this guard harassed my father. In January, he told him: "You're a terrorist. I can tell by your name."

This time there was a witness to the abuse, though he wasn't exactly a friendly one. Upon hearing his underling's outburst, the lieutenant in charge took my father aside and shackled his arms and legs. The shackles were so tight my father lost sensation in his extremities for the duration of the four-hour trip to his final destination, a detention center in Alexandria. On the way, the lieutenant joined in the abuse, unleashing a stream of obscenities at my father and repeatedly telling him to "Shut the f*** up." When they arrived, the lieutenant violently shoved my father against a wall.

The human rights group *Amnesty International* has condemned the government's treatment of my father. "The conditions under which Dr. Al-Arian has been detained both during his pre-trial detention, and since his sentencing," Amnesty wrote in a February letter to the Attorney General, "appear to be unacceptably harsh and punitive."

My father immigrated to the United States in 1975 and eventually earned tenure as a computer engineering professor at the University of South Florida. As the son of Palestinians forcibly removed from their land after the creation of Israel in 1948, he considered it his obligation to bring attention to the plight of the Palestinian people from his position of influence in the United States. He held conferences and published literature to tell the story of Palestinians living under occupation.

His activism earned the ire of some of the most reactionary figures of the right, from self-declared "terror experts" like Steven Emerson to Bill O'Reilly, whose expertise on Middle Eastern affairs apparently does not extend to the falafel.

As the shrill cries for my father's prosecution intensified after 9/11, the Bush administration arrested him. According to an anonymous FBI source, Attorney General John Ashcroft personally ordered the indictment against my father, a mandate that puzzled the many career professionals assigned to the case. The political nature of the charges was apparent from the beginning. A jury empaneled by the federal government would reach the same conclusion three years later, concluding that the Bush administration's case was not much of a case at all.

But first my father would suffer under extremely restrictive, inhumane conditions clearly meant to psychologically break him before trial, including being placed in solitary confinement for 27 months. At one point, he was denied phone calls for six months, and while convicted felons were allowed to hug their families, my father, a pre-trial detainee, had to visit us behind glass. Even then, he was strip-searched before and after our visits. The cards were stacked against us.

When my father's trial finally began in June 2005, the government presented 71 witnesses, including nearly two dozen from Israel, paraded before the jury for sheer emotional effect. Four hundred phone calls out of half a million the government recorded during a decade of relentless, indiscriminate surveillance of my family were also presented. The prosecutors acted out the phone calls on the 13th floor of a courtroom in downtown Tampa, giving new meaning to the phrase political theater.

The government's evidence against my father largely consisted of speeches he gave, magazines he edited, lectures he presented, articles he wrote, books he owned (4 out of 5,000), conferences he organized, rallies he attended, and news he heard. In one particularly bizarre instance, the prosecutors presented as evidence a conversation a co-defendant had with my father in a dream.

Some of my father's detractors say that his criticism of Israel was overly strident. Often they deliberately de-contextualize his remarks, made nearly two decades ago, to undermine the credibility of the Palestinian narrative they have long sought to suppress. But whatever you think about the Israeli-Palestinian conflict, you hopefully agree that the criminalization of political speech is un-American and violates the letter and spirit of the Constitution.

Because the government based its case on my father's expressed political views, our lawyers rested without presenting a single witness. Our defense was the First Amendment.

On Dec. 6, 2005, my father was acquitted of 8 of the 17 charges against him, though the jury voted 10 to 2 for full acquittal. Those holding out for conviction were the only two who listed themselves as readers of the *Tampa Tribune*, a paper which had slandered him for over a decade. Two of my father's three co-defendants were fully acquitted; **the jury did not return a single guilty verdict in over 100 charges.** The verdict was a testament to the hollow nature of government's case--an especially strong statement in the midst of post 9/11 hysteria.

Following the trial, the government had the option of dropping the charges against my father, but chose not to, once again revealing the political nature of his case. At the same time, they decided to casually drop tax-evasion charges against the founder of Hooters whose jury split evenly on his conviction.

Facing the prospect of a new trial that would drain my family emotionally and financially, my father decided to plead guilty to one charge of nonviolently supporting a designated terrorist group. In return, the government signed a plea agreement promising to drop the remaining charges, recommend the minimum sentence (which would have basically amounted to time-served) and allow my father to walk free on the condition that he leave the country. Disregarding the prosecutors' recommendation and dismissing the jury's verdict, the judge in the case gave my father the maximum sentence, which pushed his release date to this month. (April 2007).

Sadly, our story does not end there. An overzealous federal prosecutor with a documented record of bigoted remarks against Muslims, Gordon Kromberg, is trying to force my father to testify before a grand jury in Virginia in direct violation of his plea agreement. This is a ploy to bring further charges against my father and prolong his imprisonment and our suffering as much as possible. Kromberg himself bitterly referred to the plea agreement as a "bonanza" for my father.

Shortly before the Muslim observance of Ramadan began last October, Kromberg revealed an ulterior political motive behind his prosecution. When my father's attorney requested to delay a prison transfer during the holy month, a time he would have liked to spend with visits from his family, Kromberg responded:

> "If they can kill each other during Ramadan, they can appear before the grand jury. I am not going to put off Dr. Al-Arian's grand jury appearance just to assist in what is becoming the *Islamization of America.*"

Kromberg's racist outburst clearly calls his objectivity into question. Another reason my father has been reluctant to testify before a grand jury is because we fear Kromberg is setting up a perjury trap. The prosecutor did just that with another Muslim defendant in

Virginia, who was acquitted by a federal judge. Following his acquittal, Kromberg summoned him to testify before a grand jury and charged him with making false statements when he didn't like his answers. The man, **Sabri Benkhala**, is now facing 25 years in prison.

My father has endured a decade of surveillance and government harassment, a draining six month trial, and the demonization of his entire family by self-serving right-wing demagogues, all the while hoping his nightmare would end. It should have when he was acquitted by a jury and the government promised his freedom. Surely, the fulfillment of that promise is not too much to ask.

## THE CASE OF ASHRAF AL-JAILANI

One weekend in Ramadan (the sacred month of the fast) while enroute to a couple of speaking engagements in northeastern Pennsylvania, I decided to make a stop at the York County Prison in York, Pennsylvania. I wanted to see if a Muslim of Yemeni descent, Ashraf al-Jailani, was still imprisoned there. My hope was to be informed that Ashraf was long gone; that he had been released months ago back into the loving embrace of his family—a wife, two young daughters and a son. This, unfortunately, would not be the case.

What I discovered instead was that in addition to Ashraf still being in the custody of our "freedom" touting government, he had just received word that the December 2004 decision of the Immigration Court – which once again had ordered his release - was overturned by the Falls Church (VA) based *Board of Immigration Appeals* (BIA), on October 17, 2005. Consequently, he was subject to deportation within 30 days unless he appealed the BIA decision to the Third

Circuit Court of Appeals in Philadelphia, PA. And if he lost that appeal, Ashraf's days in America would be numbered.

Saturday, October 22, 2005, marked the third anniversary of Ashraf's unjust detention at York. The headline of an Associated Press article on page eight of the Pottsville (PA) Republican & Herald newspaper read: *"Suspected terrorist held in York: Man from Ohio faces deportation to native country of Yemen."*

While the report noted, "Federal investigators first became interested in al-Jailani in 1999, when his business card was discovered with a suspected terrorist in New York," I was pleased to see that the report also noted, "Al-Jailani has not been charged, and he says he is being held without cause." Indeed he is; and this three year detention (without charge) has taken an enormous and very personal toll on Ashraf and his family.

My short visit with Ashraf lifted his spirits; and yet the anguish of all the uncertainties was still etched across his face. What would become of him? Will he be sent back to Yemen after so many years in the United States? What would become of his family? Would he ever see them again beyond the plexi-glass of the visiting wing of a jail? Toward the end of our visit he asked me to give one of the leaders of the Islamic Center in the Kent, Ohio, area a message. If I'm sent back, ask him to please take care of my family. As he said these words, tears welled up in his eyes.

In the three years that this living nightmare has gone on, Ashraf's wife (Michelle) has been hospitalized three times. Their three young children were taken away and placed in foster-care; the first time landing in the temporary custody of an "evangelical Christian" family who were reportedly very antagonistic toward Islam and Muslims. There have also been a number of "Family Court" battles, as the agency has attempted to permanently wrest custody of the children away from their mother.

In addition to these emotional battles, there has also been the struggle of trying to make ends meet, when the primary breadwinner has been cruelly snatched away. Thank God that there has been a small, but very committed, network of friends, especially non-Muslims, who have formed a ring of support around this beleaguered family. (Of special note is a grassroots organization known as the *Immigrant Support Network*.)

On Saturday, October 22nd a support rally was held at the Islamic Center of Akron-Kent (OH) to mark the third anniversary of Ashraf's wrongful imprisonment. Ashraf prepared a statement to be shared at the gathering. At the conclusion of our visit the day before, Ashraf gave me his original copy, which reads as follows:

Dear Friends:

I would like to thank you all very much for all of your prayers and support for me and especially for my family. It has been three years now that I have been in Prison, separated from my lovely wife Michele, my daughter's Amina and Laya, and 'Mr. Sami' my dear son. I really miss them all beyond your imagination.

It is hard to believe that those kids were just 6, 4 and 2 years old respectively, and now they are growing up so fast before my very eyes. It was hard missing my children's first day at school. It is hard to not be able to hug and embrace my family. My wife Michele, what can I possible say about her. She is my best friend. She has endured much for the sake of our family and I would always cherish her, love her, care and honor her.

This predicament has taken a heavy toll on my family whom I have not seen now in over a year, and that was even behind a glass screen, unable to even touch them. It is hard to believe that I am still going through this dilemma, after being granted a full pardon by the governor of this great State of Ohio, granted the least bail amount of $1500 by the Immigration Court three times. I must also mention that after this bail amount, I won my case before a competent judge that found me not to be a threat to the community, and in his last decision of December 17, 2004, he ordered that I be released after granting the relief. Yet still the government does not want to release me; however, on the other hand they release other people with very serious crimes.

I must say, it is difficult to fathom such abuse and denial of fundamental due process in a great country like the United States of America. I quite understand the mentality that was derived after 911, but I must again reiterate that my only dilemma is being a Muslim Arab. One must remember that we all came from the same patriarch father, Abraham, thus we are all related by blood, despite our ethnic differences. There are moments when I get lost in my thoughts, unaware of my surroundings, then suddenly the sound of handcuffs and clanking keys brings me back to the reality of my situation, which saddens and makes me miserable, and leaves me with a deep yearning for my family.

It appears that the United States government is discriminating against a certain class of U.S. citizens. These classes of U.S. citizens are those that have built their families with foreign nationals. Why should my wife Michele be subjected to this treatment just because she is married to a Muslim Arab? What is at stake here is "forcible separation" of a non-citizen or spouse (infringing upon) the absolute right to familial integrity and violating marriage law. What about the *family values* that has been widely spoken about? What about the so called *faith based initiative* and so-called *compassionate conservatism* that this administration has so widely spoken about? What do these statements really mean?

It is about time that the government admit to their errors, among which was a quick rush to judgment, and allow me to be reunited with my family, to begin the healing process, because I am a person who is detained without any charge.

My heart-filled thanks goes out to you, all the volunteers who have relentlessly supported my family and I all these years. I am especially very appreciative of the *Immigrant Support Network, Akron and Kent Islamic Society*, my wonderful attorney, Farhad [Sethna], whom I cannot thank enough for his expertise and devotion in this matter.

Thank you so very much and God bless the good people of America.

Sincerely,
Ashraf Al-Jailani

Not long after writing this letter, Ashraf al-Jalani was deported from the United States back to Yemen, resulting in the permanent breakup of a formerly intact family. So much for the Bush Administration's commitment to *family values* and *compassionate conservatism!*

On a final note, the political scandal that the U.S. Department of Justice finds itself embroiled in at present, brought Ashraf Al-Jalani's case to mind (along with a number of others). Of particular note was the reported litmus test that was placed before prospective judges for the *Board of Immigration Appeals* (BIA). Now I understand why, to the best of my knowledge, Muslims who have come before this court have generally had such *consistently* negative outcomes—even when lower immigration courts have ruled repeatedly in their favor. Something to think about.

## THE TRIALS OF DR. ABDELHALEEM ASHQAR

Dr. Abdelhaleem Ashqar is another prominent Palestinian academic who has incurred the wrath of pro-Zionist forces in America. He is a brother in the struggle that I have known for a number of years (I was among those who met him at the airport upon his return from unjust imprisonment in New York, for civil contempt, several years ago). He is a man for whom I have a very deep and abiding respect.

Abdelhaleem is a gentle and peaceful man, of resolute and noble spirit. He is not a terrorist! Despite the threat of being turned over to the Apartheid State of Israel and tortured for information on others, he has consistently refused to allow his words to be used to facilitate the detention and torture of other innocent Palestinians—who want nothing more than to be able to *breathe free*, and live in peace and security like other human beings.

Twice he has been summoned before a federal grand jury (with a guarantee of immunity) if he would only testify to what he knows about the Palestinian resistance. I've been informed that there were also efforts to bribe him for valuable disclosures; yet he has consistently remained steadfast in faith and determination. What follows is Dr. Ashqar's statement to the second grand jury, which was convened on June 25, 2003. It is a long affidavit. But we decided to publish it in its entirety for a couple of reasons: (1) so that the reader can become acquainted with who this man is (and when his case comes before the court in Chicago, he will be able to enjoy the community support that he so richly deserves; (2) It is our hope that the reader will acquire a deeper understanding of, and empathy for, the Palestinian struggle against a brutal, U.S. supported occupation.

**The Affidavit**

Abdelhaleem Hasan Ashqar, being duly sworn, deposes and says under penalty of perjury that the following statement is true and correct:

1. My name is Abdelhaleem Hasan Abdelraziq Ashqar. My address is 6170 Old Brentford Ct., Alexandria, VA, 22310. My wife, Asmaa Ashqar, and I are Palestinians from the Occupied Territories. Before coming to the United States in 1989, my wife and I lived under the brutal and illegal Israeli military rule in the West Bank and the Gaza Strip. I was employed as an Assistant Professor of Business Administration at Howard University, in Washington, D.C., through the just finished spring, 2003 semester, where I taught undergraduate classes in Operations Management and Quantitative Business Analysis, Management of Information Systems, and Software Design. The publicity surrounding the allegations made by the government against me has cost me my teaching position, as the

University has declined to renew my contract for the fall semester. I am presently unemployed.

2. I submit this Affidavit in support of my refusal to testify before the Grand Jury in the above-captioned matter before the Court.

3. I am a devout Muslim and a politically active Palestinian nationalist, as well as a teacher, writer and academic. Both my father and his father before him were ardent Palestinian nationalists—my father was an outspoken cleric jailed by the British during the period of Mandatory rule before the illegitimate founding of the State of Israel; my grandfather was jailed for six years by the Ottoman Turkish rulers of Palestine for agitating for home rule. My family's tradition is one of struggle for a homeland for our people, free of rule by oppressors. The teachings of the Koran are our guide in this struggle. I will not, under any circumstances, testify before this or any other Grand Jury, whose proceedings I believe to be politically orchestrated against the cause of freedom and independence for Palestinians. I consider myself a patriot, and I will never give testimony that may be used against others who struggle in the cause of freedom for Palestine.

4. In November, 1997, I was subpoenaed to appear before the Grand Jury in the United States District Court for the Southern District of New York, in a case, which purported to investigate money-laundering activities. I complied with the subpoena and appeared before the Court; however, I refused to answer any questions based on my religious, political and personal beliefs. I made the following statement to the Court at that time:

I respectfully refuse to answer any questions put to me other than my name, address and occupation on the grounds that to do so would violate my long-held and unshakable religious, political and personal beliefs and that my answers will be used against my friends, relatives and colleagues in the Palestinian liberation movement. I would rather die than betray my beliefs and commitment to freedom and democracy for Palestine. I will never give evidence or cooperate in any way with this Grand Jury, no matter what the consequences to me.

I was held in civil contempt for my refusal to testify, and in an effort to coerce my testimony; I was jailed on 23 Februrary 1998. I began a hunger strike the first day of my incarceration and continued it until my release 180 days later, as a means of protesting the way the FBI and U.S. Attorney's offices in Mississippi and New York treated me. My case received publicity in leading newspapers, TV and radio around the world, especially in the Arabic-speaking countries. I was force-fed the entire time that I was in jail.

5. My experience with the Court five years ago came at a time of relative calm and hopeful, if illusory, progress in Palestine. It seemed for a brief moment that the Israeli military occupation might soon come to an end. Yet even then, I was adamantly unwilling to testify before the Grand Jury. Today, in the third year of the new intifada against the racist Israeli army and its relentless brutality against Palestinian men, women and children, my hopes for a just resolution to the conflict have been all but shattered. And while many in the world welcome the recent, Bush Administration's so-called "Roadmap to Peace," it is viewed largely by Palestinians as a vehicle to ensure Israeli security and little more, calculated to make the illegal settlements permanent, and achieve the expansionist aims of the occupation under the fraudulent guise of a "peace process." Because of this, I am more resolved than ever to resist any attempts

to force me to testify. I will never acquiesce in the Court's coercion to make me violate my religious and political beliefs. If my incarceration in 1998 taught me anything, it is this: I possess the inner strength of mind and spirit, even if the body should fail, to withstand iron bars and stone walls. No amount of jailing by the Court will compel me to testify against others struggling for Palestinian freedom.

6. Let me be clear: **I view this grand jury, as I did the one in 1998, as a vehicle of the United States government to further the aims of Israel.** As in 1998, my refusal to testify here is not the expression of a desire to obstruct justice or otherwise to interfere with an "investigation." I view this proceeding as an illegal abuse of process designed to chill dissent and to criminalize legitimate and lawful resistance against the Israeli designs on my homeland. As in 1998, the prospect of jail does not diminish my resolve in any way.

7. I was also jailed by the Israeli military in Ramallah in 1981, for participating in a peaceful, lawful demonstration at Beir Zeit University in the West Bank, where I was a student. On that occasion, I was beaten, kicked, struck repeatedly in the head and body with rifle-butts and fists, and soldiers stomped on my bare feet for hours. I was questioned repeatedly, with beatings administered, and ultimately I passed sixteen days in a tiny cell with as many as six other students at a time, and only a small jar in which to urinate. This jailing was far more violent and inhumane than anything the Court is likely to contemplate for me now.

8. It is my view that the current subpoena is only the latest installment of a campaign of harassment orchestrated against me by the Israeli government and mostly carried out by Israeli and U.S. investigators. This ordeal stretches back many years to when, after receiving my

MBA degree, I became a public relations administrator for the Islamic University of Gaza, at the start of the first intifada (1987-1993). At that time, I represented the University on an ad hoc committee of academics publicizing and exposing the Israeli closure of Palestinian universities during an earlier uprising, and trying to rally support for our students among the international academic community. In this respect, I cannot cooperate with the investigation of this Grand Jury because to do so would betray my cause and my people.

9. *It is written in the Koran and in the commentaries on Islamic Law (Sh'aria) that an honest and just person must never give testimony against another if that testimony might hurt that person unjustly, or hurt the witness himself.* This is my religious conviction, and as I am accused of no crime here in the United States, and I have followed the secular laws of this land, I consider myself both honest and sincere. To give testimony before this Grand Jury in a case motivated by Israel to hurt the cause of Palestinian liberation would be to violate that Koranic precept.

10. Both my family and my community support me in my decision not to testify before this Grand Jury. My wife understands my decision and, as in 1998, she knows that I cannot go against my religious and political convictions by giving testimony to help this unjust persecution by Israel of Palestinian and Islamic activists. In 1998, my wife understood the dangers of my hunger strike, and knew that I could possibly die from my incarceration, yet she stood by my decision then and strengthened my resolve. Likewise, the community of my mosque supported my refusal to testify and discussed it in sermons and study groups, praising my resolve and praying that I would have strength to do what had to be done. I know that I will meet with the same level of family and community

support if I am again incarcerated, and I am confident that this support will be as a shield to me against my oppressors.

11. More recently, in Chicago, I gave the following statement to the Grand Jury at my first appearance in this matter, on June 25th, 2003:

I respectfully refuse to answer any question put to me other than my name, address and occupation on several grounds: most important, to do so would violate my long-held and unshakeable religious, political and personal beliefs. Second, any answer I might provide could and would be given to Israel and would be used by Israel against me in an unfair, illegal and politically motivated prosecution for my beliefs and associations and my religion. Third, having been tortured before by Israel for my beliefs, associations, and religion, any answer I might provide could and would be given to Israel which would once again torture me as a result of such answers; and fourth, I have been for years the subject of widespread electronic surveillance which is illegal and being used by the Grand Jury to prepare for and to question me. Approximately, five years ago, I was subpoenaed to appear before a Grand Jury in New York regarding what I believe to be is the same subject matter as this. At that time, I refused to testify and I was held in contempt and jailed for six months. I began a hunger strike as soon as I was jailed and maintained that strike until my release leaving me with permanent medical problems. It is not my intention to obstruct justice or to interfere with any matters under consideration by this Grand Jury. As I said, I cannot answer any question today, just as I refused to do so five years ago for the reasons I have set forth. I cannot and will not permit my answers to be used against my friends, relatives and colleagues who have committed no crimes or wrongs but are being singled out for their involvement in the struggle for our legitimate political rights as recognized under international law. I would rather die than betray my beliefs and commitment to freedom, justice and democracy for Palestine and Palestinians who have been homeless for more than 50 years. I will never give evidence or cooperate in any way with this grand jury, or any other, no matter what the consequences to me.

12. Israel is the only country I can travel to at this time. Though I possess a Jordanian passport, I am not a Jordanian citizen. This passport bears no serial number. It is solely to be used as a travel document, provided by the Jordanian government, with an explicit limit of only thirty days' admittance in the country per entry. The privileges conferred by these documents have since been rescinded. In addition, *my passport expired in March of this year, and Jordan has declined to renew it, even as a travel document.*

13. In December, 1998 *I applied for political asylum* on the grounds that I had a well-founded fear of persecution and worse in Israel. While I was initially granted asylum, subsequently as a result of adverse publicity and government harassment on the part of the United States and at Israel's behest, my interim asylum was suspended. In the years since, we prepared for a full hearing on the question of my political asylum. The work undertaken in that regard was very expensive and time-consuming. It required procuring evidence from the Occupied Territories and experts from throughout the world. On the eve of the hearing, my immigration lawyer advised me that while she thought I had a meritorious claim and a chance of prevailing; in order to do so, it was absolutely necessary that I testify on my behalf. My immigration lawyer was emphatic: if I did not testify I could not prevail. I refused to testify at that

proceeding though it meant that years of effort were wasted, though it meant that I could not receive political asylum, and though it meant that I would have to leave the United States for an uncertain future overseas. I refused to testify at the hearing for the same reason that I refused to testify at the 1998 grand jury proceeding in New York, and for the same reason that I refuse to testify here. I will not be examined about the Palestinian movement for justice, independence and statehood. I will not allow the enemies of my people, whether it be Israel, or in this case, its surrogates here to use me against my people.

14. Because I could not prevail in the absence of my testimony on the application for political asylum, we negotiated a settlement on my status and claim in the United States. I agreed to forfeit any rights that I had to remain in the United States, and I agreed to voluntarily depart the country within a sixty-day period (which I understand has been continued until the resolution of this grand jury and its related matters.) Although my settlement does not dictate that I go to Israel, in reality, as stateless people, without permanent travel documents, Palestinians largely exist under the specter of being forced eventually to return to Israel. (Just a week ago I received a limited visa to travel to the United Arab Emirates for Because of this, and inasmuch as Israel controls all ports of entry to the West Bank and Gaza, I expect eventually to go to Israel. And once there, I fully expect to be questioned, charged, jailed and tortured for my political beliefs.

15. In addition, although I have received immunity for testimony in this proceeding, the immunity of this Court will not in any event under current law prevent Israel from getting access to my testimony before the grand jury, and will not prohibit Israel from using my

own words against me in a proceeding, which will eventually ensue, in that country. Any statements I might make here would certainly be utilized in an Israeli persecution of me. I therefore cannot give any testimony here that might prejudice any future defense I may have to mount against their charges; additionally, any testimony I might give here would certainly be used against other Palestinian nationalists in Israel.

16. The foundations for my belief in an Israeli campaign against me are long-standing and credible. The Israelis have continually targeted me since my arrival in the United States in 1989. The FBI has admittedly acted on their behalf in questioning me on many occasions and the Israeli Army searched the homes of my extended family in the West Bank on two occasions while I was in the United States, in April, 1995, telling my family that they had a warrant for my arrest. There is no way to hide, nor is their any judicial means to protect me if I return to Israel. As established by the material in Appendices A and B1-3, as well as the Affirmation of my attorney Stanley Cohen, there has been an inextricable connection between Israel and the United States in their efforts to target me, and I have been the subject of wholesale electronic surveillance in the US, at the hands of government agencies and at the behest of Israel.

17. The biographical details of my life I set forth here in order to demonstrate that my religious and political beliefs are long-held and unshakable. I was born August 18, 1958 in Seida-Tulkarm in the West Bank, which was then under Jordanian rule. The Israelis captured my town in 1967 when I was nine years old, and since then we have lived under continual Israeli military law and occupation. My father Hasan died of high blood pressure in 1971 at the age of 75 years. He ran the family business in Seida, using the family's

small landholdings to grow olive, black plum, fig, almond and apricot trees. The business grew until 1967 when the Israeli invasion occurred, causing a sharp downturn in fruit prices as Israeli regulations and curfews made transport and delivery to market nearly impossible. Sometimes my father used to sell the black plums at a price far below the transport cost, rather than lose his whole crop in the sun. Though my family had been growing fruit on this land since the 18th century, my father watched his trees slowly wither and die as Israeli water rationing choked off the ability to farm and make a living. My father had spent six months in jail when Palestine was a British colony because of his actions against the British Army, as well as for his political and national views. My grandfather spent six years in jail during the Ottoman Turkish rule for his political views. My father had three sons and three daughters from his first marriage. My eldest brother Rashed passed away in 1991 at 65 years of age. He was arrested for two weeks during the first days of occupation, and he left behind five daughters and two sons. My brother Mohammed who passed away last year at 67 years of age was fully paralyzed since 1990. He had four daughters and a son who all helped his mother in caring for their crippled father while he was alive. My brother Helmi, 60 years old, was a school teacher at Kuwait and had to leave in 1990 after the Iraqi invasion of Kuwait. He is unemployed and has two boys and three girls. My eldest sister Rushdeih, 70 years of age, suffers from heart problems has ten boys and two girls. My sister Rasheeda, who I saw only once over the last twenty-five years, lived in Kuwait from 1968 until earlier this year when she passed away. And my sister Shafiqa who passed away in June of 2001 had four children-two boys and two girls.

18. My mother, Amneh who died in 1989 at 75 years due to breast cancer, was my father's second marriage. She was a widow at the

time of her death and is survived by her daughter, Samira, and myself and a second son. My sister Samira is 50 years of age and has three sons and three daughters; two of her sons are unemployed. My younger brother Moayed 37 years of age, who has been living in Jordan since 1978, has four boys.

19. I attended Seida Elementary School where we used to have three classes in one room and only one teacher in the room. After 1967, all six classes were kept in one room and only one teacher for all six grades. I finished the middle school at Illar's Boys School, which was a four-mile walk each way, every day. I attended high school at Atile Secondary School, finishing in 1977, where I had sometimes to walk 10 miles every day since there was no regular transportation.

20. When the war erupted in 1967, the Israeli army again seized the West Bank, Gaza Strip, the Sinai Peninsula, and East Jerusalem (which they would later annex as part of Israel), striking terror into the community of Palestinians living in these areas. Terror inflicted on non-combatants in the occupied territories in the first weeks of the occupation hastened a mass flight of many camp-refugees. Most of those who fled went to neighboring Jordan, while the bulk of the refugees, numbering nearly three quarters of a million people, were left under army control. But to leave Palestine or to be caught outside the country at the commencement of hostilities, in most cases meant leaving Palestine forever. Israel's policy then forbade re-entry by native Palestinians, as today they will not permit alienated Palestinians to re-settle in the Occupied Territories, effectively completing for them the systematic expulsion from their homeland begun in 1948.

21. Our life became incredibly difficult in 1967—no running water, limited electricity, no sanitation, curfews, limited schools and school

closings and shortages of the basic necessities. We are governed by the occupier's law, much of which had not been committed to writing until very recently; it remains however totally arbitrary often with young soldiers exercising outright power over our lives and aspirations. Israelis have the right to stop us at any time, to detain us and to imprison us without the right to see a lawyer, all in the absence of any due process. We are tried in military courts where the language is Hebrew, though we speak Arabic. There are limited jobs available and most Palestinians work in Israel as industrial or agricultural workers. The per capita income for the Palestinians in the Israeli occupied territories is $1,000 U.S. dollars compared to $16,000 for the Israelis just a few miles away.

22. The Palestinian people, as a whole, are among the best educated in the world, and virtually all of life's instruction for young boys in the 1960's and 1970's took place in the mosque. Attending classes year-round, Islam is the foundation on which all knowledge is built, and grounding in the Koran is a necessary prerequisite to studying any other subject. A Palestinian boy is expected to take his place in the spiritual life of the community alongside the men, and he must be prepared to this end. By day, I would study my lessons, and by night, I often attended lectures by prominent sheiks and religious leaders at the mosque. Often the discussions were about the future of my people, and our duty to live our lives for Allah and an eventual peaceful future for the Palestinians.

23. My father, who was a prominent cleric in my town, was a great early influence on me. He was in charge of a mosque and taught religious instruction, led prayer and gave speeches. Sometimes, I used to lead prayer groups at the mosque, and at other times I volunteered in charitable and service activities.

24. At school, younger instructors, who explained for the boys the concept of Zionism, and the history of Jewish settlements since the 1890's, and expansionist goals of the state of Israel, constantly reinforced Palestinian nationalism. My education at the mosque included ceaseless invocation to love my people, and to cherish the cause of statehood and that only Allah could guide the struggle. I have been a political activist since the day of the Israeli occupation. I fervently believe in the liberation of Palestine. I also am a devout Muslim and hold fervent religious convictions. The teachings from the Koran are my mandate. These values have shaped my opinions and are the overarching determinants of how I live my life and conduct myself.

25. I attended BirZeit University, BirZeit, West Bank in 1978. It is 20 miles north of Jerusalem, in the Ramallah area. I participated in many student demonstrations against the Israeli occupation. I was summoned many times to the Israeli military offices because of my activities. The Israelis closed my university and the other universities in the West Bank and Gaza on a regular basis in the 1970's and 1980's. Also, I was part of the leadership of the student movement at BirZeit. I was a candidate in the Islamic Block for the election on the student council.

26. In one particular demonstration on November 2, 1981 at BirZeit University commemorating the Balfour Declaration (a 1917 British position paper which expressed the Crown's commitment to creating a state for the Jews of Europe in Palestine), the Israelis besieged the University from early morning to the evening. The Administration reached an agreement with the Israelis to let the students leave peacefully and the Israeli military would not intervene. But, after we left the University, the Israelis started to break

into the student's houses to arrest some of us. I was arrested. The Israeli military came to my house, which I shared with 3 roommates. They accused me of participating in the demonstration and protesting. They handcuffed me, did not allow me to put on my shoes, and shoved me into the military car. They were hitting me and kicking me with their hands and the butts of their guns on my body including my knees, head, hands and feet. They stomped on my feet and I did not have shoes to protect them. The Israeli military took me in a military truck with 16 other students to Ramallah Central Jail. They continued to beat us all that night. My feet were bleeding because they kept stomping on them with their military boots and my head was throbbing because they kept wacking it with the butt of their guns. They processed us at the Ramallah Central Jail where other students were being held and accused us of participating in the demonstration and throwing stones. They told us we had 3 choices—plead guilty and go free, identify other students, or face jail. 16 of us went to jail. After 4 days they took us to court. My lawyer was Leah Tsemel who was the attorney for BirZeit University. Leah Tsemel is an Israeli who represents Palestinians because she believes that the occupation is wrong and Palestinians are treated inhumanely. I would not plead guilty and I would not eye witness against others. Those are not my principles. I remained in jail.

27. I was in a cell with 5 other people. The cell was very tiny, maybe 3 yards by 3 yards. It contained mattresses and a jar for use as a bathroom. We were allowed out of it two hours a day. After 6 p.m., we could not leave the cell. There was one shower in the jail where about sixty people were housed. After the student leaders were arrested, the students conducted further protests and the Israelis closed the University for 2 months. The student movement in other Universities conducted demonstrations in support of us. Finally,

there was a lot of pressure on the Israeli government to release us. We were released on the equivalent of $2500 bail. Dr. Hanan Ashwawi—a former chief minister for education in the government of the Palestinian Authority and then the head of the English department at Birzeit University—posted my bail at that time, after sixteen days without charges. I was called to court twice during that time, but my case was postponed and I was never called to the dock.

28. I was summoned many times by the Israeli Intelligence services between 1979 and 1982. I never obeyed their summonses, based on my attorney's advice. On many occasions, my apartment was searched and before certain anniversaries, the Israel military would round up some activists, including myself, in anticipation of protests. I graduated with a Bachelor's Degree in Business Administration in 1982. However, like most Palestinian graduates, I could not get a job in my area. I went to the University of LaVerne, in Athens, Greece, from 1982 -1985. There I obtained a Master's in Business Administration and then returned to the West Bank to become a Lecturer at The Islamic University of Gaza, Gaza Strip. I became Director of the Public Relations Department from September 1986 to November,1989. During this time I was the formal spokesman for the University. I also was the Editor of the University Magazine and presided over the university's editorial committee for the 1987 Annual Book and the university's catalog.

29. I met my wife, Asmaa Jamal Muhanna, in Gaza in 1986, while I was working at the Islamic University of Gaza. My wife comes from a large Gaza City family and was a student at the Islamic University of Gaza.

30. I was appointed at that time by the Islamic University Administration to represent the university in an ad hoc committee

established by the Council for Higher Education in the Israeli Occupied Territories to expose the Israelis procedures against Palestinian academic institutions. The Israelis since the beginning of the uprising in December, 1987 until October, 1991 closed down all academic institutions—universities, schools, community centers, grammar schools and kindergartens. The committee tried to rally support from the western democracies in Europe and the Americas to pressure the Israelis to reopen the schools.

31. I was summoned to the Shin Bet, the Israeli security service, and questioned about my role as the spokesman for the Islamic University and my writings as Editor of the University magazine. I was detained by them and questioned at length. I was threatened with jail and deportation constantly. In January, 1986, the deputy of the Israeli Commander in Gaza invaded my apartment and ordered me to leave Gaza within 24 hours. When I asked him why, he said that he was issuing a military order and that no explanation was necessary.

32. In November of that year David Hakhami, Israeli Deputy Commander for Gaza, interviewed me. He asked questions about The Islamic University and wanted specific information. I told him I was not in a position to answer the questions and suggested he should ask the President. He told me that we would be seeing each other frequently. He called sometimes every day, and at least once each week. High ranking Israeli officials in Gaza, including Ms. VeraTamara, interviewed me many times between November, 1986 and November, 1989. They typically threatened me with jail and deportation at these meetings.

33. In May, 1987, the Israelis issued a military order banning the publication of the University magazine of which I was the Editor. I

had written articles describing Israeli actions and treatment of Palestinians and their institutions. One action in particular had occurred on April 19, 1987. The Israelis had broken into the University. They broke the windows, gates, and doors. I wrote an article about it and described the Israeli occupation forces and their actions. Ms. Tamara again called me to the Israeli head office in the Gaza Strip. She told me that I "had crossed the line and we know how to discipline you." She said that they knew that I was a newly-wed and that they could hurt me. She said that what I wrote was lies, a provocation, and that I should not have written it. She also told me not to refer to the Israeli army as Israeli occupation forces. She threatened me with jail and deportation.

34. In July, 1987, a Delegation of Academics from the United States visited the Islamic University. It was published in the newspapers. I was called into the Shin Bet again at Abu Khadera. They wanted to know all about the Delegation, who they were, what I told them about the Israelis, or anything else. I was interrogated by them for a long time. They threatened me again with jail and deportation.

35. In December, 1987, after the beginning of the intifada, all academic institutions were closed. Gaza and the West Bank were designated Military Zones under martial law. No one was allowed to enter the University. The Universities offered classes in other locations for the 3rd- and 4th-year students.

36. In 1989 I was awarded a Thomas Jefferson Fellowship financed by USAID and the Fulbright Program, and administered by a group called AmidEast, so that I might obtain my Doctorate at the University of Mississippi. My admission was for fall 1989 but I was unable to attend classes because the Israelis would not allow me to leave the Occupied Territories. I was finally allowed to leave through

the intervention of Mr. Abraham Milameed, an attorney and the former Interior Minister of Israel in the Begin government. He was on the Executive Committee of Mefdel Party, the National Religious Party. He convinced the Shin Bet to let me leave. They told him that I was a political activist and they did not want me to become an activist in the United States because it hurts the Israelis more when Palestinians come to the United States and expose Americans to the Palestinian viewpoint.

37. I came to the United States in November 1989 to attend the University of Mississippi as an exchange student. Nearly two years after I arrived at the University, the FBI and the U.S. Attorney's office in Mississippi contacted me; apparently they had been in communication for some time with Nancy Rogers, the Assistant Director of International Programs at the University, with regard to my activities at the University. She introduced me to the FBI and the Assistant U.S. Attorney at a meeting at the University. She asked if I would talk to them and told me that the person was pro-Palestinian. I was encouraged by Ms. Rogers to talk to the government, and I was eager not to displease the University, which had been such a good host to me. The government then maintained contact with me from approximately December 1991 to 1997, making contact between ten and fifteen times. Some of these contacts led to meetings.

38. My first interview was with FBI Special Agent Steve Taylor in Oxford, Mississippi in December 1991. He told me that he was asked by the State department to interview me. Ultimately, I was interviewed by the FBI and U.S. Attorney's office perhaps as many as fifteen times. On one occasion, October 26, 1994, I met with Steve Taylor and E. Avery Rollins, FBI Supervisory Special Agent

from Jackson, Mississippi. He told me that the FBI was acting on behalf of the Israeli government and that they had targeted me. He made accusations and asked questions about Palestinian organizations such as Hamas, fundraising, and my work at the Islamic University of Gaza. At the end of the meeting, he told me I had nothing to worry about and to get back to my daily life.

39. I was contacted on a regular basis beginning September, 1996. At that time I was completing my studies and working on my dissertation, while planning to move to New Jersey, where my wife had found a job. I was contacted by John Hailman, Chief, Criminal Division, U.S. Attorney's Office, Northern District of Mississippi. He advised that me they had concluded their investigation and told me I had four options: that I would be deported; that I would be charged with crimes; that I would help them build a case against Mousa Abu Marzook; or that the FBI and other U.S. government agencies would release materials portraying me as an informant, in the hopes that I would be discredited with Palestinian groups. I was scared to death. I asked why the government was contemplating such a campaign against me at that time—was it because I was going to New Jersey? Mr. Hailman told me that they did not want me to go there because Jews who are pro- Israeli dominate the FBI office in New York and New Jersey and they didn't want anything bad to happen to me. Also, I had recently broken my coccyx in a fall down a staircase, and I had begun treatment for the pain at a clinic in Memphis; that very day I had a severe pinched vertebral nerve. I was not to do anything for 24 hours but they insisted on talking to me.

40. U.S. Attorney, John Hailman called me again on October 1, 1996. He wanted to meet on October 2, 1996. I met with him and the following persons: Steve Taylor; Avery Rollins; Richard

Calcagno, FBI Supervisory Special Agent, Oxford, Mississippi; and James Feier, FBI Special Agent in Charge, Jackson, Mississippi; at the Ramada Inn, Room 222, Oxford, Mississippi. They threatened me with deportation. They talked about money laundering, the Palestinian resistance movement Hamas and its leadership in the U.S. They mentioned at one point Mousa Abu Marzook, the Hamas activist. They were trying to build a case against him and other activists. They offered me inducements such as full-time employment, U.S. citizenship, money, and even a ministerial post in the Arafat government of the Palestinian Authority. They told me to talk to my wife and bring her with me the next day. I met with them again on October 3, 1996 with my wife. It was the same type of conversation.

41. I continued to meet with this group of investigators. I told them I would not cooperate with them to incriminate anyone, testify or identify anyone. John Hailman said the Department of Justice would not bring charges but that they needed me for educational purposes about Palestine, various groups, settlements, refugees, Jerusalem, Israeli actions, etc. I told them I would meet with them for educational purposes.

42. On December 5, 1996 I was introduced by John Hailman and Richard Calcagno to John Atkins, FBI Special Agent, Washington, Metropolitan Field Office. He advised me that he was from the National Security Division. He told me to deal with him. He said the other men were from the criminal investigation. He wanted more information. He also told me he could help with my back injury and send me to the Mayo clinic. I met with him three more times before Christmas and again in January and February, 1997. Also, I was contacted many times by John Hailman through Mrs.

Rogers, who advised that they would not let me live peacefully and normally unless I would meet with him.

43. During this time my phone was wired, I was receiving strange calls, my doctor's appointments were canceled, my mail was tampered with, and someone was using my credit cards. Strange things were happening to me.

44. I was awarded my Ph.D in Business Administration from the University of Mississippi in May, 1997.

45. Finally, I was subpoenaed to appear before the Grand Jury in the United States District Court for the Southern District of New York investigating money laundering and I complied with the subpoena voluntarily. However, I refused to answer any questions based on my religious, political and personal beliefs. I was held in civil contempt for refusal to testify in an effort to force me to testify. I started a hunger strike the first day of my incarceration, 2/23/98 and continued it until my release on 8/21/98 (180 days later). I was force-fed while I was in jail on civil contempt charges.

46. During my hunger strike, I took only water, and was force-fed by the prison medical staff. It was very painful to have my veins constantly probed by needles and catheterized—my veins were difficult to isolate, and became progressively so as the hunger strike wore on. At one point, the medical personnel catheterized me via the vein in my neck, which was incredibly painful, so much so that I constantly had to think upon those in the history of struggle for religious and political beliefs who had withstood torture, burning, and unimaginable torment. I continually buttressed my convictions by reminding myself that they were men, as am I, and that pain and discomfort is part of the struggle. This thought was my only comfort.

47. I had broken my back falling down a staircase in February 1995, while still completing my studies at Ole Miss. My coccyx was broken in this accident, and has caused chronic pain since then. This pain was greatly increased during my incarceration; not least because of the uncomfortable conditions I was kept in, and because it remained untreated. In addition, as my body weight declined, the discomfort of the coccyx break became more acute, adding a further measure of pain to my hunger strike.

48. After Judge Cote found that I would never testify before the grand jury and ordered my release, I resumed my professional life in Virginia, taking an adjunct teaching position in Business Administration at Strayer University in Loudon, VA. Simultaneously, I became a Research Fellow at the United Association for Studies and Research, in Springfield, VA, where I conducted original research on development and technology transfer; in addition, I reviewed and edited articles for the Association's Journal, and consulted with the organization on its business management practices.

49. In the fall 1999 and spring 2000 semesters I was employed as an adjunct instructor at the University of the District of Columbia, teaching undergraduate business classes. During the spring 2000 semester I also taught Operations Management as an adjunct at Towson University in Maryland.

50. Although most of the medical conditions that I suffered from before my incarceration in 1998 have abated, I have experienced new ailments that arose as a result of my hunger strike, and my other untreated conditions during the term in jail. Needless to say the conditions of my confinement and their effect on my health were nothing short of devastating and, among other things, included:

• Placement in solitary confinement at the MCC for commencing a hunger strike
• Repeated punitive strip searches
• Unnecessary placement in shackles and black boxes;
• Being moved to hospitals without anyone knowing of my where-abouts;
• Enduring extremely unsanitary hospital conditions at the Westchester Co. Medical Center jail ward;
• Enduring an approximately six month hunger strike, despite plates of food being left at my bedside all day long;
• Enduring the overwhelming stench of mentally disturbed and termi-nally ill inmates urinating and conducting bowel movements in the bed next to me (and not being permitted to open the windows);
• Enduring the excruciating pain of repeated unsuccessful jabs of needles and IV's into my damaged, collapsed, shrunken and unreachable veins in my hands, arms, elbows, knees, legs and neck;
• Enduring swelling and pain from bad IV placement and vein sensi-tivity;
• Enduring burning, thick gelatinous matter put into my veins;
• Enduring the excruciating pain of three tubes being shoved into my internal jugular vein;
• Enduring the extreme pain and tightness of the popping of stitches and dressing and redressing with painful tape of the holes in my neck;
• Enduring re-stitching of my neck without anesthesia;
• Enduring dangerously low potassium, magnesium, glucose and blood pressure level due to my hunger strike and diabetes;
• Enduring infection; severe headaches; fainting; dizziness; severe diarrhea; dehydration; sever acid reflux; inability to sleep; fevers; chills; sweating; rapid weight loss; and the possibility of other sever medical conditions and death due to the catheter tubes in my inter-nal jugular vein and my hunger strike;

• Enduring extreme chronic back pain worsened by the refusal to provide me with any physical therapy, or two of the three medications for my back (withheld to force me to give up my hunger strike);
• Enduring constant noise from a loud television, belligerent disturbed patients, and relentless moaning, groaning and fighting among roommates;
• Deprivation of ju'maah (communal ritual prayer);
• Deprivation of exercise or physical therapy;
• Enduring racist and ignorant people, among the staff and other patients, who continually called me a terrorist;
• Failure of my feeding tubes rammed down my nose into my throat and stomach repeatedly against my will;
• Severe muscle and weight loss; and being shackled to my bed at all four points forcibly, due to my hunger strike.

51. Since my incarceration, my health has further declined, as a result of my hunger strike and the strain that occurred from my time in jail. I now have a chronic, ulcerated stomach as a result of the ordeal, and I must take Prevacid twice daily for the irritation to my stomach. My knees suffer from chronic arthritis, and I have back pain, which is related to the injury I suffered from falling down a staircase before my incarceration, which exacerbated it through the discomfort of my cell and my bad nutrition. I presently take Relaafin for my arthritis. I also suffer from severe migraine headaches, which occur daily, and I presently take Zoloft to treat the pain of these episodes. Finally, I suffer from Type II adult-onset diabetes, which is controlled at this time. Despite all this, as is shown by my resolve in my last incarceration nothing about my current medical conditions or changes in the future will affect my resolve.

52. I will not testify. I was prepared to die in jail in 1998 rather than to testify before the grand jury. The same holds true today. Alexandria, VA

On this 12th day of July 2003

## THE CASE OF BRANDON MAYFIELD

*"The FBI apologizes to Mr. Mayfield and his family for the hardships that this matter has caused," the bureau said in a statement issued from Washington.*

On May 25, 2004, a federal court threw out the case against an American lawyer once linked to the Madrid (Spain) train bombings, and the FBI apologized for a fingerprint-identification error that led to his arrest. The former Army lieutenant was released from custody after the fingerprint announcement by *Spanish authorities*, which cleared him of any involvement. He was not altogether cleared of suspicion at that time, however, for in the eyes of the U.S. government he remained a "material witness." Consequently, restrictions were placed on his movements until a short time later when they were    lifted by the court.

A statement posted on the U.S. District Court's Web site stated:

> Due to the misidentification by the FBI of a fingerprint, the court orders the material witness proceeding dismissed. The court orders all property seized to be returned to the material witness.

The court's action lifted a cloud of suspicion that had surrounded Brandon Mayfield since his arrest on May 6. The court also decreed that all documents in the case would be unsealed. An Associated Press Report had this to say about the documents (FBI Apologizes to Wrongly Accused Lawyer, by Andrew Kramer, AP):

> One of the documents, an affidavit filed by FBI Special Agent Richard K. Werder in support of the material witness arrest warrant, sheds some light on the case. After a fingerprint analysis of the detonator bag, Werder said he was "advised that the FBI lab stands by their conclusion of a 100 percent positive identification."
>
> The affidavit also notes that Mayfield's wife, Mona, was born in Egypt, and that Mayfield represented Jeffrey Leon Battle in a child custody case. Battle later was among a group of Portland men who pleaded guilty to conspiring to help al-Qaida and the Taliban fight U.S. forces in Afghanistan.

The 37-year-old convert to Islam sharply criticized the government after the announcement, calling his time behind bars "humiliating" and "embarrassing," and insisted he was targeted because of his faith. "I am a Muslim, an American, and an ex-officer of the U.S. military," he said at a news conference. "I believe I was singled out and discriminated against, I feel, as a Muslim."

FBI officials had maintained that Mayfield's fingerprint matched a fingerprint found on a bag of detonators near the train station at the March 11th bombing in Madrid, which killed 191 people and injured 2,000 others. But Spanish investigators concluded the fingerprints belonged to an Algerian man.

There is no doubt in my mind that Brandon Mayfield was singled out for investigation and prosecution because he is a Muslim, and there was probably an additional animus directed towards him because he is a white American convert (or revert) to Islam with a military background. This man was cleared because Spanish authorities discovered the fingerprint identification to have been in error!

It is also worth noting that the FBI LAB has a history of ineptness and corruption; and while the full extent of its impact on high profile criminal cases has not been fully divulged, it is an accepted FACT (among those-in-the-know) that many innocent people—many of whom are still behind bars (including Muslims)—have been adversely impacted over the years.

This case is but another example of why we have consistently held that whenever a Muslim is accused of a crime (esp. related to "terrorism" in post-9/11 America), it is imperative that people of good will accord the accused his (or her) right to a *presumption of innocence* until all of the facts come in!

Brandon Mayfield was very fortunate. Should he decide to sue the government over this highly bigoted affront, we wish him God-speed.

**Update**

Brandon Mayfield *did* sue the U.S. Government and won a *sizeable* monetary judgment!

## The Case of Jose "Abdullah" Padilla (The Dirty Case of the alleged "Dirty Bomber")

In a June 1, 2004, Associated Press release ("Government Says Padilla Targeted Apartment Buildings"), reporter Larry Margasak noted the following:

> Jose Padilla, a former Chicago gang member held as a terrorism suspect for two years, sought to blow up hotels and apartment buildings in the United States in addition to

planning an attack with a "dirty bomb" radiological device, the government said Tuesday. The Justice Department, under pressure to explain its indefinite detention of a U.S. citizen as an 'enemy combatant,' detailed Padilla's alleged al-Qaida training in Afghanistan and contacts with the most senior members of the terrorist network, his travel back into the United States and preparations to rent apartments and set off explosives. Deputy Attorney General James Comey called the chronicle of Padilla's plotting 'remarkable for its scope, its clarity and its candor.'

The department released documents, based in part on interviews with Padilla, saying he and an unidentified al-Qaida accomplice planned to find as many as three apartment buildings supplied with natural gas. "Padilla and the accomplice were to locate as many as three high-rise apartment buildings which had natural gas supplied to the floors," the government summary of interrogations said. The alleged accomplice is in custody. 'They would rent two apartments in each building, seal all the openings, turn on the gas, and set timers to detonate the buildings simultaneously at a later time,' the papers alleged.

The summary also stated that top al-Qaida officials "wanted Padilla to hit targets in New York City, although Florida and Washington, D.C. were discussed as well." To convey an appearnce of balance, the report also quoted one of Padilla's lawyers, Andrew Patel, who characterized Comey's information as "an opening statement without a trial. We are in the same position we've been in for two years, where the government says bad things about Mr. Padilla and there's no forum for him to defend himself."

The report further stated:

> Comey said release of the information had no connection to criticism from some members of Congress and some administration officials that Attorney General John Ashcroft overstated the al-Qaida threat. Rather, Comey said, he acted "because every place I went to speak, people would say, 'We agree with you with the war on terror but we've got a problem with this Padilla thing. I wish I knew more about it.' And I very much wanted people to know what I knew about Jose Padilla to address those questions."

Immediately after seeing the AP report, The Peace And Justice Foundation sent out the following release:

*There are certain things about these new disclosures that should be viewed as suspect by any objective and fair-minded observer, such as:*

1. The timing of these quasi-official allegations. Padilla (an American-born citizen) has been held incommunicado, and without charge as an "enemy combatant," for TWO YEARS; and despite this highly publicized and sensationalistic disclosure, a huge question mark still looms heavily over the merits of the government's case.

2. Deputy Attorney General James Comey's assertion that there are no plans to file the [new] information as an addendum to the government's arguments, nor to use the material to try to seek a criminal indictment against Padilla. If the government's accusations are indeed a fact, and they have evidence to support them, why wouldn't that information be used in the case against Padilla?

As far as we are concerned, the government's claims against this young man are without merit. We agree with Padilla's lawyer who stated, *"We are in the same position we've been in for two years, where the government says bad things about Mr. Padilla and there's no forum for him to defend himself."*

The dictates of both conscience and just law demand that we continue to accord this young "American citizen" (for Muslims: our brother in the deen of Islam) the presumption of innocence until all of the facts prove otherwise.

In June 2004, Comey also informed attendees at the news conference that when Padilla stepped off the plane in Chicago in May 2002, he was a highly trained and fully equipped "soldier of our enemy," who had accepted his al-Qaida assignment to kill hundreds of innocent people in apartment buildings. "We have decided to release this information to help people understand why we are doing what we are doing in the war on terror and to help people understand the nature of the threat we face," he said.

Now, over a year later, a curious thing has happened. Padilla has been ordered remanded to the custody of civilian authorities, and a formal indictment has now been lodged against him. The federal indictment against Padilla, however, is perhaps more conspicuous for what he wasn't charged with.

**To briefly recap: He was arrested at the Chicago's O'Hare International Airport in May 2002, after the government alleged that he was plotting a radiological dirty bomb attack in the United States. Two years later this internationally publicized unofficial charge was followed by the allegation of his being part of a conspiracy to blow up apartment buildings. The newly minted 31 page indictment includes NEITHER of these charges! Instead, the heart of the indictment alleges that Jose Padilla is part of a violent terrorism conspiracy rooted in North America.**

According to the government Jose Padilla attended the al Qaeda-affiliated al-Farouq training camp in Afghanistan in 2000, under the name Abdullah al-Espani; and in 2002 approached al Qaeda leaders in Afghanistan with an offer to commit terrorist acts in the United States. On May 8th he reportedly arrived in Chicago with over $10,000 in cash and the names of "al Qaeda operatives." On June 9th he is listed as an enemy combatant and placed in the custody of the Defense Department.

On December 4, 2002, U.S. District Judge Michael Mukasey ruled that a federal court has authority to decide whether Padilla was properly detained as an enemy combatant. On December 18, 2003, the U.S. Court of Appeals (2nd Circuit) ordered Padilla's release from military custody within 30 days; and further stated that he could be tried, if the government chose to do so, in a civilian court. On January 27, 2004, the appeals court agreed to suspend its ruling after the Bush administration appealed the case to the U.S. Supreme Court.

On September 9, 2005, the 4th U.S. Circuit Court of Appeals ruled that Padilla could be held indefinitely; and on October 25, 2005, attorneys for Padilla asked the United States Supreme Court to limit the government's power to hold him (and other terrorism suspects) indefinitely and without charges. Consequently, the Bush Administration's deadline for filing arguments was Nov 28, 2005.

**Subsequent to all of this, an indictment by a federal grand jury in Miami was unsealed, charging Padilla (and four alleged accomplices) with a conspiracy to "murder, kidnap and maim" people overseas. There was no mention of a "dirty bomb" or "natural gas" attacks in the U.S.** (In light of so many recent disclosures of a long line of administration officials, both past and present, speaking with "forked tongues" on a host of critically important issues, a reasonable person should wonder if this American born citizen, Jose Padilla, has also been the victim of a vicious campaign of LIES.)

As a consequence of being held for three years without formal charge as an "enemy combatant," Padilla has been at the center of a fierce legal and political battle for much of this time. His lawyers—who he met for the first time on March 3, 2004 - have argued his military confinement was unconstitutional under a 2004 U.S. Supreme Court ruling, in which the court found that another U.S born citizen held as an enemy combatant, Yaser Hamdi, had a right to contest his incarceration.

*The government was under pressure to either "charge him, or release him"*—and thus, the government's recent indictment appears to some as nothing more than a thinly veiled strategy of the Bush administration to avoid another adverse Supreme Court ruling. Indeed, Attorney General Gonzales is reported as saying, "Since he has now been charged in a grand jury in Florida, we believe that the petition is moot and that the petition should not be granted."

Again, it is significant to note that **Ahmed Abu-Ali** wasn't charged with a crime until pressure was successfully brought to bear on the government to have him returned to the United States. And, like Abu-Ali, Jose "Abdullah" Padilla also faces the possibility of LIFE in prison if convicted by "a jury of his peers."

We should also state for the record that the mere fact that the first Hispanic U.S. Attorney General of the United States, Alberto R. Gonzales, was the one to formally announce this politically driven indictment (against a fellow Latin-American), in no way legitimizes these charges. It merely confirms how much value, Alberto Gonzales, like other minority "firsts," accords to the corrupting requisites of political expediency. (Gonzales is a team player.)

On a concluding note, a representative of one of the U.S. based human rights organizations (Human Rights Watch), according to the November 23, 2005, *Washington Post* newspaper, offered "guarded praise" about the indictment. "It's a welcome development, albeit three years too late," the activist reportedly said. "Anybody captured outside the battlefield should be charged or released."

**At this writing Jose "Abdullah" Padilla is on trial in Florida, after spending *five years in solitary confinement without charge!***

## The Case of Imam Warith Deen Umar

On Feb. 11, 2004, I traveled to Albany (NY), at the request of one of my many brothers in the fold of Islam, Warith Deen Umar. The former New York State prison chaplain had been under siege (he and his family) for some time, and now he was fighting back. The occasion was a press conference to announce his intent to file a multi-million dollar lawsuit against the *Wall Street Journal,* and a number of other parties. The press release read as follows:

> The Relief sought is to recover damages for defamation based on numerous false statements pertaining to plaintiff in *Wall Street Journal* article of Feb. 5, 2003, written by defendant Paul M. Barrett entitled **"How A Chaplain Spread Extremism To an Inmate Flock."** The article exposed Imam Umar to Public Hatred, Contempt, Scorn, Ridicule and Disgrace, and has been re-published in various forms, and made widely available on-line and broadcast by public officials, i.e., Gov. George Pataki and especially Senator Charles Schumer in an irresponsible disregard for truth, inquiry, investigation or examination.

Defendants published said statements in a grossly irresponsible manner without consideration for the standards of information gathering and dissemination followed by responsible parties. Plaintiff (Imam Umar) was injured as a direct and proximate result of the action of the defendants. The relief sought is $5,000,000 plus costs and disbursements of this action.

I have personally known Imam Warith Deen Umar for about 20 years, and I've always known him to be a decent and committed man, who has contributed much in the way of good to the Muslim community and to the community-at-large. It is in this spirit that I invited Imam Umar to state his case, for the readers of this publication, in his own words.

*We praise Allah, seek His Guidance and beg for His Forgiveness. We seek refuge in Allah from the evil of our own souls and what wrong we do. Whoever Allah guides, will not go astray. Those astray have no one to guide them. I bear witness there is no god but Allah. He is Unique and has no associate, and I bear witness that Muhammad of Arabia (saws) is the Universal Prophet. O Muslims who Believe, Fear Allah as he should be Feared and die at the end of life as a Muslim.*

I thank the author El Hajj Mauri Saalakhan for his continuous striving to reach the truth and for allowing me to share with the readers something of my case and my life. I was asked to write a brief profile on my "case": (a) The Injustice done to me, and (b) How it impacted me and my family. "Cases" are usually of persons who are accused of some violation of law, like Imam Jamil Al-Amin, or Dr. Sami Al Arian, or Dr. Rafil Dhafir or New York City's martial artist Tariq Shah. They are arrested, held, tried, convicted and sent to prison on the flimsiest of evidence. These cases and others like them deserve our attention and immediate support.

First, I am not in prison. I have not been arrested. I have not been charged with doing anything wrong. I have not been accused of any violation of law. Al humdulillah. In fact I am accusing "them". I am accusing government, media, and politicians for having wronged me and used me (my "case") to frighten, oppress and abuse Muslims.

Warith Deen Umar, pro se Plaintiff
|v.| Index No. 557-04 Dow Jones, Inc, Dow Jones, Inc, d/b/a |The *Wall Street Journal* and Paul|Honorable Judge Barrett, Writer| |Joseph J. Terisi|Defendants|

This appears to be a case of me against The Wall Street Journal. But it is not about me. I'm a very private person. My 28 years of da'wah work behind prison walls, beyond the eyes of the public, testifies to my desire for privacy. However, after 9-11 too much is at stake to remain private. The times are too serious. The weak are too endangered, the leaders too inept, the followers too blind, and those who see, too fearful. The enemy of truth is too vicious, the people too afraid, and the truth is too necessary to go untold.

Our religion of Islam is under attack. Moderation, quietism, or neutrality in the face of fitna (tumult, oppression, decadence) is haram so we must act in accord with the guidance of Prophet Muhammad. He said to change things we must act, with our hands, or our mouths or our hearts.

It might be helpful to present this over-view of my case as I prepared it for court. In a nutshell this is an action for libel. Warith Deen Umar is the subject of defamation and subsequent slander, as the result of a front page article in the world famous *Wall Street Journal.*

Imam Umar is the former Chaplain and Ministerial Program Coordinator for the New York State Department of Correctional Services (DOCS). He is one of the first of two Muslim Chaplains hired in America. He supervised and trained Chaplains of all faiths including 56 Muslim Chaplains in New York.

At the time the Article was published (2-5-03). Umar was a retired employee of DOCS for two and a half years, retiring after 25 years of civil service in 2000. He was pursuing a second career as a writer and providing Chaplaincy services for the Federal Bureau of Prisons. He also conducted a weekly Program for ex-prisoners with the Albany Public Library as a means of income to supplement his state pension. He was the President of the Environmental Awareness Network for Diversity in Conservation and in line for major contracts that would provide substantial income.

The *Wall Street Journal* published the Headline *"Captive Audience: How a Chaplain Spread Extremism to an Inmate Flock."* Sub-headlines stated that Imam Umar was the "Radical New York Imam who Chose (Sunni Wahhabi) Clerics for State Prisons; who had Praise for 9/11 'Martyrs;'". The paper stated that Imam Umar was a Wahhabi agent and "Saudi Arabia's Helping Hand." All of these statements and headlines were libelous, slanderous and untrue.

The Article caused injury and tremendous harm to Imam Umar, his wife of 26 years and their family of 9 children. On TV, radio and in newspapers, he was condemned and vilified by New York Governor George Pataki, U.S. Senator Charles Schumer, Senator Dianne Feinstein, and his name was used at a number of Congressional hearings to give justification to the suppression of Muslim Chaplains in the military and in the prisons, and to blunt the tremendous growth of Islam in American prisons.  Umar was fired from his employment, banned from all American prisons and jails, black-balled from all state contracts. Umar was castigated to such a degree that the Imams would not come forth to defend him.

There was fear among the Imams. Muslim Chaplains were told by the F.B.I. not to even call Umar or associate with him. And they complied! He was banned forever from entering the Harlem Mosque for Jumah on the 1st day of Ramadan (Oct. 2004). He was told simply that he was in disfavor of the government. His litigation was abandoned by Attorney Stanly Cohen who later gave false information to the New York Appellate Court to defend himself against Umar's legal complaint for malfeasance. Umar was forced to defend himself without counsel. The writer Barrett reported that Umar, said that the September 11 hijackers should be honored as martyrs. ..."This is the sort of teaching they don't want in prisons," he said. " But this is what I'm doing." This was an outright lie.

Writer Barrett took the license to add words to my actual writing causing libel.

In my legal discovery we have found that this is a case of conspiracy to support the government agenda of suppressing the Islamic movement in prisons and in the military. These are the two places where sanctioned Muslim government workers (Chaplains) are feared by government as being or becoming Muslim sympathizers. A questionable Law Firm (Sullivan & Cromwell), an overly aggressive lawyer (J. Andrew Kent), and a writer (Paul M. Barrett who is looking for the material to publish a sensational book) went into the New York prison system joined with so-called Shi'ah inmates who were suing for separate services, made accusations against Imam Umar that would give the government justification to investigate all

Muslim Chaplains, or fire all of them as was called for by Senator Schumer.

At the least they would strike fear into Muslim Chaplains, the New York Majlis Shuurah, local Imams, and prisoners. Imam Umar was known for standing up for Muslims and strongly defending the da'wah work. The thinking went like this: Knock the leader down and discredit him and the rest will submit. This is not a case about what a Chaplain did during his illustrious 25 year career. The media published 336 articles that made false and malicious claims against Imam Umar. The government stepped in to fire Imam Umar. The politicians were the mouthpieces that would keep "investigations" going. The battle is not over, in sha'llah.

November 15, 2005

## THE CASE OF JAMES "YUSUF" YEE

An objective review of the case of James "Yusuf" Yee, retired officer of the U.S. Army Chaplain Corps, should be an eye-opening experience for any Muslim contemplating service in the U.S. Military; for it is the story of a patriotic West Point graduate who found himself faced with capital charges, subjected to abusive treatment, and unjustly imprisoned in solitary confinement under the color of "law," for no other reason then being Muslim in a post 9/11 world. His story also provides a gripping inside view of the U.S. Military operation at Guantanamo Bay (Cuba), where Yee was assigned in 2003. His duties as chaplain (and his responsibility as a Muslim) required him to minister to the detainees being held as "unlawful combatants." He came to know their miserable condition well.

The reward of Chaplain Yee was to be labeled a "Chinese Taliban," and to be persecuted by anonymous briefings to the media and by a parade of accusation and innuendo. None of the accusations were ever substantiated; all of the charges against him would be dropped, but only after his career was ruined and his reputation left behind in shreds!

In the words of his publisher, the saga of James "Yusuf" Yee is the "story that shows the dark side of an unregulated and overzealous war on terror, in which danger is anticipated everywhere and a true American patriot becomes indistinguishable from a shadowy enemy." In my humble opinion, this characterization is only partially true—for it is really about much more than that.

By this time, most of you reading these words have heard something about the case of the Muslim chaplain at Guantanamo Bay. Well, a book has come out titled, For God And Country: Faith And Patriotism Under Fire, (a fitting title).

The back cover reveals a gripping exchange that took place between Captain Yee, upon his arrival at Guantanamo Bay, and the Muslim chaplain that he was about to replace:

> There are other things about this place that will be a little harder to take," he [Chaplain Hamza, Yee's predecessor] said, turning toward me in his seat and growing more serious. "I don't want to discourage you on your first night, but you need to be prepared. This is not a friendly environment for Muslims, and I don't just mean for the prisoners." He told me that this assignment had been one of the most difficult that he had ever endured, and not because of the long hours or the disorganization, but because of the anti-Muslim hostility.

"You need to watch your back," he said. He explained that when he arrived at Guantanamo three months earlier, the Command Sergeant Major had warned him to be careful, implying that many people who worked in interrogations often took special interest in Muslim personnel, and the chaplains in particular. "It was helpful information," he said, "and it's worth passing along." He [then] opened his door. "You'll be fine, but be aware."

The book is authored by James Yee, with the help of freelance journalist Aimee Molloy (published by Public Affairs). Needless to say, we consider it a must read!

## THE CASE OF ADAMA BAH & TASHNUBA HYDER

The case of Adama Bah and Tashnuba Hyder, two 16 year old Muslim sisters, who were brutally snatched away from their families in March of 2005, was one of the most heart-wrenching cases this writer had ever become involved in. When I first heard about the case I immediately thought about my own teenage daughter, and how I would feel if she were snatched away from the loving and protective embrace of her family.

After hearing about the abduction, and responding to a few calls and e-mails about the case, I sent messages to a number of Muslim leaders and organizations in New York City, with a simple message: *With this unwarranted detention of two young sisters, rogue elements within the government were pushing the envelope, testing the waters to see just how far they could go. A strong and immediate response from the Muslim community was needed*!

The two teenage *practicing* Muslims—Adama Bah and Tashnuba Hyder, of Guinea, West Africa and Bangladesh respectively—were taken into custody for the official reason of being "illegal immigrants," but unofficially they were labeled "**imminent threats to the national security of the United States.**" The ridiculous assertion was made that these girls were contemplating becoming suicide bombers. Both Adama and Tashnuba grew up in the United States.

The French philosopher Voltaire once said, *"Those who can make us believe absurdities can also cause us to commit atrocities."* This troubling case afforded a textbook example of that quote; an atrocity of the highest order!

The response from the Muslim establishment was typical, and largely ineffective. Efforts were made to mobilize the community around a "legal response" to the crisis—meaning raise money to hire attorneys and let the process play itself out. It was our belief, based on years of observation and experience, that if this was the only response, these two sisters would share the same fate as hundreds (if not thousands) of other young Muslim males in post 9/11 America. They would remain in detention indefinitely!

Following their unwarranted arrest – along with the early morning detention of Adama's father as he left the 96th Street Masjid in New York City after fajr prayer—not only did the government not disclose the basis for the unofficial "imminent threat" designation that was leaked to the media, it requested a "gag order" on the case! Meanwhile, there were already some intimations given to the media from government sources that the U.S. was prepared to hold them until they were 18 years of age and then deport them back to their respective countries of birth.

We decided that the most effective response would be to follow the admonition of our Prophet (pbuh), who advised: *"Tie your camel (meaning do all that you can do), and have trust in Allah."* Our response began with a lecture at the *Islamic Cultural Center of New York* (also known as the 96th Street Mosque) on Sunday, April 17, 2005, titled "PROTECTING OUR DAUGHTERS IN POST 9/11 AMERICA." The announcement for the forum read, in part:

> In January 2002, in a speech to an American Bar Association conference in Naples, Florida, [then] Assistant U.S. Attorney General Viet Dinh reportedly said, "We are reticent to provide a road map to Al Qaeda as to the progress and direction of our investigative activity. We don't want to taint people as being of interest to the investigation simply because of our attention. We will let them go if there is not enough of a predicate to hold them. But we will follow them closely, and if they so much as spit on the sidewalk we'll arrest them. The message is that if you are a suspected terrorist you better be squeaky clean ... if we can, we will keep you in jail."

> The admitted targets for this new and more insidious form of [ethnic and religious] profiling had been young immigrant Muslim men between the ages of 18 and 35. The arrest of Adama and Tashnuba took the targeting of the Muslim community to a new low, and has raised serious concerns for all persons of good will.

The Sunday following the April 17th lecture, a newly formed coalition held a protest rally at 26 Federal Plaza in New York City. In addition to The Peace And Justice Foundation, other supporters of the initiative were from a varied array of grassroots organizations — i.e., *The Coalition for Peace & Justice thru the Due Process of Law, The Islamic Thinkers Society, The Justice for James Yee Ad-hoc Committee, The Not In Our Name Project, Voices in the Wilderness, and The World Human Rights Service Council.*

The April 24th rally was then followed by a press conference on Thursday, April 28th, at the National Press Club in Washington, DC. An official from the Bangladeshi Embassy attended the press conference, and was invited to share his views. We later learned that the General Consul of Bangladesh pressed the U.S. Government for an explanation, and the Department of Homeland Security responded that the girl, who entered the United States with her mother at the age of 4, was being held solely because she was in the country illegally. It was then that the girl's parents formally asked the government to let the whole family leave the country voluntarily.

In addition to these important initiatives, we went on radio talk shows in different parts of the country to discuss the unprecedented and dangerous nature of this case. Another critically important factor that helped with the resolution of this crisis was the (comparatively speaking) good press that the case received. (By good press I mean balanced, fair-minded reporting). God rewarded us for our efforts when after 6 $^1/_2$ weeks of unjust detention, Adama Bah and Tashnuba Hyder were released!

Nina Bernstein of *The New York Times* authored most of the articles I read on the case. What follows is an excerpt from her report following the release of Adama Bah. (*"Elation in Harlem as Girl Held in Terror Inquiry Is Released,"* 5/7/05)

> It began with two 16-year-old immigrant girls arrested at dawn, detained far from home, and, in a chilling government assertion, called would-be suicide bombers who posed "an imminent threat to the security of the United States." But now, after holding the girls for six weeks in a Pennsylvania detention center, the government has quietly released one of the girls and is allowing the other to leave the country with her family.

One girl, an immigrant from Guinea, was back in her East Harlem high school yesterday among the jubilant friends and teachers who have insisted all along that the accusation was absurd. The other girl, who grew up in Queens, was still in detention, but was granted an order from an immigration judge that will allow her and her parents to return to their native Bangladesh as soon as the trip can be arranged.

Truth be told, it was the government that was granted the deportation order; for this was a "voluntary deportation" in name only—the price of freedom for a wrongfully detained 16 year old Muslim girl.

As Bernstein noted, many questions remained unanswered in a case that was marked from the very beginning by secrecy - including closed hearings, sealed F.B.I. declarations, and orders barring the lawyers from disclosing government information. Even after Adama and Tashnuba's release from detention, their attorneys (Natasha Pierre and Troy Mattes, respectively) remained under the gag order.

Adama's release came with conditions that Ms. Pierre said she was prevented from discussing; but what is known is that the conditions included Adama's being available to government investigators and reporting to immigration authorities. Her father, Mamadou Bah, a former cabdriver, remained in a detention center in Elizabeth (NJ) facing deportation for immigration violations. According to Bernstein:

> Jessica Siegel, Adama's English teacher, was among many adults in the girl's life who had described her as a vibrant, popular teenager who wore jeans under her Islamic garb, ran for student body president, and hung out with the daughter of the PTA president, a Christian girl, when she was not baby-sitting for her younger brothers and sisters. Her return

was a joyful celebration. "She's seeing everybody, and she's smiling because people are jumping up and down and ecstatic," Ms. Siegel said in a cell phone call from school. "She's like a little bird that just got out of a cage."

Fellow students began laughing and crying at the same time when they saw her walk in, said a friend, Yolanda Lawrence, 15. Many had tried to send Adama letters of support, but were told that *she was not allowed to receive or send mail in the maximum security juvenile detention center, in Berks County, Pa.*

Adama did reveal how the experience impacted her during her days of captivity: "I cried a lot," she said. "You just feel depressed, you just feel like nothing when you're in there."

Asked if she understood why she had been detained, the girl replied, "Honestly, no." She added, speaking of federal agents, *"They asked a lot of questions."*

Mr. Mattes also noted that his client, Tashnuba, was no would-be suicide bomber, "just a regular teenager devoted to her Islamic faith." Tashnuba was being home schooled, and was highly thought of by all who knew her.

Tashnuba's parents, who had lived in Queens for more than a dozen years, had their longstanding applications for political asylum closed administratively in the late 1990's. What is important to note, however, is that *there were no outstanding deportation orders* against them. In normal circumstances, they might have fought to legalize their immigration status; however, their daughter's detention changed all that.

## Lessons Learned

When we collectively formed the ad-hoc coalition to work on this troubling case, we set what many thought at the time was an overly ambitious agenda - the release of these two young sisters within a 90 day period.

We knew there would be impediments along the way (both *internal* and *external*), but we were convinced that if we had faith and determination—as the Prophet (pbuh) said, **"Tie your camel and have trust in Allah"**—the goal was achievable. After a combination of efforts made in the "court of public opinion" by activists, and argumentation in the Immigration Court by attorneys, the worst part of the nightmare came to an end after about six weeks. (I sincerely believe that the most critical factors were the activism in the street and the fair press that this case received.)

For far too long the Muslim community, generally speaking, has been content to hire overly cautious attorneys and then blindly follow their dictates. More often than not these attorneys function like self-serving, politically naive, "officers of the court"—advising their clients, at considerable expense, to quietly allow "the system" to work. When the truth is, *the system* has been malfunctioning for Muslims since the tragic attacks of 9/11.

When we began our campaign on behalf of these two young sisters (and their respective families) we were criticized from certain quarters for publishing their names, for holding a demonstration in New York City on April 24th, and for attempting to get family members to speak (or just be present) at a press conference held about a week later at the National Press Club in Washington, DC. But we are absolutely convinced (surely Allah knows best), that these initiatives factored prominently into the outcome.

Even after the sisters' release, however, we still had lingering concerns which were outlined, in part, in the following press release.

### Activists Schedule Press Conference to Respond to Government's Conditional Release of 16 year old Muslim Girls

WHEN: Wednesday, May 11, 2005...3PM
WHERE: CITY HALL - 1 City Hall Plaza (at the base of the Brooklyn Bridge)

A coalition of activists concerned about the detention of two 16 year old Muslim girls from New York City on March 24, 2005 - and the father of one of the two girls - will hold a press conference this coming Wednesday, May 11th, at 12 noon, at 1 City Hall Plaza.

The purpose of the press conference will be to publicly respond to the government's "conditional release" of both girls, and to raise a number of important concerns emanating from this very troubling case. Among these concerns are the following:

– Concerns about "conditions," imposed by the government, which may be injurious to the psychological well being of 16 year old Adama Bah;

– Concerns about the imposition of a deportation order against the family of 16 year old Tashnuba Hyder, as a condition for her release;

– Concerns about the veil of secrecy that still surrounds this case;

– Concerns about the grave injustices done to both girls; their families; and to the community as a whole

And further, concerns that a formal apology and some form of substantive compensation (such as Amnesty for the "illegal" members of both immediate families) is in order.

To date, these concerns have remained unanswered.

**Update**

With the last report that I received concerning Tashnuba, she was not doing so well. She, her mother, and her American-born siblings are reportedly residing with relatives in Bangladesh, in cramped circumstances. She misses the place of her earliest memories—the land that she used to think of as home (America).

As for Adama, she and her family (absent her father, who was deported back to Guinea) are still embroiled in struggle. The promising student has left school to go to work, and she still wears a monitoring device on her ankle. She is also attempting to secure political asylum in the U.S. At the time of this writing she awaits an immigration hearing on that issue.

# A FEW FACES BEHIND THE MASKS

*American-born Ahmed Omar Abu-Ali*
*[faces possible life imprisonment]*

*American-born Seifullah Chapman*
*[the Paintball Case: sentence 85 years]*

*American-born Masaud Khan*
*[The Paintball Case: sentence – LIFE]*

*American-born Hammad Abdur-Rahim*
*[The Paintball Case: 8 years]*

*Dr. Abdelhaleem Ashqar during his*
*detention ordeal in New York*

*(Retd.) Captain James "Yusuf" Yee*
*[Fmr. Chaplain at Guantanamo Bay]*

*American-born Dr. Ali al-Tamimi with trial Attorney (left) McMahan, Sentence: LIFE*

*Dr. Ali al-Tamimi at fund-raising dinner with Attorney Ashraf Nubani*

*James "Yusuf" Yee with young daughter*

*The Parents of Ahmed Omar Abu-Ali*

# Part 3

# WHY DO
# THEY HATE US?

## AMERICAN PRISONS:
## AND THE DELIBERATE USE OF TORTURE

The America of the new century has achieved a truly dubious distinction. We have gone from being the nation with the highest incarceration rate of its own citizens in the industrialized world, to being the nation with the highest incarceration rate of the *global community's citizens* in the world! And by no means has this proven to be for the better.

The late British Prime Minister Winston Churchill (Speaking at the House of Commons–1910) reportedly said:

> The mood and temper of the public in regard to the treatment of crime and criminals is one of the most unfailing tests of the civilization of any country. A calm dispassionate recognition of the rights of the accused, and even of the convicted criminal against the State—a constant heart-searching by all charged with the duty of punishment—a desire and eagerness to rehabilitate in the world of industry those who have paid their due in the hard coinage of punishment: tireless efforts towards discovery of curative and regenerative processes: unfailing faith that there is a treasure, if you can only find it, in the heart of every man. These are the symbols, which, in the treatment of crime and criminal, mark and measure the stored-up strength of a nation, and are a sign and proof of the living virtue in it.

Has America been a benevolent jailor of its own, or the global community's, citizens? I think not; and this, perhaps, is one of the reasons why…there is so much anger felt toward America.

On November 5, 2005, a very informative discussion occurred on the Diane Rehm Show, broadcast out of the WAMU-FM studios of American University in Washington, DC (a National Public Radio

Affiliate). The featured guest on this particular day was the former commanding officer at the Abu-Graib Prison in Iraq, [now retired] General Janice Karpinski.

Janice Karpinski was the first female general to ever command troops in a combat zone. She received this command after 24 years of service in the U.S. military, and during the broadcast spoke fondly of her military service.

In April of 2004 her career came to an abrupt end when CBS showed photos of Iraqi prisoners being abused by American soldiers at Abu-Graib. Karpinski has recently published a new book titled, One Woman's Army, that provides some eye-opening perspective from her side of the Abu-Graib prisoner abuse scandal.

The day before the broadcast, five American soldiers with the 75th Ranger regiment in Iraq had been charged with abusing three detainees, as they were about to transfer them to a prison (in September 2005). The embarrassing development came on the same day that President Bush announced, "We do not torture." What follows are excerpts from that provocative WAMU-NPR broadcast.

*Regarding the present-day roots of prisoner torture in the U.S. Military:*

Response: I believe we can find a direct connection to the original discussion with Alberto Gonzales and other people in the Attorney General's office, and the vice president of the United States—authorizing a departure from the Geneva Conventions in dealing with terrorists or people who have association with terrorists. Even if you consider that a slight departure, or one degree of departure, you've set the stage for other departures and a gray area starts to develop.

Today, or in the news of yesterday, when we see our most highly skilled trained soldiers in the military, Rangers, these are the elite forces, and if they are confused by instructions they're receiving, or if they are being directed to use more aggressive techniques, it's a condemnation of the situation and the instructions that have been given to our soldiers.

*Regarding her Mission in Iraq*

Response: I never expected that U.S. forces would be running any kind of a detention operation on the grounds of Abu-Graib. Mostly because the 800th Military Police Brigade is really a prisoner of war brigade—we handle refugee operations, internment resettlement, and prisoner of war operations. And those operations were for the most part completed by the time I arrived in Iraq because the war was declared over on the first of May, and prisoners of war released, we had a very small prisoner population. But they assigned a new mission to the 800th Military Police Brigade, involving restoration of Iraqi civilian prisons throughout Iraq, and Abu-Graib was one of them.

Our plan never included using Abu-Graib for a long term facility at all, for many reasons. It's contrary to good order and discipline to run any type of detention operation in the middle of the most dangerous location in a combat zone. This is a prison that was located in the Sunni Triangle, there was no protection overhead, so this is not a good location for any detention operation. It's notoriety under Saddam contributed to that problem.

*On the number of prisoners held at Abu-Graib:*

Response: While the prison was under my control, when we were just holding Iraqi prisoners there, our prisoner population stayed around three to five hundred during a month.

*On the question of where she was in relation to the prisoners being held at Abu-Graib, and the makeup of the facility:*

Response: I didn't live at Abu-Graib, it was one of 17 prison facilities under the 800 Military Police Brigade control, [but] I had full access to anywhere on Abu-Graib. Actually a very small percentage of the compound was being used for prisoner operations. The prison had been largely looted, in disrepair, rendered disabled for all practicable purposes—and there was an awful lot of money that had to be invested to make it minimally acceptable.

The prison grounds encompassed about 60 acres, and most of the buildings that were operational under Saddam were in terrible disrepair, or were actually taken all the way down to their foundations—possibly there were improvements that were planned if Saddam had remained in power. So we're talking about a cell block complex; there was long building that had a hospital facility in the middle of it and a mess hall, and a warehouse that was originally a milling operation. And then we had this large open area that was prepared by the Army Corp of Engineers for these outside compounds to be constructed; and these outside compounds would be the typical prisoner of war blueprint for holding prisoners.

*On the question of morale among the Military Police Brigade:*

Response: The unit that was running operations out of Abu-Graib when I first arrived was a National Guard unit, run by a very capable and bright company commander, a captain. He took me for a walk around the grounds of Abu-Graib and I absolutely did not think there was any way of making any type of detention operation out of the grounds of Abu-Graib. We were walking in near knee deep rubble, pieces of concrete, glass, metal, looted infrastructure—no running water, no electricity—and when I said to him, 'Do you think you can make a prison out here of any kind?' he said, 'If we have the right support, yes ma'am, we can.'

His soldiers were fired up to do that; no training, they weren't engineers; but of course at that time, they were visualizing a population of a few hundred Iraqi prisoners, at the most. So, we had some funding; we had a plan to use it as an interim facility, and those military police personnel made it happen.

*On the question of the extension of deployments (and its effect):*

Response: It was the most devastating impact on morale, throughout, not just the 800th Military Police Brigade, but all reserve and National Guard soldiers in particular. But the active component units were not exempt from it; they left their home stations with the idea that they would be in Iraq for 90 days or less. The difference is when you extend a National Guard or Reserve component soldier, without proper planning, without advising them, they feel, justifiably so, that they have been hoodwinked, that they've been taken hostage.

Their first concern was, 'Our families back in the states did not sign up for any of this, and we are abandoning them.' They didn't have telephones that they could pick up and call and say, 'Don't worry, they're going to cut an amendment to our orders so your ID cards will remain valid, your medical benefits, your dental benefits will remain in place'—so terribly disruptive to family members who were told, as the soldiers were told at the mobilization stations, that they were going for six months or less. And they left with a piece of paper that said so—179 day orders.

So when they made this decision with a stroke of a pen, it didn't have a tremendous effect on the active component, but it certainly had a devastating effect on Reserve and National Guard soldiers.

*Had the Reserve and National Guard Soldiers been trained for that assignment?*

Response: Absolutely not. Again, we rely very heavily in circumstances' like this on National Guard and Reserve component soldiers civilian skills. Some of them are police officers, some of them are firemen, some of them are bank managers, some of them are prison wardens—and we rely on them to establish the rules and the program for how we're going to continue and succeed, and that's what we did in this case. The soldiers that were in the unit out at Abu-Graib were no better trained than any other MP unit to handle prisoner operations.

*When asked to talk about some of the problems that led up to the abuse at Abu-Graib, and how she learned about them:*

Response: Well, Military Police personnel were succeeding against great odds, and encountering unbelievable challenges, but they knew detention operations. They took their lessons from prisoner of war operations, made some modifications, depending on their facility, and continued to succeed. Detention operations do not involve interrogation operations. So, in our prisoner of war camp, at another holding facility, there were some interviews being conducted by the Military Intelligence interrogators. They asked them a standard set of questions; it was a fairly routine interview, to determine if they had any knowledge of WMD, or if they knew where Saddam was; or if they knew anything about Osama Bin Ladin, or terrorism—fairly routine questions.

It continued in that direction at two facilities, but it was the only time where Military Intelligence personnel actually interfaced with Military Police personnel—until September 2003; when General

Miller, who was the commander of Guantanamo Bay, and was responsible for not only detention operations there, but also for interrogation operations—he was sent to Iraq to work with the Military Intelligence personnel to teach them more *aggressive* techniques to use in interrogations.

Apparently it means there were techniques that were approved for use in interrogations when you were interrogating terrorists or suspected terrorists, or people with information about terrorism —such as *hooding, sleep deprivation, longer periods of standing in uncomfortable positions, insults to their culture and religious beliefs*—certainly harsher techniques than were ever used in interviews—and authorized in a memorandum from the Pentagon.

I did not see any information about interrogation techniques, or harsher interrogation techniques, until after I heard about an ongoing investigation out at Abu-Graib.

*Diane Rehm than raised the question: Yesterday, we learned about this new policy directive governing interrogations. The eight page directive signed without any public announcement last Thursday, by acting Deputy Defense Secretary Gordon England, will allow the Army to issue a long delayed field manual for interrogators that's supposed to incorporate the lessons gleaned from the prisoner abuse scandals last year. Did you have a manual of any kind that talked to you about how your people would glean information?*

Response: Absolutely not, because interrogation operations are a separate mission altogether; it is the responsibility of the Military Intelligence personnel. They did not work for me, they were not subordinate to me, the commander actually lived at Abu-Graib, supervising his interrogation teams. But they are separate and apart from Military Police Operations.

*So are you saying that no members under your command were involved in these torture tactics, the photographs of which we've all seen?*

Response: Well, we've seen some of the soldiers that were assigned to a company subordinate to the 800th MP Brigade, we certainly have seen them in some of the photographs; but I was shocked when I saw the photographs, for many reasons—and amongst them was why are the MPs working with the interrogators like this? MPs are not trained in interrogation operations, they have never received training in how to enhance interrogations. And the first mention I ever heard of such a combination, was when General Miller came to work with the Military Intelligence personnel in Iraq.

*What about the role of Colonel Papas at Abu-Graib?*

Colonel Papas was the commander of the 205th Military Intelligence Brigade. He was an active component commander; career Army officer; worked in previous military intelligence assignments at the strategic intelligence level. I asked him one time—very early on after he had moved to Abu-Graib—'What about release procedures, how does it work in other locations?' And he said, 'Ma'am I don't know, I've never worked interrogations before. So I asked, 'How were you selected for this assignment?' He said, 'I wanted to command. I was at the War College, and they selected me and sent me here.'

*But it was his unit that was responsible for the detainees in Block A, which is where an awful lot of this occurred:*
Response: That's correct. At Abu-Graib there were two specially constructed interrogation facilities outside of Cell Block 1A, and outside of what we called the heart site—they were specially constructed outside. And the process was, the Military Police personnel

remove a prisoner from a cell, sign him over to a Military Intelligence interrogation team, the Military Intelligence interrogation team then takes that prisoner to the interrogation facility, speaks to them, interviews that individual, and then returns the individual, after the interrogation, back to the Military Police personnel – who then examine him, make any annotations if there's any bruising, or change in the person's demeanor, specifically, and then return that individual to a cell.

I first saw the photographs on the 23 of January 2004—it was eleven days after I received a classified message stating that there was an ongoing investigation out at Abu-Graib. I wasn't even aware of an investigation, let alone an ongoing investigation at Abu-Graib. They were ultimately going to hold me responsible, but in the very beginning, they forgot to make me aware that there was actually a problem.

*You knew absolutely nothing of any kind of torture, or of any kind of shaming of prisoners, or forcing them to pose in hideous, naked positions, you knew nothing of it?*

Response: I knew nothing of it, and I believe, I am convinced, it was done intentionally. Those activities were designed and conducted on the night shift. I, like many other people, was not essential travel—we were not allowed to travel on the roads at night. Insurgents were obviously very effective setting ambushes and IUDs at night; and I was specifically not allowed to remain at Abu-Graib, because it was an extremely dangerous location. When were the photographs taken? [They were taken] on the night shift; on the 14th of November, if you believe the date stamped on some of the photographs.

General Miller, who came from Guantanamo Bay, said "TREAT PRISONERS LIKE DOGS." *Did you hear him say that?*

Response: I did. General Miller was sent to Iraq to work with the Military Intelligence personnel, to teach them more effective interrogation techniques. There were operations underway from the end of August to arrest and detain specific individuals that they believed were connected to Saddam Hussein, or to terrorist cells. And these individuals were targeted by information that was developed at the site where Uday and Qusay, Saddam's sons, were killed. So toward the end of August they were undertaking these raids, and they were arresting record numbers of these so-called security detainees. So General Miller was sent to—right from the beginning of these interrogation operations, with these newly arriving security detainees—to teach the interrogators how to be more effective in getting information.

*There is in your book, a memo from Donald Rumsfeld. Can you talk about that?*

Response: I can. When I found out about this ongoing investigation I was not in Baghdad, in fact I was about an hour and 45 minutes outside of Baghdad very close to the Iranian border, we left at daybreak the next morning and went directly to Abu Graib. We asked when we got out there, what's going on, what investigation? People directed us to Cell Block 1A, I went over to Cell Block 1A, I spoke to the sergeant that was over there on shift, he didn't know anything —he said, 'I just know that there is an investigation, ma'am. I'm only working here because the other people were taken away from their positions.'

I said, 'Let me see your information,' [His response] 'The logs had been secured by the investigators, we really started a new log; we just have this field file.' And he pointed out a memorandum that was posted on a column just outside of this small administration office that they were using—and he said, 'And there's this memorandum.' So I went over to look at it, and immediately my eyes were drawn to the signature on it—it was signed by the Secretary of Defense. And it was the memorandum authorizing harsher techniques; to include *prolonged standing, stress positions, disruption of sleep patterns, late meals, hooding, that kind of thing—and an annotation in the margins, 'Make sure this happens.*

So I said, 'Where did this come from?' He said, 'Ma'am I don't know; it was here.' I thought that it was rather unusual that there would be an interrogation memorandum right outside the little administration office of the Military Police personnel, but it really was the only document of any sort that was still available in Cell Block 1A when I got out there.

*So do you believe that, in effect, Secretary Rumsfeld was ordering these military intelligence people to carry out—beyond even what is specified in this memo—techniques that he would have approved?*

Response: You know, Diane, I think that it was the original memo that did not define limits, did not establish parameters; did not say, you can put a person in a stress position for no longer than 10 minutes, for example. Did not say, you can be disruptive to sleep patterns for two hours, there were no limits. They just gave examples of what could be done. And perhaps those techniques were used and tested in Afghanistan and Guantanamo Bay, and found to be somewhat effective, but without limitations people expand those authorizations to become what they did become.

And the reason I say that is because in September of 2003, after General Miller's visit, General Sanchez signed an eight page memorandum authorizing far more aggressive techniques to be used in interrogations— to include, in the memorandum, the use of dogs in interrogations; *insults to culture; humiliating positions*, and the use, specifically, of un-muzzled dogs with his permission. So he was clearly aware, and was authorizing far harsher techniques than any used anywhere before.

*On the question of non-disclosure statements given to military personnel:*

Response: I can tell you that I would have been alarmed if anybody handed me a blank non-disclosure statement and told me to sign it. I would never have given the same to my soldiers; I would never have signed such a non-disclosure statement; but in fact…**soldiers serving now in prison operations throughout Iraq, and also Guantanano Bay, have in fact been required to sign a non-disclosure statement,** to say they will not discuss anything that they are ordered to do, or doing, in those facilities.

*You are specifically of the belief that those who were there at Abu-Graib knew long before January of 2004 that those photographs existed, and that kind of treatment had taken place. What makes you so sure?*

Response: Well, of course they weren't sharing the information with us at the time but sworn statements that have been released under court order, from interrogators and some of the *contractors*, say specifically that in November of 2003, General Fast was out at the Intelligence Coordination Element—which was the top secret facility built on the grounds of Abu-Graib for interrogators—she walked into the facility and saw one the pictures of the pyramid style pile of naked detainees being used as a screen saver on somebody's laptop computer. And they said, in their words, not mine, that she went ballistic.

Shortly after that event took place, a new spokesperson for General Sanchez and the CJT of Seven arrived in Iraq. I believe that they took that time—November, December, and part of January—to decide who exactly was going to be the fall guy in this, who exactly was going to be the scapegoat in all of this, and how they were going to construct or craft plausible denial, or actual denial, or responsibility. So they settled on these seven soldiers who were part of the 800th MP Brigade, and they settled on the commander, meaning me, at the time.

*Did you have any sense that this was coming?*

Response: Absolutely not. As I said, the first I knew of it was when I was sent an e-mail making reference to an ongoing investigation; and then eleven days after I saw the e-mail was the first time I saw the photographs.

[The following question came into the studio, via e-mail, from one of the listeners identified as "Tom in Utah"]

*I'm perfectly happy to believe that the general's superiors and subordinates were unforthcoming with their actions and decisions, but isn't the responsibility of a general to know what's going on under her command? Is there no one in our armed forces, civilian or military, who's willing to take responsibility? Maybe the systematic refusal to accept accountability for gruesome and inhuman behavior is part of the reason we're fighting such an aggressive insurgency; we've earned their hatred!*

Response: Well I don't disagree with what you're saying, but I can tell you this, I have said from the very beginning, I will take full responsibility for those things I could actually control; and what I know today—and I'm more determined than ever to pursue the truth—people above me have been cleared of any wrongdoing, persons between me and these soldiers have been cleared, for all practical purposes, of any wrongdoing. And that means soldiers and officers and civilians. There were too many players sent specifically to Abu-Graib to undertake specific things, to prevent the blame from being shared or equally distributed.

And I'm afraid that this failure to take responsibility and be held accountable, is promoted by the Pentagon, by our Secretary of Defense, who has, through his actions, made it very clear to officers, seniors soldiers, [that] if you disagree with him, if you disagree with the direction that he is going, you will find yourself out of a job, out of a position, and out of the Army.

## The "Black Sites"

President G.W. Bush reportedly signed a top secret presidential finding within six days of the 9/11 attacks, authorizing an unprecedented range of covert action, including the lethal use of force, renditions, disinformation campaigns and cyber attacks against the enemy in America's newly declared "war on terror."

The opening paragraph of a revealing report published on the front page of the December 4, 2005, edition of *The Washington Post* newspaper speaks volumes about one aspect of this controversial preemptive program (*"Wrongful Imprisonment: Anatomy of a CIA Mistake,"* by Dana Priest):

> In May 2004, the White House dispatched the U.S. ambassador
> in Germany to pay an unusual visit to the country's interior
> minister. Ambassador Daniel R. Coats carried instructions from

the State Department transmitted via the CIA's Berlin station because they were too sensitive and highly classified for regular diplomatic channels, according to several people with knowledge of the conversation.

Coats informed the German minister that the CIA had wrongfully imprisoned one of its citizens, **Khaled Masri**, for five months, and would release him, the sources said. There was also a request: that the German Government not disclose what it had been told even if Masri went public. The U.S. officials feared exposure of a covert action program designed to capture terrorism suspects abroad and transfer them among countries, and possible legal challenges to the CIA from Masri and others with similar allegations.

According to the report the interior minister did keep the secret, but other former and current intelligence and diplomatic officials have spoken publicly about the program, run out of the **CIA's Counterterrorist Center** (CTC). The combination of what these anonymous sources, and Masri himself, have said sheds some much needed light on a deeply flawed and oppressive covert operations program. Priest writes:

> To carry out its mission, the CTC relies on its Rendition Group, made up of case officers, paramilitaries, analysts and psychologists. Their job is to figure out how to snatch someone off a city street, or a remote hillside, or a secluded corner of an airport where local authorities wait
>
> Members of the Rendition Group follow a simple but standard procedure: Dressed head to toe in black, including masks, they blindfold and cut the clothes off their new

captives, then administer an enema and sleeping drugs. They outfit detainees in a diaper and jumpsuit for what can be a day-long trip. Their destinations: either a detention facility operated by *cooperative countries* in the Middle East and Central Asia, including Afghanistan, or one of the CIA's own covert prisons—referred to in classified documents as **"black sites,"** which at various times have been operated in eight countries, including several in Eastern Europe.

Khaled Masri was taken into custody by Macedonian authorities on New Years Eve 2003. He was taken off a bus at the Tabanovce border crossing by police because his name was reportedly similar to an associate of a 9/11 hijacker. In short order the Macedonian authorities drove him to the capitol, Skopje, and contacted the CIA station there. In the first weeks of 2004, an argument reportedly arose within the CIA over what should be done with him. The female director of the Counterterrorist Center (CTC) won the argument and ordered Masri captured and flown to the CIA prison in Afghanistan (a process known as "rendition").

According to *The Washington Post* report, the first night of his arrival Masri was "kicked and beaten and warned by an interrogator: *'You are here in a country where no one knows about you, in a country where there is no law. If you die, we will bury you, and know one will know.'*"

For the five months that he was held captive, his family, nor anyone else, had any knowledge of his whereabouts. He simply disappeared. It turns out Masri's detention was based on "speculative evidence" that proved to be unfounded. He was not the person that he was mistaken for, and the passport in his possession was legit.

It's been reported that the CIA working with other intelligence agencies has captured an estimated 3,000 people in its campaign to dismantle terrorist networks, but it's impossible to know how many "mistakes" have been made. Thus far, after a careful (and long overdue) vetting process, to date an estimated 180 prisoners have been released from Guantanamo Bay (a reported dumping site for CIA "mistakes"); but there is no tribunal or judge to check the evidence against those picked up by the CIA and delivered to "black sites."

It is now clear that what happened at Iraq's **Abu-Graib Prison** was *official policy*, and that it was not restricted to Abu-Graib alone. What should also be clear, for any thinking person, is that the atrocities that are being committed in the name of "national security" at Abu-Graib, Guantanamo, and at black sites scattered around the world, are not in "America's interest."

Khaled Masri, who is now planning to sue the U.S. government, had this to say after his up close and personal contact with agents of the land of the free: "I have very bad feelings about the United States. I think it's just like in the Arab countries; arresting people, treating them inhumanely and less than that, and with no rights and no laws."

Something to think about!

**Update**

After months of denying the practice of "extraordinary rendition," and the existence of "secret prisons," the Bush Administration has finally admitted to their existence, but continues to fudge on the admission of torture.

# Iraq: Was It Really Worth the Price?

*"Whoever recommends and helps a good cause becomes a partner therein; and whoever recommends and helps an evil cause, shares in its burden. And Allah has power over all things." - The Noble Qur'an (4:85)*

Gideon Rose, managing editor of the Foreign Affairs section of *The Washington Post*, in a book review of <u>The Assassin's Gate: America in Iraq</u> by George Packer (10/9/05), wrote the following:

> Denial, anger, bargaining, depression, acceptance: The psychiatrist Elizabeth Kubler-Ross came up with her famous five stages of grief to describe how patients react to the discovery that they are terminally ill, but these phases apply to other traumas too. With regard to the debacle playing out in Iraq, for example, the White House and its diehard supporters are still in denial, while most of their Democratic critics are stuck in anger. Policy wonks have moved on to the bargaining phase, debating how much of the original mission to sacrifice in return for a way out. Depression is likely to set in as the full extent of the calamity becomes clear; acceptance is a long way off.

> How did this happen? How could the strongest power in modern history, going to war against a much lesser opponent at a time and place of its choosing, find itself stuck a few years later, hemorrhaging blood and treasure amid increasing chaos? Americans will be debating the answer for decades...

Conscientious Muslim Americans won't be among those debating this issue. For them the answer is already written in the Qur'an: *"Satan plots, and ALLAH plans; and ALLAH is the best of planners."*

It is this writer's humble view that today's quagmire in the Gulf actually has it roots in September 1980, when Saddam Hussein was discreetly encouraged to attack the newly established *Islamic Republic of Iran,* while the revolution was still in its infancy. When [then] National Security Adviser Zbigniew Brezenski was asked for an official US reaction to Iraq's unwarranted aggression against its neighbor, he reportedly said, *"There are no incompatibility of interests between the U.S. and Iraq."*

With the incoming administration of President Ronald Reagan, that stance became official; as did Saddam Hussein. He was "our man in Baghdad," and America supported him (covertly) to the hilt. During the eight year period that Saddam prosecuted his war against Iran, the "Butcher of Baghdad" received full diplomatic, logistical and material support from the United States and its allies. Indeed, in addition to being our man in Baghdad, he was the darling of other corrupt Arab regimes in the region!

When his regime perpetrated the horrific chemical massacre in Halabcha - and a host of other *crimes against humanity* against Iraqi and Iranian civilians, in violation of well established international law—he did it with full U.S. support. The U.S. knew what he was doing and we sanctioned it!

But as the saying goes —"what goes around, comes around." It was only a matter of time before a used up Saddam Hussein would suffer the same fate as other corrupt, despotic, and willing tools of American foreign policy (i.e., Duvalier, Marcos, Mobutu, Noriega, Pinochet, the Shah of Iran, etc). And it was only a matter of time before our national duplicity would come back to bite us as well.

Saddam's time came at the end of the war, when certain interests signaled that it was time for the second most powerful military in the region (courtesy of United States largess) to be dismantled. The Frankenstein Monster had to be destroyed; and for this task, one of the most classic setups in modern history was put into motion.

At the conclusion of the Iran-Iraq war, Iraq's economy was in a shambles, and Iraq was deeply in debt. The image of Saddam Hussein, as the great modern day Arab conqueror, had suffered as well. Meanwhile Kuwait (one of Iraq's leading financiers during the war) had reportedly purchased some slant drilling equipment from Europe, and was using this equipment on the disputed territory that bordered the two countries. This, coupled with a host of other domestic pressures, reportedly infuriated Saddam – and the rest, as they say, is history.

**Ambassador April Glaspie,** a career officer in the U.S. Department of State, was only the second American ambassador to be named to Iraq since the closing of the U.S. embassy in 1967, a result of the 67 "Arab-Israeli War." This seasoned diplomat would be the instrument used by her own government to lay the trap. Ambassador Joseph Wilson, at the time the number two officer in Baghdad, wrote in his book, *The Politics of Truth* (pg 104):

> On July 31, State Department Assistant Secretary of State John Kelly appeared before an open session of the House International Relations Committee, chaired by Congressman Lee Hamilton, an expert on Middle East affairs. Hamilton asked Kelly a question point-blank to which he must already have known the answer: Did the United States have a mutual defense pact with Kuwait that would necessitate an automatic American response should Iraq invade?

The State Department spokesman had already addressed the question several weeks previously, but Hamilton asked it anyway. John Kelly gave the correct answer, the only answer that he could give: *"We don't have any defense treaty with the Gulf States. That's clear.* We support the independence and security of all friendly states in the region. Since the Truman administration, we've maintained naval forces in the area because its stability is in our interest. We call for a peaceful solution to all disputes, and we think that the sovereignty of every state in the Gulf must be respected."

**This was the same essential message that Ambassador Glaspie reiterated in her face-to-face meetings with Saddam Hussein.** What Saddam heard is precisely what the behind the scenes orchestrators wanted him to hear—in fact, knew that he would hear; in short, that your dispute with Kuwait is fundamentally an *Arab-Arab issue*.

As soon as Iraqi President Saddam Hussein invaded Kuwait—and despite the absence of any mutual defense pact, American President George Herbert Walker Bush (aka, Bush I) declared war; and when that declaration of war was issued there was nothing Saddam Hussein could do to reverse that decision!

What followed was more than a decade of unending war—turning what was once one of the most materially developed countries in the region, into one of the most devastated and dependent countries in the region. Iraq and its ruler went from being America's darling, to America's favorite whipping post—and both Democrats and Republicans had their turns. When **Clinton** needed cover for some of his unseemly presidential shenanigans, he bombed Iraq. When **Bush II** decided that it was time to complete unfinished business, and advance his father's vision of a "New World Order" (with an evangelical spin) he declared full scale war on Iraq.

The real weapon of mass destruction turned out to be the U.S. imposed (American-British enforced) sanctions, which reportedly took the lives of over a half million Iraqi children under the age of five, while stunting the development of millions more.

In what will no doubt remain one of the most memorable and disturbing images of that unending conflict, [Clinton Administration] Secretary of State Madeline Albright was asked, in a nationally broadcast interview, if the human devastation in Iraq was worth the price? After pausing for a moment she responded in the affirmative—and to this day (to this writer's knowledge) there has never been a statement of correction, clarification, or apology from any high level official of that administration, nor the one that succeeded it.

Given present day realities in Iraq, I wonder if the powers-that-be still feel that the romance and breakup was really *"worth the price?"*

# THE ARROGANCE OF POWER
## Mercenaries on the Battlefield

The Qur'an says: *"Corruption has appeared on the land and on the sea, on account of what men's hands have wrought; ALLAH (God) will make them taste a part of what they have done so that they might return (to a state of God-consciousness)."*

American Founding Father, Thomas Jefferson, once said: "I tremble for my country when I reflect that God is just; His justice cannot sleep forever."

One night I caught a few minutes of Bill O'Reilly's show on the Fox television network. (I truly believe that it's a little difficult for any *thinking and balanced* person to tolerate this show for a full hour). On this particular night he had as a guest, a retired U.S. general who was operating as a private contractor in Iraq. As the two of them put on what must have been the standard fare for O'Reilly's dedicated viewers—arrogantly pontificating (in a biased one-sided manner) on the ongoing carnage in Iraq—I decided that it was time for me to pick up the pen. A few days earlier I had written a commentary on the Virginia Tech University tragedy. It was now time for me to revisit my thoughts on its deeper significance.

A well known Muslim scholar of another age, Sheikh ibn Taymeeyah, impressed upon his students the following: "Civilization is rooted in justice, and the consequences of oppression are devastating. Therefore, it is said ALLAH aids the just state even if it is non-Muslim, yet withholds His help from the oppressive state even if it is Muslim."

As America still struggles to understand the carnage that erupted on the campus of Virginia Tech, nestled up in the commonwealth of Virginia's picturesque Blueridge Mountains, our nation's actions (both here and abroad)—i.e., the culture of violence that permeates life and living in the USA, and the violence that we shamelessly *export* to other parts of the world - must be factored into the equation.

For purposes of this writing we will focus our attention on the violence that America exports to other corners of the world. While volumes could be written on the destructive impact that American foreign policy has had on Africa and Asia, or Central and South America, we will devote our attention to the corner of the world that is constantly in the news these days: Iraq and the Middle East.

We begin with a simple question: *Is an American life of greater value than a life that is not "American"*—particularly if that life happens to be found in one of the developing countries of the world? We invite the reader to honestly ponder this question for a few moments before proceeding any further with this commentary.

In a featured article published in the April 2007 edition of Vanity Fair Magazine, titled "Iraq's Mercenary King," former C.I.A. agent Robert Baer provided some valuable insight into the world of high paid, U.S. financed mercenaries currently operating in Iraq. Baer began his article with a provocative question: "As a former C.I.A. agent, the author knows how mercenaries work in the shadows. But how did a notorious former British officer, Tim Spicer, come to coordinate the second largest army in Iraq—the tens of thousands of private security contractors?" How indeed? Baer continues:

> [Spicer] popped up on the C.I.A.'s radar after he retired from the British Army and went to work, in 1996, as the C.E.O. of **Sandline International**, a private military company offering 'operational support' to "legitimate governments."

A year later Spicer was in Papua New Guinea, where he fielded a mercenary army for the government in order to protect a multi-national copper-mining company. After Spicer was expelled, he moved to Sierra Leone, this time helping to ship arms to coup plotters. Spicer's name resurfaced in 2004 in connection with a putsch aimed at Equatorial Guinea...

But then, somehow, two months later, Spicer's new company, known as **Aegis Defence Services**, landed a $293 million Pentagon contract to coordinate security for reconstruction projects, as well as support for other private military companies, in Iraq. This effectively put him in command of the second largest foreign armed force in the country—behind America's but ahead of Britain's. These men aren't officially part of the Coalition of the Willing, because they're all paid contractors—the Coalition of the Billing, you might call it—but they're a crucial part of the coalition's forces nonetheless.

What is the going rate for mercenaries these days? The Government Accountability Office released a report in February 2006 which stated there were approximately 48,000 private military contractors in Iraq, employed by 181 different companies. (No doubt, the numbers have increased since then.) The bulk of the military contractors are American and British—many retired from elite units such as the *British Special Air Service* or the *U.S. Special Forces*—with a sprinkling of other nationalities thrown in for good measure. A report in *The Economist* opines that mercenaries are Britain's largest export to Iraq—before food, medicine, or even construction material!

Soldiers with an elite military background can make up to $1,500 per day! More typically a western military contractor will earn

$180,000 a year - while a contractor from one of the "developing nations" (i.e., Bosnians, Chileans, Filipinos or Nepalese, etc.) can be acquired for considerably less.

Case in point: Baer references the *hot water* that **Blackwater USA** (one of the largest private military contractors in Iraq) got itself into because of its own unscrupulous hiring practices. About three dozen former Colombian soldiers are suing Blackwater USA for breach of contract, because Blackwater reportedly reduced their rate of pay at the last minute to $34 a day (a virtual slave wage in comparison to what an American or Brit receives)!

These "contractors" often operate with depraved indifference toward the lives and property of the indigenous population. Baer wrote that one of their habits—aka "tactics" in the field—is to shoot first and ask questions later; but it doesn't stop there. Some of America's paid mercenaries "have been accused of shooting Iraqis for sport." Case in point: In November 2005 a disgruntled Aegis ex-employee posted a "trophy video" on the Internet, featuring some of Aegis's employees speeding down the highway and indiscriminately shooting at civilian cars, against Elvis Presley's "Mystery Train" soundtrack.

The company's internal investigation of the video concluded that the actions depicted represented "legitimate operations," undertaken in compliance with *rules of engagement.* "The Pentagon looked into the video and declined to take further steps," Baer writes. It should also be noted that many of these contractors come with murky backgrounds, to say the least.

**Hart Security**, for example, is a private military company with roots in Apartheid South Africa (once known for having one of the world's most ruthless counter-insurgency forces). According to Baer, "One of Hart's men was Gray Branfield, a former covert South African operative who spent years assassinating leaders of the African National Congress. After Branfield was killed in Kut during the 2004 uprising of the Mahdi Army, and his history became public, Hart Security said it had been unaware of his past."

After another subcontractor named Francois Strydom was killed by Iraqi insurgents in 2004, the private military company Erinys discovered that it too had an Apartheid South African problem. Strydom, it turns out, was a former member of the notorious **Koevoet**—formerly an arm of Apartheid South Africa's counter-insurgency campaign in the territory now known as Namibia.

These contractors operate as small military units. They routinely carry automatic weapons, rocket launchers, and travel at high rates of speed in heavily armored SUVs. They are known to shoot at any civilian vehicle that appears even remotely to be a threat. Nowadays when a contractor gets into trouble over its head, it can call for assistance in the form of military air support, or a quick reaction force. (Contractors also carry transponders, which supposedly facilitates the military being able to locate them in an emergency.)

Baer notes:

It's easy to imagine how a young man in Fallujah, where the unemployment rate is now perhaps 70 percent, views private military contractors. They arrive in the form of an armored GMC Suburban, with smoked windows, bearing down at high speed. The closest thing to a visible human being is the turret gunner. But in his kevlar helmet and blue-mirrored wrap around Oakleys, the gunner doesn't seem all that human. The young Iraqi knows that the gunner makes more

money in a year than he will in a lifetime, that he is effectively IMMUNE FROM PROSECUTION [emphasis
mine], and that he won't hesitate to shoot if people don't get
out of the way fast enough.

Private military companies are said to represent a $30 billion a year
industry. A lot of lobbying clout comes with that kind of money;
needless to say, the industry has friends in high (or low places
depending on your point of view.) Baer revealed that Steve Kappes,
the current deputy director of the C.I.A., came from **ArmorGroup,**
a private military company with contracts in Iraq; Cofer Black,
formerly with the C.I.A. and the State Department, is the vice-
chairman of Blackwater. (The industry reportedly has many other
friends who routinely flow in and out of government.)

Baer also makes mention of a revealing address that Mr. Black delivered to an audience in a predominantly Muslim country in 2006.
"Last year Cofer Black addressed a convention of mercenaries in
Jordan, and he floated a plan to create a full-size Blackwater brigade,
ready to be deployed virtually anywhere, for a price. 'It's an intrigu-
ing, good idea from a practical standpoint because we're low-cost
and fast. The issue is: *Who's going to let us play on their team?*"

Ponder for moment the mentality such language reflects: "Who's
going to let us PLAY on their team?" Let us cite (by way of example)
the form that such PLAY can take in a country like Iraq.

We often hear about the despicable and fundamentally un-
Islamic insurgent warfare that deliberately targets civilian
non-combatants in Iraq—but we seldom hear about the
innocent Iraqi lives that are routinely snuffed out by the
occupiers at PLAY! The April 15, 2007, edition of *The*

*Washington Post* newspaper featured a front page article titled "A Chaotic Day On Baghdad's Airport Road," by Steve Fainaru, that provides a case in point. The article begins with the following words:

On the afternoon of July 8, 2006, four private security guards rolled out of Baghdad's Green Zone in an armored SUV. The team leader, Jacob Washbourne, rode in the front passenger seat. He seemed in a good mood. His vacation started the next day. **'I want to kill somebody today,'** Washbourne said, according to the three other men in the vehicle, who later recalled it as an offhand remark. Before the day was over, however, the guards had been involved in three shooting incidents. In one, Washborne [a 29 year old former U. S. Marine from Broken Arrow, Oklahoma] allegedly fired into the windshield of a taxi for amusement.

When you factor this one incident against the backdrop of over 48,000, military contractors in Iraq—many of whom coming from questionable backgrounds and psychological states—one gets some sense of the magnitude of destructive pathology on the ground in Iraq; and why many Iraqis have nick-named the private mercenaries, *black death*! And to date, not a single criminal case has been brought against a security contractor operating in Iraq or Afghanistan!

Private contractors were granted immunity from the Iraqi legal process in 2004 by the former head of the U.S. occupation government, Paul Bremer. That the nominally independent Iraqi government has not moved to amend this oppressive provision, speaks volumes about its "independence."

The private military firm that employed the four contractors involved in the aforementioned July 8 incident, **Triple Canopy,** conducted an inquiry that led to the firing of three of the men—Jacob C. Washborne, Shane B. Schmidt and Charles L. Sheppard III. The fourth contractor, Isireli Naucukidi, reported the incident to his superiors immediately and left the company on his own volition. Schmidt and Sheppard filed reports on the incident days later, and attempted to distance themselves from any culpability.

Naucukidi described the taxi driver as a 60 to 70 year old man. *"From my point of view, this old man, he was so innocent, because he was ahead of us with a normal speed. He couldn't have [been] any danger for us."* He also noted that "the three Americans were laughing," and that Schmidt reached over, tapped Washbourne on the shoulder and said, "good shot." All three soldiers of fortune are now back in the states, spending their ill-gotten gains.

(It should also be noted that Naucukidi is a Fijian Army veteran who earned $70 a day—as compared to Washborne's $600 a day and Schmidt and Sheppard's $500 a day, for the same work. He has reportedly returned to the Fiji Island of Ovalau, where he farms. I strongly encourage the reader to pull up *The Washington Post* article and read it for yourself. It is very revealing, indeed.)

In closing, I'd like to revisit the rhetorical question raised by President Bush at the recent Virginia Tech memorial ceremony, as he wondered out loud what had the victims done to deserve such a fate. As individuals they did nothing. But nor have the people of **Iraq**, the people of **Palestine**, the people of **Somalia**, the people of **Darfur** (Sudan), etc, etc—they have done nothing to deserve the ongoing externally-imposed carnage in their lands. (Regarding Darfur, my strongest criticism is directed at those who armed the rebels and then encouraged them to remain recalcitrant at the negotiation table; thus prolonging that very unfortunate man-made crisis.)

In IRAQ, there are several massacres equivalent to the Virginia Tech massacre EACH DAY! (We only hear about the Arab-on-Arab perpetrators. But what of the others?) Where are the memorials for these slaughtered innocents? And why aren't the foreign perpetrators held accountable to the fullest extent of the law, for these atrocities? The collective conscience of the nation, from which most of the young victims of the Virginia Tech tragedy were born, should be raising these challenging questions of itself. For only then can we begin to institute urgently needed, *spiritually-based* reforms before it is too late.

The Bible says, "*As a man soweth, so shall he reap.*" As it is for men, so it is for NATIONS!

# THE SECRET WARS OF THE CIA

In Bob Woodward's Book titled, <u>Veil: The Secret Wars of the CIA 1981-1987</u>, we get a glimpse into the murky and violent world of state-sponsored terrorism, *American style*. The "Cast of Characters" listed on page 17 of the book, the book's description, and a quick review of the index, is sufficient for providing a good sense of things past and present.

The 543 page book is basically about the dubious exploits of the CIA under the late William J. Casey, who served as the presidential campaign manager for Ronald Reagan in 1980, before being named Director of the CIA in 1981. Woodward notes that Casey helped define the foreign policy aspirations of the Reagan Administration in a way "that will come to be seen as defining its era. And some era it was!

The book's description reads as follows: "This is a classic study of the relationship between the management of the world's most sophisticated espionage apparatus and the making of foreign policy. Treachery, deception, bribery, even assassination were tools.... Veil is the story of the covert wars that were waged in a secretive atmosphere and became the centerpieces and eventual time bombs of American foreign policy in the 1980s."

For example, the description of a CIA orchestrated (and Saudi financed) attempted assassination of a Muslim leader in Lebanon in 1985 (pg. 397):

> On March 8, 1985, a car parked with explosives was driven into a Beirut suburb about fifty yards from Fadlallah's highrise residence. The car exploded, killing eighty people and wounding two hundred, leaving devastation, fires and collapsed buildings. Anyone who had happened to be in the

immediate neighborhood was killed, hurt or terrorized, but Fadlallah escaped without injury. His followers strung a huge 'MADE IN THE USA" banner in front of the building that had been blown out."

Case study number two (pg 289-290)—the military invasion of the tiny Caribbean island of Grenada, only 133 square miles in area, with a population estimated at the time to be 110,000; producer of about a third of the world's annual consumption of nutmeg. Its leader, Maurice Bishop, a young, charismatic Marxist had reportedly become one of Reagan's many obsessions:

> Casey and [George] Shultz saw an opportunity. The absence of a government on Granada provided a rare chance to invoke mutual-security agreements the United States had with other small Caribbean islands. "Hey," Casey said at one point, "fuck it, let's dump these bastards." Shultz was at first inclined to a less ambitious scheme, but he favored readiness for possible military action. Reagan's other normally fractious and divided senior advisers and Cabinet officers agreed. The Administration needed a firmer grounding, more legitimacy…

The solution surfaced the next day, Friday October 21. Prime Minister Eugenia Charles of Dominica, another small Caribbean island, headed a group called the *Organization of Eastern Caribbean States*. They were meeting that day in Barbados, and word was sent to them that the likelihood of U.S. military action would be substantially increased if they requested it. The OECS decided to do so, phrasing their request for U.S. assistance to restore order and democracy on Granada.

Case study number three (pg 281)—the covert war against Nicaragua:

On October 11, CIA-trained speedboat teams with their own force of CIA Latino assets conducted a pre-dawn raid against the Nicaraguan fuel storage depot at the port of Corinto on the Pacific side. Five storage tanks that supposedly had most of the Nicaraguan oil reserves were blown up. About twenty thousand residents of Corinto had to be evacuated because of fires. Casey was elated. This was big time, not trivial cross-border op. He carried reconnaissance photos to Reagan immediately, and the White House aides found him [Reagan] like a schoolboy with a good report card.

Case study number four—what investigative author and television producer James Bamford had to say in his book titled, <u>Body of Secrets</u> (pgs. 78 & 82):

The pall cast over the CIA as a result of the botched invasion did nothing to dampen the Kennedy administration's obsession with Castro…

"The Bay of Pigs fiasco broke the dike," said one report at the time. "President Kennedy was pilloried by the superpatriots as a 'no-win' chief…The Far Right became a fount of proposals born of frustration and put forward in the name of anti-Communism…Active duty commanders played host to anti-Communist seminars on their bases and attended or addressed Right wing meetings elsewhere."

Although no one in Congress could have known it at the time, [Joint Chiefs Chairman Lyman L.] Lemnitzer and the Joint Chiefs had quietly slipped over the edge. According to secret and long-hidden documents obtained for Body of Secrets, the **Joint Chiefs of Staff** drew up and approved plans for what may be the most corrupt plan ever created by the U.S. government. **In the name of anticommunism, they proposed launching a secret and bloody war of terrorism against their own country in order to trick the American public into supporting an ill-conceived war they intended to launch against Cuba.**

**Codenamed Operation Northwoods**, the plan which had the written approval of the Chairman and every member of the Joint Chiefs of Staff, called for innocent people to be shot on American streets; for boats carrying refugees fleeing Cuba to be sunk on the high seas; for a wave of violent terrorism to be launched in Washington, D.C., Miami, and elsewhere. People would be framed for bombings they did not commit; planes would be highjacked. Using phony eveidence, all of it would be blamed on Castro, thus giving Lemnitzer and his cabal the excuse, as well as the public and international backing, they needed to launch their war.

Now, the significance of Bamford's explosive revelation is two-fold. First: the late William "Bill" Kunstler, in his thought-provoking book titled, <u>My Life As A Radical Lawyer</u>, had some very revealing things to say about an Egyptian informant/agent-provocateur by the name of **Emad Salem**, and the World Trade Center bombing of 1993 (pg, 335):

> Ron Kuby and I had evidence that Emad Salem, the government's confidential informer, was himself involved in the WTC bombing. Not only had he confessed to the crime during a conversation with an FBI agent he had secretly recorded—as defense attorneys, we were given copies of transcripts of these and other conversations – but HE WAS HOSPITALIZED LESS THAN THREE HOURS AFTER THE BLASTS with a middle ear attack. We had information that Salem was prone to these attacks when exposed to shots or explosions; he had suffered a similar attack when he fired a rifle on a practice range without wearing earplugs.

This writer has heard the taped recording of which the late Bill Kunstler spoke, as have thousands of listeners of *Pacifica Radio*'s affiliate in the New York City tri-state area (WBAI-FM)—and it's clear to me that if the 1993 bombing of the World Trade Center was not orchestrated by rogue elements of the U.S. government (thru their "confidential informant" Emad Salem), they at least knew that it was on the horizon before it happened; yet they allowed it to happen in order to achieve a political end!

It should also be an outrage to the American public that this man (Emad Salem) was paid over a million dollars and given a new identity at the con-clusion of that politically-driven legal lynching of the blind Egyptian cler-ic, Sheikh Omar Abdur-Rahman (and his co-defendants) in 1995. It is this writer's humble opinion that if something of this nature could be con-ceived in the 1960s, and carried out in the 1990s, it stands to reason that such thinking could also achieve frightening fruition on **September 11, 2001!**

Secondly, there is another equally important point to be made. What became of the Joint Chiefs who conceived of that treasonous plot against the American people during the Kennedy Administration? If I were a bet-ting man I would wager the house on the premise that they all retired with attractive pensions and respectability; and those who passed on were buried at the *Arlington National Cemetery* with full military honors.

Now, I know that some readers might be inclined to opine—'Even if what Mr. Bamford says is true, it was never carried out. So what's the fuss?' Simply this: In section two of this book, there are a number of young Muslim men who the government has alleged were planning, or *thinking* about planning, acts of terrorism against the United States or its interests. Most of these young men, upon conviction, were given sentences that will result (at minimum) with them spending most, if not the rest, of their productive lives in prison. (That is if these barbaric sentences are not over-turned on appeal.) That's the point!

# Part 4
# The Role of
# The Media

## NEO-CONS IN THE NEW ROOMS

On the wall of the National Press Club in Washington, DC, is an inspiring treatise entitled *The Journalist's Creed*, written by the late Walter Williams, the former Dean of the School of Journalism at the University of Missouri. The "Creed" reads as follows:

I believe that the public journal is a public trust, that all connected with it are, to the full measure of their responsibility, trustees for the public; that acceptance of a lesser service than the public service is a betrayal of this trust.

I believe that clear thinking and clear statement, accuracy, and fairness, are fundamental to good journalism.

I believe that a journalist should write only what he holds in his heart to be true.

I believe that suppression of the news, for any consideration other than the welfare of society, is indefensible.

I believe that no one should write as a journalist what he would not say as a gentlemen; that bribery by one's own pocketbook is as much to be avoided as bribery by the pocketbook of another; that individual responsibility may not be escaped by pleading another's instructions or another's dividends.

I believe that advertising, news and editorial columns should alike serve the best interests of readers; that a single standard of helpful truth and cleanness should prevail for all; that the supreme test of good journalism is the measure of its public service.

I believe that the journalism which succeeds best—and best deserves success—fears God and honors man; is stoutly independent, unmoved by pride of opinion or greed of power; [is]

constructive, tolerant but never careless; [is] self-controlled, patient, always respectful of its readers, but always unafraid; is quickly indignant at injustice; is unswayed by the appeal of privilege or the clamor of the mob; seeks to give every man a chance, and, as far as law and honest wage and recognition of human brotherhood can make it so, and equal chance; is profoundly patriotic while sincerely promoting international goodwill and cementing world comradeship; is a journalism of humanity, of and for today's world.

I personally believe, and I think most reasonable people would agree, that if today's journalism practitioners were to follow the aforementioned blueprint, the global community would be a much better place in which to live. American citizens would be far more educated, informed and conscientized on the requisite duties of citizenship within—what we like to call, "representative democracy."

Unfortunately, in today's corporate controlled, ego-driven media culture, far too many journalists (of questionable allegiances) are content to serve as the hired guns of whoever is in a position to financially secure their allegiance. In such a climate truth is indeed found in the eye of the beholder, as ethics and principles morph into expediency. And for this we all pay the price.

What follows are two brief examples of injustices that were aided and abetted by reporters, journalists, columnists, "talking heads," etc. One occurred in 1998, and the other in 2002—(Pre-9/11 and Post-9/11).

In August 1998, a terrorist attack was launched against American embassies in two East African countries. Despite the fact that these attacks were committed by persons unknown, and high level U.S. officials and investigators were stating (*on the record*) that it would take a considerable amount of time to carry out a careful and thorough investigation, military attacks were ordered by the Clinton Administration on two sovereign nations within two weeks of the tragedy. While politics no doubt factored into Clinton's decision to order the attack, mainstream media clearly had its agenda as well.

With the passing of time some truth would emerge. It would be discovered that the destroyed pharmaceutical plant in the Sudan was just that—a pharmaceutical plant! However, while a formal apology has quietly been made through "diplomatic channels," the last time this writer inquired on the matter (which was approximately a year before this writing) no restitution had thus far been made by the U.S. government to the Republic of Sudan.

What follows is the fact sheet that was prepared on the incident by The Peace And Justice Foundation, shortly after the U.S. military strike in 1998.

## A FACT SHEET ON THE BOMBINGS IN EAST AFRICA BY PERSONS UNKNOWN; AND THE SUBSEQUENT MISSILE ATTACKS ON SUDAN AND AFGHANISTAN BY THE U.S. MILITARY

• On August 7, 1998, two almost simultaneous bomb blasts occurred at U.S. embassies in Nairobi, Kenya and Dar Es Salaam, Tanzania, resulting in the deaths of 257 and over 5,000 injured. While no one immediately claimed responsibility, speculation by anonymous government sources, "terrorism experts," and media organizations pointed the finger of responsibility at "extremist Muslims" and "militant Islam."

• Israeli military/investigators were the first foreigners on the scene. An American (Fairfax County, Va.) rescue team arrived hours later and were prevented by the Israelis from working in the area where the bombs exploded outside the embassies. Local Kenyans, who were not aware of these details considered this to be flagrant insensitivity toward the welfare of Kenyan people. (They felt the U.S. was only concerned about "Americans inside the embassy." The commander of the Fairfax team held a news conference to explain that they were under Israeli constraints. Despite this explanation, the American rescue squad reportedly had to be moved from one hotel to another undisclosed location every two days for their safety.

• On August 10, Secretary of State Madeleine K. Albright addressed a meeting of several hundred State Department employees, in which she said: "We are not a nation that retaliates just in order to get vengeance, nor do we forget our own legal system while searching for those who have harmed us. Even if we would like to go out right this instant and bomb somebody, I think that we've got to be careful about what were doing and why we're doing it, and if we're doing the right thing so that we can be true to ourselves."

• White House spokesman P.J. Crowley cautioned that "this [investigation] could very well take a number of years."

• News organizations, syndicated columnists, think tank analysts, etc., systematically increased the tempo of assigning blame and instigating reprisal. Within 48 hours U.S. government officials had already labeled Osama bin Laden—and an alleged "network" of terrorist links—the leading suspect, based upon unidentified U.S. intelligence sources. (One senior European intelligence official, who spoke on condition of anonymity, was quoted as saying: *"If bin Laden did not exist the U.S. would have to invent him."*)

• Of seven nations consistently listed as "state sponsors of terrorism" (Iran, Iraq, Libya, Sudan, Syria, Cuba and Korea), five are predominantly Muslim nations. The U.S. State Department's 1997 Report stated that state-sponsored terrorism had declined in favor of freelance groups not backed by any government.

• There were reportedly 304 acts of international terrorism in 1997, with 221 killed and 693 wounded worldwide. Of this number seven of the dead and 21 of the wounded were U.S. citizens. Most of the anti-American attacks consisted of "low grade bombings" of American-owned pipelines in Colombia, involving no loss of life.

• By August 11, a group (previously un-heard of) calling itself "The Islamic Army for the Liberation of Holy Places" is alleged to have taken responsibility for the blasts.

• The bombing of the Federal Building in Oklahoma City and the crash of TWA Flight 800 were also initially blamed on Muslims; and in the Oklahoma City case there were also reports that a previously unknown Muslim entity had claimed responsibility for the attack. It is now a known fact that "the worst act of terrorism on American soil" up to that time, was committed by individuals born and bred in the U.S.A. (There are Native Americans and African Americans who might differ with the oft-repeated characterization, the "worst act of terrorism" in American history.)

• While accepting the principle of just war (for defense and the elimination of oppression when all reasonable attempts for resolution by peaceful means fail), Islam imposes strict and clearly defined limits on the conduct of Muslims during times of war.

• Some experts opined that the East Africa attacks had the look of government sponsorship, because the bombs and their transportation were so sophisticated they would have necessitated preparations by people with either *diplomatic* or commercial ties. Daniel Pipes, editor of Middle East Quarterly and often stated "expert on Middle East terrorism," reportedly said: *"Bin Laden may have lots of money, but there are many things that money can't buy. It cannot buy extensive intelligence networks needed to study targets and plan sophisticated, carefully synchronized attacks. It cannot buy certain kinds of weaponry, including Semtex explosive. It cannot buy diplomatic pouches which representatives of states use in many cases to smuggle weapons and money freely into countries to launch attacks."* (8/14/98 *Washington Times*)

• By August 14, a total of 215 FBI agents, lab examiners, evidence technicians, computer specialists, photographers and translators were in Nairobi and Dar es Salaam. The agent in charge, Assistant Director Thomas Pickard stated: "It will take at least four more weeks to complete examination of both bomb sites and witness interviews, and from that we will develop leads." Pickard reportedly said there were 700 interviews to conduct in Nairobi and 200 in Dar Es Salaam.

• On Monday, August 17, **President Clinton** testified before the **Monica Lewinsky** grand jury and was forced to provide testimony, under harsh questioning and new information, which dramatically differed with information provided during his January 17 deposition under oath. President Clinton then gave a brief (damage control) television address to the nation, following his testimony before the grand jury.

• On Thursday, August 20, the Clinton Administration authorized a military strike on two sovereign nations, violating the airspace of a third. Approximately 75 Tomahawk cruise missiles targeted a pharmaceutical plant (responsible for an estimated 50 percent of medicines needed) in Sudan, and alleged "terrorist camps" in Afghanistan. The attacks were justified on the basis of "mounting evidence" that both sites were connected to bin Laden and his "terrorist network, and further, were described by Administration officials as a preemptive strike against another terrorist attack.

• The U.S. assault was conducted less than two weeks after the East Africa bombings, and three days following the President's embarrassing address to the nation, in which he confessed to "an inappropriate relationship" with former White House intern Monica Lewinsky. (It has also been published in the media that the President approved the assault on Friday 8/14, and gave the final go ahead on the morning of the attack.)

• Despite repeated and widely circulated high level U.S. government assertions that there was "mounting" and "credible" evidence to  support the attack (based on CIA and Pentagon gathered intelligence), FBI Director Freeh, in Nairobi overseeing the investigation of the Kenyan bombing, said he had come to "no final conclusion concerning who was responsible." (Washington Times 8/22/98)

• The Sunday 8/23/98 edition of *The Washington Post* (A25) diagramed, "**A Global, Pan-Islamic Network,**" in which the opening paragraph of the sub-caption read: "Saudi born millionaire Osama bin Laden has been linked to terrorist acts and militant Muslim organizations across the globe and is said to command forces numbering 3,000..." **Eighteen countries** (the majority  with predominantly Muslim populations) are listed on the chart in this Post report as being within bin Laden's sphere of influence.

• Anti-American demonstrations erupt in several Muslim countries, while the Sudanese government appealed to the United Nations for an impartial investigation, insisting that it could prove the bombed pharmaceutical facilities innocent purpose.

• Pakistan filed a complaint with the U.N. Security Council, offering the discovery of an un-exploded cruise missile on its territory as proof that the U.S. violated its airspace during the attack on Afghanistan.

• In the wake of mounting world criticism, a U.S. intelligence official detailed the physical evidence which in their words "justified" the lethal strike on the pharmaceutical plant in Sudan—a soil sample, "obtained by clandestine means."

• The front page headline in the August 27, 1998, edition of the *Weekly Urdu Times* reads, "The person arrested in Pakistan may be related to [Israeli] **Mossad...**" This report was based upon "reliable sources" within Pakistani intelligence.

• The 1954 "Lavon Affair" in Egypt proves that it is not beyond the scope of Israel to conspire to bomb a target (in this case, reportedly, an American Embassy and British Consulate) and make it appear that Arabs did it.

• According to the *Organization for the Prohibition of Chemical Weapons*, the international agency that oversees the treaty that bars chemical weapons, the chemical known as Empta, cited by the U.S. to justify its missile attacks on Sudan, could be used "in limited quantities for legitimate commercial purposes." (*New York Times*, 8/27/98, "Possible Benign Use Is Seen for Chemical At Factory in Sudan")

• In the same report, Defense and intelligence officials (speaking on condition of anonymity) revealed that the soil sample was secretly collected outside the factory "several months ago."

Was the U.S. Attack on Afghanistan and Sudan justified, or was it a case of life imitating art ("Wag the Dog") with corporate media instigation? Were U.S. actions just another example of the arrogance of power? Just another illegal act of state-sponsored terrorism (by international law standards), and a manifestation of the Clausewitz theory: *"War is an extension of politics carried out by other means?"* You be the judge!

**Example #2**

On Wednesday, March 20, 2002, a gross violation of our nation's alleged commitment to "life, liberty and the pursuit of happiness" occurred when U.S. government agents, under the influence of foreign interests (Israel), trampled upon the constitutional rights of its own citizens, in the shadow of the very institutions and monuments that have come to symbolize beacons of hope for people around the world.

In Northern Virginia, law abiding citizens of the Islamic faith were terrorized by agents of the government; affirming once again that religious and ideological bigotry have been accorded the mask of legitimacy at the highest levels, in post 9/11 America.

In conclusion, life is short. It would behoove the nation's spineless and self-seeking politicians (*not all* of them are, *but most* appear to be), and the neo-cons in the newsrooms, to consider the good counsel found in a passage of Alan Paton's, <u>Cry The Beloved Country</u>, wherein he wrote:

*"I shall no longer ask myself if this or that is expedient, only if it is right. I do it not because I am noble or unselfish, but because life slips away, and I need for the rest of my journey a star that will not play false to me, a compass that will not lie. I do it because I can no longer aspire to the highest with one part of myself, but deny it with the other."*

# JUDITH MILLER AND ME

by John Sugg

OK, for a start, there really is no "Judith Miller and me," at least in the sense that I'd invite her to my birthday party. But I have talked to her on the phone a few times (nothing to do with Valerie Plame, Scooter Libby or Karl Rove, however). For a time, our lives were remotely in each other's gravity, drawn together by a pseudo-journalist—indeed, a model for what Miller has become—named Steven Emerson.

I don't like what Miller represents in journalism. She is not, to my mind, a journalist. She forfeited that claim when she became a conduit of propaganda for the neo-conservative cabal that has its bloody hands on the control levers of the nation. In a stunning declaration this month, Miller admitted that she'd been granted a Pentagon security clearance. She tried to backpedal on the assertion, claiming the clearance was routine. But she couldn't spin away the disclosure that she'd been blindsiding her editors and colleagues. She had become a shill for the Bush administration; her employment at the New York Times was merely a cover.

She boasted in a self-serving article two weeks ago that she "had everything to be proud of and nothing to apologize for." That bombast was in the same edition as a companion piece where the Times admitted to censoring reporters who had written an article that would have exposed details about Libby and his role in outing Plame's work as a covert CIA agent. In short, the Times' publisher, Arthur Sulzberger Jr., had turned his newspaper into a public relations vehicle for an out-of-control pet reporter. If burying the truth was the price, Sulzberger was willing to pay.

Miller's 85 days in jail elicit no sympathy from me. She was made to appear a martyr for "protecting sources," a cynical attempt to repair her slime-adorned reputation after she contributed to the serial misleading of America on Iraq's weapons of mass destruction. When the Times issued an after-the-fact semi-confession that it had on at least a half-dozen occasions failed to do its duty in vetting articles that credulously backed George Bush's war propaganda, all but one of the stories was a Miller job. The newspaper, oh-so protective of the woman, did not mention her name, however.

The reality behind her jailing is that she was merely carrying water for the Bush administration in its (likely criminal) efforts to punish former Ambassador Joe Wilson, who had exposed one of George Bush's chief fabrications in support of invading Iraq, the wild tale that Saddam Hussein was trying to buy "yellowcake" uranium from Niger. Revenge was exacted by the Bushies in the form of outing Wilson's wife, Plame, as a CIA operative.

The Bush machine spin—relentlessly echoed by the right, from Pat Buchanan (who knows a few things about seeing White House colleagues indicted) to Sean Hannity—is that the Plamegate (or Treasongate, as Bush's more trenchant foes call it) affair is just politics as usual. In Washington, information is currency that is traded among factotums and scribes, the Bush apologists claim. Actually indicting someone, as seems likely will happen, will as Hannity screeched recently, "criminalize politics." Of course, the spin was different when Bill Clinton was dropping his pants, but was not, as is happening in the current administration, betraying the nation.

Information bartering is, indeed, part of journalism, but it's clear that what Miller was up to was far from anything that even remotely could be called newsgathering. She was simply spreading the smear the White House wanted spread. The WMD lies exposed by Wilson were integral to the whole scare-and-deceive-the-public strategy to bolster support for the war. The famed British *"Downing Street Memo"* spoke of the Bushies' efforts to "fix" intelligence. Miller was nothing more than one of the fixers.

The incredible fact that no [one] at the Times or almost any other mainstream media outlet has addressed is that all of this is nothing new with Miller. She's been doing carefully calculated propaganda for years. Here is an excerpt that illustrates my point. It is from a 1996 review of Miller's book, <u>God Has 99 Names</u>, by famed Arab-American academic Edward Said.

> Miller "trades in 'the Islamic threat'—her particular mission has been to advance the millennial thesis that militant Islam is a danger to the West. ... [B]ooks like Miller's are sympto-matic because they are weapons in the contest to subordi-nate, beat down, compel and defeat any Arab or Muslim resistance to U.S.–Israeli dominance. Moreover, by surrepti-tiously justifying a policy of single-minded obduracy that links Islamism to a strategically important, oil-rich part of the world, the anti-Islam campaign virtually eliminates the possibility of equal dialogue between Islam and the Arabs, and the West or Israel.

> To demonize and dehumanize a whole culture ... is to turn Muslims into the objects of a therapeutic, punitive attention. I do not want to be misunderstood here: The manipulation of Islam, or for that matter Christianity or Judaism, for ret-rograde political purposes is catastrophically bad and must be opposed, not just in Saudi Arabia, the West Bank and Gaza, Pakistan, Sudan, Algeria and Tunisia but also in Israel, among the right-wing Christians in Lebanon (for whom

Miller shows an unseemly sympathy) and wherever theocratic tendencies appear. And I do not at all believe that all the ills of Muslim countries are due to Zionism and imperialism. But this is very far from saying that Israel and the United States, and their intellectual flacks, have not played a combative, even incendiary role in stigmatizing and heaping invidious abuse on an abstraction called 'Islam,' deliberately in order to stir up feelings of anger and fear about Islam among Americans and Europeans. ...

Perhaps Miller's most consistent failing as a journalist is that she only makes connections and offers analyses of matters that suit her thesis about the militant, hateful quality of the Arab world. I have little quarrel with the general view that the Arab world is in a dreadful state, and have said so repeatedly for the past three decades. But she barely registers the existence of a determined anti-Arab and anti-Islamic U.S. policy. She plays fast and loose with fact.

Did you get that last sentence by Said: Miller "plays fast and loose with fact." Said wrote that nine years ago. The Times apparently just noticed.

Miller first surfaced on my radar about a decade ago. Her close confederate was Emerson. Both had been engaged in a furious campaign attacking virtually every Arab and Muslim voice in America. Emerson— who also at various times claimed to be a journalist—lost his foothold as a commentator among most responsible media, especially after he tried to pin the Oklahoma City bombing on Muslims.

Emerson's most noteworthy crusade has been against a Tampa professor, Sami Al-Arian. Emerson and an ally at *The Tampa Tribune* were relentless. I eventually exposed many of Emerson's and the Trib's distortions and exaggerations. More important, the top FBI counterterrorism chief told me Al-Arian had not committed any federal crimes, and the lead federal prosecutor in the case also said there was no evidence to prosecute.

My heavily documented revelations about Emerson provoked him to retaliate via a lawsuit. Noteworthy, the lawyer he went to for advice was Floyd Abrams, most recently in the news as Miller's attorney. That's only fitting. We spent four years litigating with Emerson, and finally prevailed in both federal and state courts. The final blow to his case came when we obtained an order compelling him to show proof of his allegations. He wouldn't—couldn't?—and he ran away.

During the litigation, among the most interesting insights that I gleaned were reports of meetings held that involved Miller, Emerson, arch-Islamaphobe Daniel Pipes—and a number of other people we now call "neo-cons." All of these people had strong ties to the right-wing *Likud* party in Israel. Heck, Miller had even sat in on Israeli "interrogation" sessions of Palestinians; and Emerson provided beds in his Washington apartment to Likud spooks who slipped into the United States to try and undermine peace negotiations. Keep in mind, it took 9/11 to restore a veneer of credibility to Emerson as an "expert" on terrorism.

Many people, including me, had predicted years ago that terrorism would reach our shores. If we declare we are on the road to inevitable conflict with a culture and religion, and pursue policies that reflect such belligerence, it's likely to happen. (Of course, missing from Miller's, Emerson's and Pipes' breathless predictions about terrorism striking America is the fact that it long ago had. **The Islam-haters neglect to notice the thousands of terrorist events in the United States committed by fundamentalist Christians who hate blacks or oppose abortion, not to mention the scores of bombings and murders committed by right-wing Cubans in Miami. Indeed, the only three actual Middle East-related terrorist events in Florida,** including an assassination attempt on a former Israeli prime minister, were committed by radical supporters of Israel, not by Arabs or Muslims. But you're not supposed to know that.)

Emerson's and Miller's mission had always been to depict all Muslims as likely terrorists—to foster the idea of a "conflict of cultures." One of the more enlightening explanations of that process was "The Green Peril," a 1992 Cato Institute paper by Leonard Hadar, a former bureau chief for the Jerusalem Post. In descriptions that, looking back 13 years, are near-prophetic, Hadar describes how *the "green peril"—Islam—will be substituted for the "red menace." The process,* Hadar wrote, will involve *government leaks* that, without skepticism, are *echoed by the media, creating fear and distrust* in the nation. In other words, a perfect description of the work of Judith Miller.

Prior to 9/11, the Tampa federal probe of Al-Arian had stalled. This was unacceptable to the neo-cons and their Likudnik allies; Al-Arian was arguably the most prominent advocate for Palestinians in America, and had gained audiences with many Congressmen and even the White House (George Bush welcomed him in a 2000 campaign photograph). Thus, Israel conjured up "intelligence"—not actual documents and information that could be vetted and responded to by Al-Arian, but shadowy insinuations much like Miller's WMD claims. Miller, in fact, was one of the water-carriers for the Israeli "intelligence."

The essence of the work of people such as Miller and Emerson is to blur the distinctions among Arabs. *Palestinians have adopted horribly reprehensible and self-defeating tactics, but they are nonetheless an indisputably oppressed people.* The tactic is to equate Palestinians, with their justifiable claims to nationhood, with the criminal madmen of Al-Qaida. It's an effective technique. And it's clearly the party line from Likud. **Former**

Israeli Prime Minister Benjamin Netanyahu, when asked what 9/11 would mean for American-Israeli relations, responded: "It's very good." Realizing his maladroit gaffe, he then added: "Well, it's not good, but it will generate immediate sympathy" for Israel from the United States. The fact that no Palestinian had anything to do with 9/11 is a mountain-size distinction intentionally overlooked by Netanyahu—and Emerson and Miller.

In the post-9/11 anti-Arab frenzy, Al-Arian was bushwhacked on the *Bill O'Reilly show.* The new "intelligence," thanks to Miller and *The Tampa Tribune,* led to Al-Arian's indictment. His trial has been going on for months in Tampa. The government has repeatedly been caught prevaricating - including claiming Israeli intelligence wasn't involved in the prosecution, only to be exposed by an Israeli newspaper, *Ha'aretz* (and me).

Without doubt, Al-Arian had secrets, including participation with the *Palestinian Islamic Jihad.* But that involvement appears to have been during a period when it was legal, and the government has had a hard time showing that Al-Arian actually did anything illegal. But justice was never the purpose of the trial - or of the work by Miller and Emerson. **The judge in the case has dictated that jurors are supposed to hear only about the deaths of innocent Israelis and never about the far more numerous deaths of innocent Palestinians. In this Kafkaesque setting, if Martin Luther King Jr. were on trial for civil disobedience, he wouldn't be allowed to mention Jim Crow, lynchings or the Ku Klux Klan.**

Reading the latest about Miller wasn't a surprise. I'd seen it before in her alliance with Emerson and her catering to the neo-cons behind the Al-Arian prosecution. She's not a journalist. She's a convenient tool for some very bad people.

October 24, 2005

What follows is what Dave Lindorff had to say about Judith Miller.

Revoke Judith Miller's Pulitzer Prize (10/24/05)

> Now that *The New York Times*' own ombudsman has weighed in with a scathing critique of Judith Miller's lies and deceptions about her WMD and Al Qaeda reporting, including a recommendation that the paper not allow her back in its newsroom, it's time to call for an independent investigation into her much trumpeted Pulitzer Prize, which she won jointly in 2002 with several other Times reporters for her articles in 2001 about Al Qaeda.
>
> Clearly, Miller was no independent journalist looking for truth in her incarnation as "Ms. Run Amok," pushing the Bush Administration line for war with Iraq in the post 9/11 run-up to the invasion of that country. Her breathless and terrifying stories claiming that Saddam Hussein was sitting on masses of WMDs--biological and chemical weapons and perhaps even nuclear bombs--and that his regime was tight with Osama Bin Laden and his merry band of bombers and terrorists--were at best single-sourced...

(To read the rest of this commentary go to www.thiscantbehappening.net ) The writer is the author of <u>Killing Time: an Investigation into the Death Row Case of Mumia Abu-Jamal.</u>

# AN OPEN LETTER TO MARY BETH SHERIDAN, AND THE *WASHINGTON POST*

Dear Ms. Sheridan:

May this find you well. This comes in response to your Washington Post article of August 8, 2005 ("Educating Against Extremism"). After reading your article I felt there were certain things that you and your colleagues needed to know; and I can assure you that what I am about to share is representative of the thoughts and feelings of many others.

Your informative article begins as follows: "Alarmed by the London subway bombings, U.S. Muslim activists are taking a series of steps aimed at preventing young people here from embracing extremist ideas – including producing a pamphlet on how to spot susceptible youth."

Point #1: Every Muslim (young or old) who declares, *"I bear witness that there is nothing worthy of worship except Allah (God Almighty),"* and means this in his or her heart, is capable of being "radicalized" in a world like the one in which we live in today. In a commentary that I wrote in 1999 (*Five Mistakes of U.S. Policy-makers in the Muslim World*), I noted the following: "No nation can indiscriminately bomb, maim and kill innocent Muslims without the pain, grief, and anguish, being felt on some level by Muslims the world over. No matter how many official disclaimers are issued —'This is not to be taken as an attack on Islam, or all Muslims'—the actions are going to be seen for what they are, and the impact is going to be felt."

Point # 2: You and other fair-minded journalists in the mainstream media should broaden your reference base in the Muslim community. In the aforementioned commentary we also noted: "Too often America... has misread the pulse of the people by listening to leaders of the establishment telling them all is well. Don't continue to make this mistake in the Muslim community... It would behoove American politicians and policy-makers to keep their ears to the ground in order to get the most accurate read on how the grass-roots are feeling, concerning U.S. domestic and foreign policy and its impact on the Muslim World. Our major Muslim organizations and mainstream leaders serve an important function, and are appreciated for what they do; however, they are not always the ones you should be listening to. For they will sometimes tell you what you want to hear, and not what you *need* to hear."

Ms. Sheridan, you were probably present at the National Press Club a few weeks ago for a press conference wherein the Muslim American Society-Freedom Foundation unveiled its antiterrorism campaign. If so, you may recall a voice being raised from the audience as the press conference was winding down. That voice belonged to me. I was attempting, without much success, to get the organizers to address a question that lay at the very heart of their highly touted campaign.

Mr. Bray, as you may recall, did everything in his power to prevent my voice from being heard; and this raises a very important and sensitive issue (especially within the Muslim community). If individuals and organizations like Bray and MAS find it too difficult to entertain open and frank dialogue on tough issues with well known and respected Muslim advocates like myself, what hope do they have of reaching the hearts and minds of radicalized youth, who might be inclined to view such individuals and organizations as compromised sellouts?

You quoted Bray in your article as saying, "If Muslims preach intolerance we have a responsibility to debate that person, make that opinion unpopular." That is easier said then done, Ms. Sheridan, because healthy debate, as you well know, requires give and take.

Truth be told, many of our "mainstream"organizations have been instrumental in helping to foster a climate that makes "extremist" tendencies difficult for any conscious and caring person (Muslim or non-Muslim) to resist. And again, truth be told, most of our main-stream media organizations are guilty of doing the same. I'll provide you with two relevant illustrations on the latter (and then come back to the former). The media's treatment of the "Arab-Israeli conflict," and "domestic terrorism," are two cases in point.

We all know that Israel's withdrawal from Gaza has nothing to do with altruism, or a change of heart; it was pragmatic to the core. In the words of pro-Israel commentator Charles Krauthammer, *"Gaza was simply a bridge too far; settlements too far flung and small to justify the huge psychological and material cost of defending them."*

While the media has been very sympathetic regarding the "emotional toll" this newly enforced policy has had on "displaced" Jewish settlers, little, if anything, is ever mentioned about the catastrophic toll 38 years of brutal occupation have had on the Palestinian people, and especially on the developing psyche of Palestinian children. I have yet to hear, or read, any in-depth reports on the numerous violations of well established "international law," resulting from the establishment of these universally acknowledged illegal settlements in the West Bank and Gaza! Laws such as:

**The Geneva Convention of 1949, Article 49** (paragraph 6) which states: "The occupying power shall not deport or transfer parts of its own civilian population into the territo-ries it occupies."

**Article 27 of the Geneva Accords**: "Persons under control of an occupying power shall at all times be humanely treated, and shall be protected, especially against all acts of violence or threats thereof."

**Article 53 of the Geneva Accords**: "Any destruction by the occupying power of the real or personal property is prohibited."

And then we have the issue of domestic terrorism. One of the most frightening aspects of the manipulation of this issue is the evisceration of the U.S. Constitution taking place before our very eyes, facilitated by men and women who took and oath to uphold and defend this very document! And more often than not, instead of serving as that critically important check and balance, the media (generally speaking) is complicit!

In your article, Ms. Sheridan, you referenced the so-called "Virginia Jihad Network" (aka "Paintball Case") as well as the case of Ahmed Omar Abu-Ali. It should be noted for the sake of accuracy that NOT ALL eleven defendants in that case visited a Lashkar-e-Taiba camp; of the few who did, not all visited for the same reason; lastly, and perhaps most importantly, when those visits took place, Lashkar-e-Taiba was not on the State Department's list of "Terrorist Organizations."

The Virginia Jihad Network case is often cited as the most successful government prosecution to date in America's so-called "War on Terrorism." Its prosecution and outcome, however, should make every fair-minded American lower their head in shame! (It reminds us of the words of Voltaire, *"Those who can make us believe absurdities, can also cause us to commit atrocities."*)

As for the case of Abu Ali, your article suggests that when you raised Bray's organization's support of this wrongfully imprisoned young man, Bray gave a rather tepid, almost apologetic, response: "His organization, he said, was concerned that Abu Ali's rights had been violated since he had been held in a Saudi prison for more than a year without charges..." In our view his response should have been, 'We supported him then, and we support him now, because we believe he is innocent and being victimized by his own government!' (This would have been our response, particularly given all that is known about this shameful case.)

Ms. Sheridan, some people consider persons like me "militants," or "Islamists,"or "fundamentalists," and the like; and yet, The Peace And Justice Foundation and I have been on record for years now (long BEFORE the tragic attacks of September 11th) as opposed to the targeting of civilian non-combatants ANYWHERE in the world!

The difference with us, however, is that we make little distinction between the "terrorism" of the oppressor and the "terrorism" of the oppressed! We denounce both for what they are, *"crimes against humanity"* —but we also recognize two undeniable facts: **terrorists are not born, they are made**; and secondly, that the more materially developed terrorists commit a hell of lot more terrorism! It would be of such tremendous global benefit if the world's opinion-shaping apparatus—especially here in the West—would also publicly recognize the same.

I am an American born Muslim who unabashedly recognizes the superiority of a Quranically-based governing system over what is today euphemistically called "Western Democracy." Does this make me an "extremist," a "terrorist," or even a "terrorist sympathizer?" It shouldn't.

Does being a critic of western style democracy render my thoughts and inclinations incompatible with "modernity?" It shouldn't. I have long been a proponent of *representative government*; I believe in it with all my heart. Believe it or not, Islam mandates this very important doctrine. When the first caliph (successor to Prophet Mohammed, peace be upon him) assumed office, he said, in his inaugural address to the people: *"Here I have been assigned the responsibility of being a ruler over you, while I am not the best among you. If I do right support me; if I do wrong redress me."*

Here was the most powerful leader in that part of the world (quite possibly in the entire world) calling for the people to hold him accountable in office, 14 centuries ago!

The opposition that many Muslims have to democracy, echoes some of the same concerns that a number of prominent [American] Founding Fathers had with this concept. Don't take my word for it; go back and read your history. It echoes some of the same concerns that prominent figures like Henry David Thoreau expressed about "majority rule" in early America. In one of his most memorable essays, Thoreau wrote: *"Can there not be a government in which majorities do not virtually decide right and wrong, but conscience?*—in which majorities decide only those questions to which the rule of expediency is applicable?"

In our humble view, "democracy" is analogous to two wolves and a sheep debating the question of what to have for dinner (based on majority rule).

Getting back to the need for organizations like *The Washington Post* to broaden its reference base, one of the major mistakes that western media organizations make (both print and broadcast) is in favoring a certain type of Muslim for their reports. Usually this Muslim representative is of one of three types: He, or she, is a Muslim connected to the deen of Islam only by a thin thread. This is a person who is either ignorant of, or outrightly rejects, many of the fundamental principles of Islam, and reflects an uncritical, almost slavish, commitment to American-style democracy (while presuming to help lead the charge to "reform Islam").

Another type of Muslim favored by the media is the one who can be found at the other extreme; the Muslim who's actions and rhetoric reinforce an image of hating anything, and anyone, coming from the West (and/or not Muslim). This is the type of Muslim that persons like Bush, Cheney, and Rumsfeld depend on to sell the public on the ridiculous proposition that, *"They hate us for our freedom."*

Increasingly, there is a third type of Muslim that we are beginning to see more of in the mainstream media; the type that engages in a confused and almost transparent dissimulation. This type of Muslim, unfortunately, lends some degree of credence to the accusation (increasingly heard from Islamophobes of various stripes) that Islam encourages its adherents to lie and conceal their true beliefs.

There is another type of Muslim, Ms. Sheridan; the type of Muslim that sincerely inclined journalists (like yourself, I would like to believe) should be seeking out. This Muslim is deeply and confidently committed to Islam; and believes, in the deepest recesses of his or her heart, that Islam is a divinely sent code of life and living, and a benefit for all living things.

This Muslim is not an *apologist* or hate-filled *polemicist*, nor does he or she engage in wanton dissimulation. This Muslim's attachment to Islam doesn't negate them from loving their country of birth (or naturalization); nor does it prevent them from adhering to the law of the land (as long as such adherence doesn't cause them to violate Islam). You and your colleagues, in the profession, should not ignore this type of Muslim. You will find them intelligent, articulate, and, believe it or not, committed to a better America!

Yours in the struggle for peace thru justice,

El-Hajj Mauri' Saalakhan
Director of Operations
The Peace And Justice Foundation

Special Note: While this letter was addressed to Mary Beth Sheridan, in response to something that she had written, it was in fact composed by the author with a much broader audience in mind —The *Washington Post* Company, and the broader media establishment. For the record, this writer considers Ms. Sheridan a fair-minded journalist.

# Part 5
# THE TRUE FACE
# OF ISLAM

# THE QUR'AN & SUNNAH ON JIHAD AND TERRORISM

In Sahih Muslim, a collection of the sayings and actions of the Prophet Mohammed (pbuh) that Sunni Muslims consider to be among the most authentic – in a section that is known as Kitab al-Jihad wa'l-Siyar (The Book of Jihad and Expedition), part of the commentary reads as follows:

> The word jihad is derived from the verb jahada which means 'he exerted himself.' Thus literally, jihad means exertion, striving; but in a juridico-religious sense, it signifies the exertion of one's power to the utmost of one's capacity in the cause of Allah. This is why the word jihad has been used as the antonym to the word qu'ud (sitting) in the Holy Qu'ran (4:95). Thus jihad in Al-Islam is not an act of violence directed indiscriminately at non-Muslims, it is the name given to an all around struggle which a Muslim should launch against evil in whatever form or shape it appears. Qital fi sabililah (fighting in the way of Allah) is only one aspect of jihad.

In a recently published book titled <u>Infiltration</u>, author Paul Sperry shamelessly stated the following: *"Sadly, much of anti-Western terrorism is simply Islam in practice, the text of the Qur'an in action."* How accurate is this statement? You be the judge. What follows are some relevant verses from the Noble Qur'an, and recorded traditions from the prophetic ahadith (i.e., a record of the saying and actions of the Prophet Mohammed (may the peace and blessings of God be upon him). We begin with passages from the Qur'an:

> **To those against whom war is made permission is given to fight, because they are wronged; and verily Allah is Most Powerful for their aid. They are those who have been expelled from their**

homes in defiance of right—for no other cause except that they say, "Our Lord is Allah." If Allah did not check one set of people by means of another, there would surely have been pulled down monasteries, churches, synagogues and masajid (mosques), in which the name of Allah (God) is commemorated in abundant manner. (22: 39-40)

This is widely recognized as the first ayah (verse) sent to the Prophet Mohammed (pbuh) wherein permission was given to fight back, within prescribed limits. Until this time, for a 13 YEAR PERIOD, the Islamic movement on the Arabian peninsula had been a totally *non-violent, spiritually-based resistance,* under the worst forms of persecution imaginable.

Fight in the cause of Allah those who fight you, but do not transgress limits; for Allah does not love transgressors. And slay them wherever you catch them, and turn them out from where they have turned you out; for persecution is worse than slaughter. Do not fight them at the Sacred Mosque unless they first fight you there; but if they fight you slay them. Such is the reward of those who reject faith. If they cease, Allah is oft- forgiving, most merciful.

And fight them until there is no more persecution, and the religion becomes Allah's. But if they cease, let there be no hostility except to those who practice oppression. The prohibited month for the prohibited month, for all things prohibited there is the law of equality. If then anyone transgresses the prohibition against you, transgress likewise against him. But fear Allah, and know that Allah is with those who restrain themselves. (S. 2: 190-194)

In these verses of the Qur'an the emphasis is on the following: (a) fighting solely in the "cause of Allah;" (b) responding to an aggressor, and fighting with vigor until the source of persecution has been removed (while remaining within the limits established by Allah); (c) not fighting at the "Sacred Mosque," or in the "prohibited months," unless attacked first; (d) and keeping the door open for peace and reconciliation (if the enemy comes to terms).

Islamophobes are inclined to hone in on (and distort the true meaning of) the passage, "And fight them until religion becomes Allah's." But what is meant by this?

The Arabic word used in this translated verse is *Deen*—a term that implies the ideas of indebtedness, duty, obedience, judgment, justice, faith, religion, customs, etc. The meaning here is until there is deen for Allah; a system and society free of oppressive coercion. The Prophet (s) is reported to have said that Allah said to him: *"I have forbidden oppression for Myself, and have made it forbidden amongst you; so do not oppress one another."*

The prohibited months are Dhul Hijjah (the month of pilgrimage), Dhul Qa'da, Muharram, and Rajab. Warfare was prohibited in these months, and in the sacred territory of Mecca, by Arab custom. When it came to the Muslims, however, this time honored custom was violated repeatedly, and thus, the Prophet and his followers were given permission to respond whenever this occured; but always with consciousness of the "limits."

> **Fighting is prescribed for you, and you dislike it; but it is possible that you dislike a thing which is good for you, and that you love a thing that is bad for you. But Allah knows, and you know not. They ask you about fighting in the prohibited month. Say: Fighting therein is a grave offense; but graver is it in the sight of Allah to prevent access to the path of Allah, to deny Him, to prevent access to the Sacred Mosque and drive out its members. Tumult and oppression**

are worse than slaughter. Nor will they cease fighting you until they turn you back from your faith, and you die in unbelief. Their works will bear no fruit in this life; and in the Hereafter they will be companions of the Fire, and will abide therein. (2: 216-217)

Let those fight in the cause of Allah who sell the life of this world for the Hereafter. To him who fights in the cause of Allah —whether he is slain or gets victory—soon shall We give him a reward of great value. And why should you not fight in the cause of Allah, and for those who, being weak, are ill-treated (and oppressed)? Men, women, and children whose only cry is: 'Our Lord! Rescue us from this town whose people are oppressors; and raise for us, from You, one who will help!' Those who believe fight in the cause of Allah, and those who reject faith fight in the cause of evil (tagut); so fight against the friends of Satan, feeble indeed is the cunning of Satan. (4: 74-76)

O Prophet! Rouse the believers to the fight. If there are twenty amongst you, patient and persevering, they will vanquish two hundred; if a hundred, they will vanquish a thousand of the unbelievers; for these are people without understanding. (8:65)

While there are many more verses in the Qur'an on this issue, what we've presented is sufficient to give the reader a sense of what the Qur'an has to say on this matter. The bottom line is that according to Islam fighting in the way of Allah (in Arabic: *qital fisabililah*)— in Judeo-Christian theology "Just War" - is not an arbitrary or reactionary thing! It is a very serious matter, which, when engaged, must be with an ever present consciousness and accountability toward The Almighty!

**Prophetic Hadith**

> *He who is killed under the banner of a man who is blind (to the cause for which he is fighting), who gets flared up with family pride and fights for his tribe—is not from my Ummah; and whosoever from my followers, attacks my followers (indiscriminately) killing the righteous and the wicked among them, sparing not even those who are staunch in faith, and fulfilling not his promise made with those who have been given a pledge of security—he has nothing to do with me, and I have nothing to do with him.*

Reflect over the aforementioned saying of God's last prophetic Messenger against the backdrop of what is going on in Iraq and a few other places in the Muslim world today. Clearly the "insurgents," "jihadists," whatever you want to call them, have stepped far beyond the bounds of Islam.

Prophet Mohammed (pbuh) is also reported to have said:

> *Set out for Jihad in the name of Allah and for the sake of Allah (alone.) Do not lay hands on the old verging on death, on women, children and babes. Do not steal anything from the booty and collect together all that falls to your lot in the battlefield; and do good, for Allah loves the virtuous and the pious.*

And then we have the record of what the first of the Rashidun Calpihs (successors of the Prophet, pbuh) said to his army before they departed for battle:

> Stop, O people! That I may give you ten rules for your guidance in the battlefield. Do not commit treachery or deviate from the right path. You must not mutilate dead bodies. Do

not kill a child, nor a woman, nor an aged man. Bring no harm to the trees, nor burn them with fire, especially those which are fruitful. Do not slay any of the enemy's flock, except for food. You are likely to pass by people who have devoted their lives to monastic services; leave them alone.

We also have the record of the second successor to the Prophet (pbuh), Umar, and his parting instructions to the commander of his army:

Always search your minds and hearts and stress upon your men the need for perfect integrity and sincerity in the cause of Allah. There should be no material end before them in laying down their lives, but they should deem it a means whereby they can please their Lord and entitle themselves to His favor. Such a spirit of selflessness should be inculcated in the minds of those who unfortunately lack it.

Be firm in the thick of the battle, as Allah helps man according to the perseverance that he shows in the cause of his faith, and he will be rewarded in accordance with the spirit of sacrifice which he displays for the sake of his Lord. Be careful that those who have been entrusted to your care receive no harm at your hands, and are never deprived of any of their legitimate rights.

These admonitions are so beautiful (in their inspiration), and so very profound and revealing. It is no wonder that one of the most prominent non-Muslim symbols of creative non-violence—a man known the world over for his fervent commitment to non-violent struggle - had this to say about the final Messenger of God and his devoted followers:

How their lives were transformed as if by magic; what devotion they showed to the Prophet; how utterly unmindful they became of worldly wealth; how they used power itself for showing the utter simplicity of their lives; how they were untouched by the lust for gold; how reckless they were of their own lives in a cause they held sacred, is all told with a wealth of detail that carries conviction with it. When one notes their lives, and the lives of the present day representatives of Islam in India, one is inclined to shed a tear of bitter grief.

You may have guessed (with the reference made to India) that these are the words of the late Mahatma Gandhi. And he wasn't finished. Listen to what else he had to say:

I passed from the companions of the Prophet to the Prophet himself. I became more than ever convinced that it was not the sword that won a place for Islam in those days, in the scheme of life. It was the rigid simplicity; the utter self-effacement of the Prophet; his scrupulous regard for pledges; his intense devotion to his friends and followers; his intrepidity; his fearlessness, his absolute trust in God and in his own mission. These, and not the sword, carried everything before them, and surmounted every obstacle.

How eloquent; and how true!

# DR. HINA AZAM'S ADDRESS
# TO THE ISNA CONVENTION

*The following address was delivered by Dr. Hina Azam at the 2005 Islamic Society of North America (ISNA) convention.*

One hardly needs to ask al-Qaeda (and al-Qaedaesque) operatives what they think they are doing in their suicide attacks. The pronouncements and writings of Osama bin Laden and Abu Mus'ab al-Zarqawi make it abundantly clear that they believe they are engaging in a legitimate jihad. Never mind that they break cardinal rules of jihad as laid out in the Qur'an and the lawbooks of Islam. Never mind that they confuse basic distinctions, such as the one between combatants and civilians, and between suicide and martyrdom. No, according to the architects of the World Trade Center attacks on 9/11, the ongoing explosions in Baghdad, and the London train bombings, they are engaging in the ultimate expression of human submission to the divine intent. The truth of the matter, however, is that they are engaged in the very behavior that the Qur'an and Prophet came to combat: tribalism. Despite protestations to the contrary, Al-Qaeda and similarly-minded groups are engaged in no more than the old-fashioned *tribal warfare, the hallmark of jahiliyya.*

An examination of al-Qaeda pronouncements reveals this to be true. While the texts of these pronouncements is laden (no pun intended) with religious language taken from the Qur'an, the hadith and classical fiqh, the murderous objectives of al-Qaeda is not what was intended by the authors of those texts. A knowledge of Islamic history reveals that those writings have never before been used to justify the random killing of non-combatants. While Muslim history has seen politically-motivated assassinations and traditional warfare in which armies faced armies, we have never before witnessed armed groups of Muslims who went about intentionally targeting civilians and claiming their actions to be religiously justified.

No, the motivation for their actions is not any religious command to engage in jihad as traditionally understood. In their statements and fatawa, argumentation on religious grounds is secondary to their primary argument, which is political. But it is not the political nature of their motivation in itself that is illegitimate from an Islamic perspective. The illegitimacy lies in their methods. In the discourse of the terrorists, religious texts are being twisted in order to support the pre-Islamic practice of vendetta (*tha'r*)—the very approach to socio-political conflict that the Qur'an and the Prophet outlawed.

Pre-Islamic Arabia was a society in which there was no central authoritative body to oversee justice or to mete out punishment for injustice. It was a society in which the only commonly-recognized law was the law of tribal vengeance: If someone from tribe A attacked or harmed someone from tribe B, the attack was taken as license by anyone in tribe B to retaliate against anyone and everyone from tribe A. The tragic result was bloodshed that would touch a far wider circle than the original assailant.

The Qur'an sought to put an end to this murder and mayhem through a series of moral and legal principles dictating how human beings should live with one another, both inter-tribally and intra-tribally. No longer was it legitimate for anyone from tribe B to kill anyone from tribe A, no matter how great the desire for vengeance. In the civilian realm, this is the principle behind the law of *qisas*: the only one who could be prosecuted was the one who has committed the crime, whether it be murder or injury. At the level of the state, the Qur'an laid down principles governing warfare, principles that the Prophet and the scholars interpreted as delineating fundamental laws—such as the distinction between combatants and non-combatants, and the illegitimacy of attacking the latter.

The terrorists' deepest deviation from the Qur'an, however, is not at the legal and political levels, but at the spiritual and moral level. Pre-Islamic Arabia was considered to be *jahil* not because it was ignorant, but because it was crude. In seeking to defend tribal honor at the cost of social justice, it was a society that idealized qualities such as hot-bloodedness, arrogance, quickness to anger and slowness to forgive. In contrast to *jahala*, the Qur'an advocates *hilm*, which comprises an attitude of forbearance, patience and humility:

> **The [true] servants of the Merciful are those who walk on the earth humbly, and who, when the jahilun address them, reply, 'Peace!' (Q 25:63)**

And *hilm*, it must be emphasized, is a social virtue, a quality of character. It is neither a theological tenet nor a legal doctrine, but is the manifestation of the inner transformation that occurs when the message of the Qur'an and the example of their Prophet have truly penetrated one's consciousness.

Al-Qaeda and its various branches have set aside Qur'anic spirituality and ethics as well as traditional law, however, in favor of a return to pre-Islamic condition of total war, in which all the members of the opposing 'tribe' are fair game, including old men, pregnant women, babes-in-arms, Jewish doctors, Christian teachers and Muslim engineers. The totalistic mindset of the vendetta sees only one distinction, that is between 'us' and 'them.' It allows for no cooperation and no friendship between members of different 'tribes.' It leaves no room for reconciliation and no avenue for settlement of differences. The hardness of heart demonstrated by a group that exacts vengeance on the innocent for crimes committed by others is the heart that lacks *hilm* and is dominated by *jahala*.

The irony is that the ideology of al-Qaeda and like-minded terrorists is founded on the notion that everyone other than themselves exists in a state of jahiliyya. That people - including Muslims—who are willing to coexist in a pluralistic world, according to the Qur'anic notion that God has created humanity into nations and tribes that we may know one another, are in fact disbelievers. That people—including Muslims—who are willing to distinguish between soldiers and civilians, according to the Qur'an and Sunna, are cowards and hypocrites. In the mad psychology of the vendetta, there is no escape from the domain of war into the domain of peace.

---

* I disagree with Dr. Azam's embrace of the idea that Muslims were solely, or even primarily, responsible for 9/11.

# A Muslim Response to Dennis Prager's 'Five Questions'

By Hussam Ayloush

In a recent commentary, radio talk show host Dennis Prager posed five questions "that law-abiding Muslims need to answer for Islam's sake, as well as for the sake of worried non-Muslims."

SEE: "Five Questions Non-Muslims Would Like Answered" http://www.latimes.com/news/opinion/sunday/commentary/la-op-prager13nov13,0,1904398.story

Prager said his questions were prompted in part by recent rioting in France "by primarily Muslim youths," despite the fact that neutral experts say the violence had little to do with Islam and it was Muslim leaders who ultimately helped quell the violence.

Faulty premise aside, here are answers to Prager's questions:

**Q: Why are you so quiet (about terrorism carried out in the name of Islam)?**
A: One might argue that Muslims could do more to get their anti-terror message out. But to say Muslims have been quiet about their unequivocal condemnation of terrorism is a gross misrepresentation of the facts and reeks of Islamophobia.

It was after all a coalition of American Muslim groups that issued what was perhaps the first condemnation of the 9/11 attacks. The Council on American-Islamic Relations (CAIR) also published a full-page advertisement condemning the attacks.

Muslims have consistently condemned suicide bombings in the Middle East, attacks on the London transportation system, the bombing of hotels in Jordan, and many similar outrages.

Muslim scholars recently issued a fatwa, or Islamic religious ruling, condemning terrorism and religious extremism. Muslim groups in Texas and Arizona held anti-terror rallies. In Jordan huge demonstrations were held against the recent terror attacks. Muslims in Lebanon demonstrated against the terrorist assassination of former Prime Minister Rafik Harirri.

Outrage can be expressed in many ways. Public demonstrations are merely one of many different methods available to oppose terrorism.

**Q: Why are none of the Palestinian terrorists Christian?**
A: Robert Pape in his book, "Dying to Win - The Strategic Logic of Suicide Terrorism," shows that between 1982 and 1986, 71 percent of the Lebanese suicide attackers were Christians and 21 percent Communists/Socialists. Pape states, "Of the 384 attackers for whom we have data, 166 or 43 percent were religious, while 218 or 57 percent were secular. Suicide terrorism is not overwhelmingly a religious phenomenon." It is a response to occupation.

Inquiring minds might also consider the suicide bombings carried out by non-Muslim groups such as the Tamil Tigers in Sri Lanka, the religious orientation of the abortion clinic bomber or the depredations of Serbian forces during the Bosnian conflict.

**Q: Why is only one of the 47 Muslim-majority countries a free country?**
A: Muslim majority countries such as Indonesia, Malaysia, Bangladesh, and Turkey among many others having held free elections and being governed by popularly elected governments will dispute the charge that they are not "free."

Moreover, only in the past 50 years have more than half of the Muslim-majority nations been freed from their European colonizers.

Despite winning this freedom, most continued to be client states of their former colonizers who through the imposition of dictatorial regimes maintained control, some even to this day.

Opposition to such lack of freedom is generally Islamically-oriented. *Lack of freedom in Muslim nations is in spite of Islam, not because of it.*

**Q: Why are so many atrocities committed and threatened by Muslims in the name of Islam?**
A: All major faiths have people who commit, or have committed atrocities in the name of their religion. But no faith should be held responsible for the crimes of a few individuals. It seems Prager believes that any act by Muslims should be blamed on Islam. Just as we do not blame the Crusades or the Israeli atrocities on the faiths of Christianity and Judaism, we ask others to offer the same respect for our faith.

Again quoting Pape, *"The world's leading practitioners of suicide terrorism are the Tamil Tigers in Sri Lanka—a secular, Marxist-Lennist group drawn from Hindu families."*

**Q: Why do countries governed by religious Muslims persecute other religions?**
A: While there are areas of the Muslim world in which religious freedom is not granted to all citizens, it is unfair to claim that this phenomenon is a problem unique to Islam. Blaming persecution of minorities on Islam is akin to blaming slavery and segregation on Christianity. Choosing the Taliban as an example of religious intolerance in Islam is disingenuous, because the Taliban's religious perspective has been rejected by mainstream Muslim scholars and Muslims worldwide.

Every religious group has a responsibility to challenge hate by their fringe groups. It is unproductive to single out Muslims while remaining silent about the extremists of other faiths who vilify the faith of Islam without similar repudiation from Prager and others.

Dealing with the impact of war, poverty, racism, and injustice is our collective duty. To achieve solutions to these real problems we need voices that accentuate our common humanity, not use opportunistic smears of an entire faith to further their parochial agenda.

I would offer a challenge to Mr. Prager. Are you willing to enter into a real dialogue, not an exercise in one-upmanship, with mainstream Muslims? If so, CAIR stands ready to facilitate that dialogue, just as I did when I appeared recently on his program.

We await your response.

*Hussam Ayloush is executive director for the Southern California office of the Council on American-Islamic Relations (CAIR-LA). He can be reached at socal@cair.com*

# THE MM-FACTOR:
# WHO IS THE MODERATE MUSLIM?

By Abukar Arman

*Abukar Arman is a close friend and a very active educator in the Columbus, Ohio, area.*

Since the terrorist attacks on the United States and United Kingdom and the disastrous political shambles resulting from the *neoconic* vision of world order which led to, among other things, the war in Iraq and the subsequent proliferation of insurgency and extremism, the argument that 'moderate Muslims or the MM-Factor is the only legitimate defense against Islamic extremism' has gradually found its way onto the center stage and is now finding acceptance in certain circles.

But, who are these "moderate Muslims"? What is the ideological engine driving them? What indicators are there to authenticate them? And, more importantly, who should interpret the readings of such indicators?

Before an objective debate on these and other such questions could get underway, neocon activists such as Daniel Pipes have been vociferously spinning the whole MM-Factor in order to push a certain handpicked list of what he describes as " anti-Islamist Muslims."

Not surprisingly, the list included controversial names such as: Khalid Duran, a notorious Islam basher who is a friend and an affiliate of Mr. Daniel Pipes; Irshad Manji who produced, according to her website, "the world's first program on commercial airwaves to explore the lives of gay and lesbian people" and hosted "Queer Television" on Toronto's City TV; Ayaan Hirsi Ali, a self-declared

Atheist who collaborated with murdered film-maker Theo Van Gogh on a controversial film whose most offensive scene involves Qura'nic verses on a naked female body- a scene that was attributed to Ayan; and Ibn Warraq (pseudonym) who is the author of "Why I Am Not A Muslim"—a book that is highly advertised in many special interest circles.

Granted these are individuals who are exercising their freedom of expression who may want to "shock the system" from the periphery. But neither the shocking nor being in the periphery could moderate the current trend of extremism. Bring back Islam to its original nature of being *Diin Alwasata* (a middle ground faith), as taught by the Prophet Muhammad, would require moderate tone and judicious dialogue.

Lending support and providing platforms to charlatans or individuals considered as pariahs could simply undermine the whole MM-Factor effort. Credibility and sincerity is the name of the game.

For anyone to be accepted as a moderate voice and for his or her message to resonate with the broader Muslim population in the US and around the world, one must demonstrate, among other things, the following three main characteristics:

First, that he or she is a devout Muslim with a track record of community service—an individual without any apparent ulterior motive.

Second, he or she is an independent person with an independent mind- an individual who is not predictably on the same side of any issue all the time, since neither truth nor justice is predictably on the same side. Third, he or she is a sensitive bridge-builder willing to cultivate peaceful, tolerant community life, who respects the rule of law, who supports his or her position through Islam's main authority- the Qur'an and the Sunnah (the legacy of Prophet Muhammad).

Unfortunately, there seems to be a flipside argument that defines one's level of moderation based on one's political stance on the Israel and Palestine issue. Not on the now moot question of whether or not Israel has the right to exist, but whether the Palestinian people have the right to self-determination and to resist oppression and occupation! And this is what the overwhelming Muslims in America gradually came to understand as being the real litmus test.

Muslim thinkers and activists who are apathetic, oblivious, or are supportive of the status quo are readily embraced as "moderates," while others, regardless of how moderate or liberal they might be, are declared radicals or terrorist sympathizers.

A case in point is the routine harassment of prominent Muslim activists such as Yusuf Islam- formerly known as Cat Stevens- who is famous for his peace songs and indeed activism; widely respected moderate Muslim scholars such as Dr. Yusuf Al-Qaradawi who made a career campaigning against extremism and radical literalism, who commonly preaches what is known as *middle-ground Islam*, and "liberal" thinkers such as Professor Tariq Ramadan who is known for being a pioneer in bridging Islamic values and Western culture, all of whom were, in one way or another, denied entry to the US for "national security" reasons.

Along that same trend, recently the US Embassy in Cairo has denied Sheikh Abdul Hamid Al-Atrash, the head of Al-Azhar Fatwa Committee, an entry visa to tour the US and give lectures and sermons at a number of American Islamic centers during the month of Ramadan. Other than being the oldest and the most prestigious Islamic university, Al Azhar is ironically considered as being the most moderate Islamic institution. It goes without saying, any such subjective alienation and deliberate silencing of those widely recognized as genuine moderates would only fuel more cynicism, anti-Americanism, and extremism.

But, if the ultimate goal is to tame extremism and to defeat it in the market place of ideas, both Muslims whose religion has been eclipsed by bloody extremism, and U.S. foreign policy which has been highjacked by aggressive, one-dimensional ideologues ought to find genuine Muslim moderates to support. And until a bona fide definition crystallizes, there will always be the risk of blindly embarking on yet another quixotic foreign policy endeavor!

# Part 6
# OTHER VOICES

## MESSAGES FROM OUR FRIENDS

*"You know, I don't know the doctrine of assassination, but if he thinks we're trying to assassinate him, I think that we really ought to go ahead and do it... It's a whole lot cheaper than starting war, and I don't think any oil shipment will stop."*

—Rev. Pat Robertson of the Christian Coalition

When the "Reverend" Pat Robertson brazenly called for the assassination of Venezuelan President Hugo Chavez, a U.S. Government spokesperson labeled Robertson's comments "inappropriate," and "not representative" of the Bush Administration, and then proceeded to note that his were "the views of a private citizen." (Imagine the public reaction to a Muslim leader advising the same.)

Robertson's "views" reminds me of the controversial remarks made a few years ago by a former Nixon administration insider and conservative talk show host. In the course of his daily radio broadcast, the commentator advised his virulently anti-Clinton good ol' boys in America's heartland to aim for the "heads" of federal marshals (and other federal law enforcement officers), because of the body armor they routinely wear.

If Pat Robertson were any American citizen of prominence, his comments would be cause for concern and outrage. However, Robertson is not just your average, everyday, unbalanced, yet prominent, bigot; he's a "Christian minister" who leads one of the most prominent and influential *Christian* organizations in the country.

I sincerely believe that if he were a Muslim calling for the assassination of a "friend" of the United States, he would be promptly investigated, indicted, and prosecuted under freshly minted antiterrorism law!

And for those who may not be aware of this, "Rev. Robertson" and a number of his close business associates, have been linked for years now to Africa's dirty *"blood diamond"* trade! No doubt, Mr. Robertson's mindset has served him well in that cutthroat, very lucrative, dog-eat-dog business!

What follows are very informative commentaries by a couple of non-Muslim friends: the Rev. Graylan Hagler (Senior Minister of the Plymouth Congregational United Church of Christ in Washington, DC), and Heather Gray (producer and broadcaster at WRFG Radio in Atlanta, GA).

## PAT ROBERTSON IS NOT CHRISTIAN!

Pat Robertson suggested this past Monday that the President of Venezuela, Hugo Chavez, be assassinated by operatives of the United States government! Though his comments are newsworthy because of his following in the *700 Club* and his political stature and role in the political religious right, his comments are out of synch with everything that has been handed down to us from the teachings of Jesus Christ. What I am suggesting here is that Pat Robertson and individuals of his ilk are not practicing or preaching Christ, but have become adherents of a political movement in this nation that attempts to use Christianity towards their own narrow political ends. I believe that there is a role for Christianity in the events of the world, but the teachings of Christ leads us to love one another, strain and stretch to understand each other, and dare to know each other enough that we come to an understanding of one another, and from that create a world that is not built on might and winning but on understanding and unity. Clearly the comments of Robertson defy the framework we find in the gospels of Jesus Christ.

Some may argue that Christ existed in another time and did not have an understanding of the kind of world we exist in today. But any follower of Jesus knows that as he was human, he was also fully God, and therefore his understanding of the world, humankind and our needs were not captive to a particular time but applies to all time! Knowing this, I do not see anywhere in the gospels of Christ that he condones, suggests or advocates murder or political assassination! Instead Jesus reminds us to beware of Pharisees, and Robertson, Dobson and others have become the Pharisees of our contemporary world!

What do we find in the Good News of Christ? We find love is expressed continually and unceasingly. The gospels admonish us to do unto others, as you would have them do unto you. We find words in the gospels that define the mission of Christians as the elevation of the poor, freedom for those who are oppressed, salvation for the lost, and hope for the hopeless. Jesus says come unto me all of you who are weak and heavy laden and I will give you rest. He does not say come to me those who are looking for political expediency and I will show you *who and how to assassinate*!

Sure there has been trouble in Venezuela, and some will suggest that it is communism struggling to raise it head. Others will suggest that the poor of Venezuela have been poor too long in a nation that is the 5th largest oil producer in the world. Some will suggest that too much of the resources have been in the hands of too few, and that the poor of the land have found hope in a political leader, Hugo Chavez. I would not suggest that Chavez is a saint, for no person is perfect, but I do know that Chavez was elected even while the greatest power in the world, the United States government, did everything possible to thwart his election. This is hardly the neighborliness that Jesus Christ calls us to emulate.

I am continually amazed at how so many preachers have ceased to preach Christ, or to proclaim him out of the rich simplicity of his teachings, and have resorted to a kind of theology that is not gospel based but is based on a narrow point of view that keeps the powerful powerful and the poor poor!

Therefore, it is impossible to justify the comments of Pat Robertson. His comments are not of the gospel he claims to preach, nor of the teachings of Christ that any Christian claims to love. Instead what Robertson has to say is based on a paradigm from the most conservative voices in this country, and those voices have no God except themselves, and no soul except their selfish point of view!

L

---

The aforementioned statement was issued by Reverend Graylan Scott Hagler, on August 23, 2005. Rev. Hagler serves as National President, Ministers for Racial, Social and Economic Justice & Senior Minister, Plymouth Congregational United Church of Christ Washington, D.C.

# A PERSONAL TESTIMONY
# —WILL THE REAL CHRISTIANS PLEASE STAND?

Hearing all this rhetoric about faith based this and faith based that and plans in the Bush administration to further erode the separation of church and state, the dangers of organized religion are becoming more acute to say the least. In fact, if Bush is so concerned about those who support terrorism then he probably needs to scrutinize how right-wing Christians here in the United States have supported terrorists. More on that later, but first, below is some of my personal journey with Christianity —a religion in which I was raised. It takes one to know one!!!

Christians have much to atone for in their long and egregious history. This is particularly so in the European and United States international context that I want to address here. Have they done some good as well? Probably, but you've got to look at what the Christians have done with some skepticism before affirming that statement. This community is divergent at best.

There are a lot of interpretations of Jesus. I have mine as well. To me, the guy was a revolutionary and should be considered the first of the liberation theologians. He grew up in the Middle East, during a time of stressful occupation. As a devout Jew he was obviously concerned about the corruption of his faith and of the Jewish leaders by the "pagan" Romans and their culture.

The Romans were skilled occupiers, doing what military occupiers do best—oppress and control the people socially and economically, grab whatever resources are available in the occupied land, and identify the elite in the occupied population as puppets who will serve Roman interests. (There are parallels, of course, to what the U.S. occupiers are doing now in Iraq.) The Romans, after all, selected the chief priest of the Temple in Jerusalem and other civic leaders, such as the infamous King Herod; the Romans were taking all the good farmland in the area; and they were constantly killing or oppressing Jews who opposed their rule.

No doubt the Romans, like any good occupier, and likely with the complicity of the Jewish elite, were consistently using and abusing the poor as Jesus routinely made reference to the less fortunate. Not surprisingly, uprisings (or as the U.S. prefers to call them in Iraq, insurrections) against Roman rule were frequent. (Read The Dead Sea Scrolls Deception; Holy Blood, Holy Grail; or The Messianic Legacy by Michael Baigent and Richard Leigh for more details on the historical Jesus.)

Most scholars concur that Jesus had no intention of starting a new religion. To do so would have been blasphemous against the Jewish faith. The historical task of creating Christianity was left to Paul whose credentials are mixed at best. Paul was named Saul before his conversion on the road to Damascus after the Romans had murdered Jesus. He was a Roman citizen, also Jewish and had never met Jesus. He had been persecuting his fellow Jews who opposed the occupation.

It is understandable, then, that the inner circle of Jesus' followers, such as James, did not trust Paul. Nevertheless, James, who is often referred to as the brother of Jesus, and others rather cautiously taught Paul Jesus' philosophy and then sent him to Turkey where he wrote letters back to Jerusalem about his work. Some contend that sending Paul to Turkey was an indication that he was not trusted, otherwise they would have kept him in Jerusalem to work in the heart of the movement there. Paul was recalled, however, once it was understood what he was doing. There were also plans to assassinate him as described by Baigent and Leigh. (Read <u>The Dead Sea Scrolls Deception</u> for more details on Paul).

So what was Paul doing in Turkey? Well, he was creating a new religion, which was common practice at the time. The prerequisite conditions of a new religion required a virgin birth, resurrection and, importantly, there had to be a direct link to God before anyone would believe you had a religion worthy of merit. For some strange reason, we humans seem to want miracles then as now, and what's even stranger, we are inclined to believe these miracles as fact. Paul obviously knew what he was doing. Anyway, the rest is history as they say.

To summarize, if you look at the historical Jesus he seemed to be concerned about the poor, about corrupt power, about loving your neighbors and about maintaining Jewish traditions and faith void of Roman influence—my simplistic summary. This, to me, was his revolutionary posture. It appears he chose not to side with those who cozied up to Roman power. He was not a *sellout*. Obviously, the Roman occupiers and the Jewish elite didn't like this.

While there have been all kinds of books about the wonders and glory of Christianity (the music is nice after all), when it's organized it can also be dangerous, extremely violent and oppressive. This is born out in history and impossible to recount here, but look at <u>Holy War: The Crusades and their Impact on Today's World and Battle for God</u> by Karen Armstrong or <u>Terror and Civilization: Christianity, Politics and the Western Psyche</u> by Shadia Drury for an excellent account of Christian abuses and analysis; and for more contemporary corruption by U. S. Christian conservatives look at <u>Spiritual Warfare</u> by Sara Diamond.

But, I have my own personal journey with Christianity apart from the documented historians and philosophers.

As a student at Emory University in Atlanta I was required to take a religion class. It was my introduction to the politics of religion. A church committee, I was taught, selected the books of the New Testament in 100 AD. Think about it—the committee was the scholarly elite in Europe at the time. They had a vested interest in portraying Rome in a positive light, and selected books accordingly. Some books, like that of Thomas, were left out that disputed Paul's version of the resurrection, virgin birth, etc. (read Elaine Pagel's Beyond Belief: The Secret Book of Thomas and The Gnostic Gospels). And so the Bible is supposed to be the word of God? Well, it certainly appears to have its mortal and political twist.

In 325 the Roman Emperor Constantine even called for a gathering of church leaders to meet in Turkey—known as the first *Synod of Niceae*—where the decision was to be made by these "mere mortals," whether Jesus was the son of God or not. So a committee made this decision? Well, yes, and they decided, in their rather dubious infinite wisdom three hundred years after Jesus died, that Jesus was, in fact, the son of God. Then, at this meeting, they developed the *Nicene Creed* that goes like this, *"We believe in one God, the Father Almighty, maker of all things, both visible and invisible; and in one Lord, Jesus Christ, the Son of God etc. etc."* and is recited by Christians today all over the world. This provided some clarity and unity, as the Emperor obviously wanted, for Christian leaders to conveniently sweep in and control the masses.

Then there's Michelangelo. It's a sad twist of history that he used his uncle and nephew as models for God and Jesus for his painting on the Sistine Chapel. By doing so, he created an unfortunate legacy of people throughout the world who think of *God as a white male*. This is the ultimate of white supremacy and insult. Jesus was, after all, described as dark skinned and woolly haired. Let's have some honesty here. And God as human? I don't think so.

Then I studied Latin American history where there is an abundance of historical accounts of European Catholic priests on board ships who would bless and Christianize the land before embarking from their ships. They were "shocked" and "appalled" to find that the indigenous peoples of this new land were not Christians, even after having been blessed by the priests from afar no less. This could and probably should be considered a ploy—a justification for massacring, enslaving or condescendingly oppressing the native populations, which the Europeans and their U.S. descendants have always done, without abandon, in their occupied foreign lands.

In the 1970's I lived in Singapore. In early 1973 I joined other international journalists for a tour of Vietnam during the war. In Singapore I lost a baby after 7 months of an excruciating pregnancy where I was in bed or in the hospital most of the time. I wanted to explore adopting a Vietnamese child and visited three orphanages in Saigon. The children in the first two were relatively well cared for and the institutions were clean, even in spite of what were probably relatively limited resources. Christians did not head these orphanages.

Then I visited the third orphanage administered by a Catholic priest. I was utterly appalled. The children were filthy and groveling and crawling on dirty floors. Some of them were strapped in chairs outside. One child, the mixture of a Vietnamese and Black American, was blind and screaming. My colleague told me this Catholic priest was notorious throughout Saigon. His attitude was that it didn't matter what happened here on earth because the rewards were to be found in heaven. This was, apparently, the priest's justification for the abysmal treatment of these children. Not that all Christain orphanages are likely to be problemmatic or abusive, of course, but I've wondered since how often Christians utilize this rationale.

Later, I was involved in the anti-apartheid movement. Recall that in 1975, Mozambique and Angola had finally wrenched themselves from Portuguese colonial rule. As was usually the case, the United States sided with the colonizers, the Portuguese in this case, rather than supporting the Mozambican freedom fighters. The church was also complicit, of course. The Catholic Church in Mozambique sided with the Portuguese against the freedom movement. So for some time after 1975 the Mozambicans wisely placed restraints upon the Catholic Church, much to the chagrin of American Christians.

To undermine the newly formed government in Mozambique, the European apartheid "terrorists" in the former Rhodesia (now Zimbabwe) were instrumental in creating, arming and funding the brutal *Renamo* to fight against the Mozambican Frelimo government. The Mozambican government was primarily socialist and you know what Christians would think about that! Rightwing U.S. Christians and anti-communists became associated with the support of Renamo.

The tactics of Renamo were notorious. They would often recruit their forces by kidnapping children from villages. To control these youth, Renamo leaders would, on occasion, force them back to their own villages to kill their parents and/or siblings. Occasionally these youth would escape the camps. Some say the soul is reflected in the eyes. Friends of mine spending time with these children told me the eyes of these kids were void of anything distinctly alive or emotive. *This is what American right-wing Christians were supporting in Mozambique.* There were parallels in Angola with the Christian-right, including Pat Robertson, of course, and anti-communist support of Jonas Savimbi, the infamous Angolan UNITA thug and terrorist who viciously fought against the freedom movement there.

In the late 1980's I spent some time in the Philippines. *The Philippines is another victim of a long history of European and United States colonial and, military occupation and oppression.* For 400 years the Philippines was occupied by Spain. Of course, the Spanish occupiers used their Christian ambassadors, Catholic priests, to control and "civilize" the masses. Priests fanned out throughout the Philippine islands. These early priests are legendary, in the Philippines, for their arrogant attitudes, pillaging and raping of the women.

The Filipino resistance to Spanish colonial rule was finally becoming productive in the late 1800's. At this time Spain was devoting its resources to the Spanish-American war that was won by the Americans. As the United States forces landed in Manila Bay in 1898, the Filipinos erroneously thought the Americans were there to help them fight the Spanish. Not so! The Americans wanted the former Spanish colony for themselves. From 1898 to 1902 the Filipinos valiantly fought the American forces.

The human cost of the war was immense. Some scholars estimate one million Filipinos ultimately died in the Philippine-American war. The US President William McKinley justified this brutality, however, saying that after praying to "Almighty God", a message came to him that Americans were in the Philippines to "uplift and civilize and christianize" Filipinos. He was obviously not aware that the Filipinos had been "christianized" for 400 years by Spain. I'm sure the Filipinos would have rather done without this violent Christian "civilization."

After 1902 the United States occupied the Philippines until after WWII and thus began the first major imperial venture of the United States outside its region. The U.S. military bases in the Philippines were retained, however.

In the mid 1980's retired U.S. General John Singlaub, president of the World Anti-Communist League, led an aggressive and violent anti-communist campaign in the Philippines to counter the growing anti-US bases movement in the country. Countless leaders, including Christian pastors, working for the poor in the rural areas were labeled as communists and subject to harassment or summary execution. Like the Spanish use of Catholic priests, the U.S. evangelicals flooded the Philippines to bolster the U.S. image and likely to dilute the movement against the U.S. bases. So the Filipinos not only had to struggle with endless human rights abuses from the government and the U.S. supported Philippine paramilitary, but also the arrogant, flagrant and well funded Christian evangelicals.

In 1989, I visited a refugee camp in Negros—the poorest island in the Philippines. The camp was filled with people who had been evacuated from the hinterlands by the Philippine government to root out the members of the New People's Army. The NPA was engaged in armed struggle against the Philippine government and was a strong proponent of the Philippines ending the military bases agreement with the United States. This camp was the largest refugee community in the Philippines since WWII. Thousands of families lost everything. Children and the elderly were dying. I talked with a mother who angrily told me that American Christians were there selling Bibles. She said, *"I don't have enough money to feed my children, much less to purchase a Bible."*

In Negros, a German collegue  and I had joined an international group in the dire task of exhuming  the graves of suspected resisters (adults and children), that  had been assassinated by the Philippine paramilitary, so an investigation   could be pursued regarding this atrocity. Shortly after, we happened upon a church in Dumaguete, in Negros. An American evangelical was preaching. He warned the people that the rapture could come at any time. If, for example, you were on a plane and not "born again" and the pilot was, you would be left to suffer a  dubious fate as the pilot would immediately be swept from the  plane and sent to heaven. We left in disgust. U.S. evangelicals were creating all kinds of characteristic havoc in the Philippines. Was this meant to dull the senses from the anti-communist violence that saturated the countryside?

The above are some of my personal experiences internationally that I know can be echoed by other witnesses throughout the world. Our domestic Christian community also needs serious scrutiny. The history of Christianity, organized or not, is fraught with tragedy, yet in some instances kindness and compassion. Where's the balance? I'm not sure.

There are people who call themselves Christians who do courageous work for the poor and who fight for justice and liberation. The *United Church of Christ* in the Philippines, for example, has routinely been in the forefront of the freedom movement. Countless liberation Catholic priests were doing incredible work for the poor, working for land reform and an end to oppressive policies generally in Asia and Latin  America. Christians played an instrumental role in the movement for abolition in the United States.

*The South African Council of Churches* took profound and courageous stands against the apartheid state. In the 1900's a Spanish Catholic priest was the founder of *Mondragon* in the Basque area, which is the most profound and successful cooperative movement in the world. *The Catholic Maryknolls* in the United States and elsewhere have done profound work for the poor and liberation efforts all over the world. The role of many of the U.S. Black churches and leaders in the freedom movement are legendary. To me, these are the real Christians and the list goes on and on.

While thousands of Christians are likely doing good work, I still say proceed with caution. History has shown that many Christians are inclined to easily side with the powerful elite against the people and to wreak havoc on indigenous beliefs and traditions that are often enforced by military and economic muscle. Greed and power are invariably at the core of it all.

Can these folks be trusted? I'm not sure. I also ask, does the good and compassionate work of some Christians outweigh the historic and contemporary tragedy, death and destruction from other Christian behavior? I'd say the jury's out on that one as well. Christians seem to wear many hats. Perhaps without the "real Christians," briefly described above, there would be no check on the dark side of this religion.

---

Heather Gray is producer of "Just Peace" on WRFG-Atlanta, 89.3 FM, covering local, regional, national and international news. She lives in Atlanta, Georgia and can be reached at justpeacewrfg@aol.com .

# EPILOGUE

## The Challenge to Concerned Citizens of America and the World

*"Three classes of men are cut off from the blessings of Paradise: the oppressors, those who aid and abet oppression, and those who tolerate oppression."* –Ali ibn Abu-Talib (raa)

I pray that through this modest book we've been able to answer a few important questions, correct a few misperceptions, and provide a little clarity where it was needed. Islam is not the "threat" that some demagogues have made it out to be. In fact, quite the opposite, Islam was revealed as a mercy and a healing for all humanity (not just for the Muslim Ummah (community). And thus, it behooves the reader to pursue his or her own independent investigation of Islam. I can assure you that if you embark upon this journey of discovery with a sincere heart and truly objective mind, you'll be pleasantly surprised at what you find.

I caution the reader, however, not to be unduly influenced by the present state of the Muslim Ummah itself; for the adherents of this faith are human beings, with human failings, just like the members of any other faith. Some Muslims you come across will be knowledgeable of and deeply committed to their faith, while others will not. Generally speaking, the Muslim Ummah of today (like the Jewish and Christian communities) is not what it once was; and this present-day reality was foretold by the Prophet himself (pbuh), wherein he said:

> A time is soon coming to mankind when their learned people will be the worst people under heaven's skies; corruption will come from them, and return back to them as smoke returns to the hole—and this will be a time when knowledge departs. One of the companions asked, "O Messenger of

Allah, how can knowledge depart, when we recite the Qur'an and teach it to our children, and they will teach it to their children up to the Day of Ressurrection?"

The Prophet looked at this companion and responded: "O Zaid, I'm astonished at you, I thought you were one of the most learned men in all Madinah. *Do not the Jews and Christians teach their children the Torah and the Injil (Gospel), and yet they know nothing of what it contains?*"

In this prophecy the last prophetic Messenger from The Almighty was speaking of a time in the future when the adherents of all three Abrahamic faith traditions—Jews, Christians, and Muslims—would have their respective books, but the manifestation of that knowledge in the lives of the people would be absent. In the case of the Muslims the loss would be even more significant, because it would be the only faith community left with uncorrupted divine revelation still in its possession (The Qur'an).

It is for this reason that I again emphasize that yours, dear reader, must be an independent journey—via research of the Qur'an, the Prophet's *sunnah* (oral traditions), and the study of Islamic history (sirah). In the course of your journey you will discover why Professor Michael Hart (a non-Muslim scholar), in his book entitled <u>The 100: A Ranking of the Most Influential Persons in History</u>, ranked the Prophet Mohammed (pbuh) as *the most influential person* in history. You will also discover why the great human rights activist Mahatma Gandhi had such glowing things to say about the Prophet (pbuh) and his generation.

You will be inspired by the great civilizations that sprung up and flowered in different parts of the world, at different times, under "Muslim rule." Unlike today, you will see vivid examples of how

Christians, Jews, and Muslims lived harmoniously side-by-side in the lands of the Qur'an. For example, in a book titled <u>Moses Maimonides And His Time</u> (edited by Eric L. Ormsby, and published by the Catholic University of America Press), can be found an essay by Professor Norman Roth, with an excerpt that reads as follows:

> In a recently published book on Maimonides, I noted that were he to have been born in another land, France or Germany, for instance, he would at most have become another one of those almost anonymous rabbis who wrote endless commentaries on commentaries on the Talmud. In that case, he would be of interest to no more than a small handful of Jewish scholars who specialize in such matters. Instead, this man became the greatest genius ever produced by the Jewish people. His productivity and creativity were prodigious.

Where did this great Jewish scholar and theologian live? The answer: Maimonides was born and raised, and led Jewish communities, in Muslim ruled lands—Al-Andalus (aka, "Muslim Spain"), and historic Palestine (under Muslim rule)!

I could cite many more examples of the benefits which have accrued to Muslims and non-Muslims alike, when Muslim societies were in an Islamic state; but space and time limitations will not allow such an endeavor at this time. Instead, I would like to conclude with a look at present day America.

In 1967, in his final address to a convention of the Southern Christian Leadership Conference (SCLC), the Rev. Dr. Martin Luther King, Jr., said the following:

I want to say to you as I move to my conclusion, as we talk about 'Where do we go from here,' that we honestly face the fact that the movement must address itself to the question of restructuring the whole of American society. There are forty million poor people in America. And when you begin to ask that question, you are raising questions about the economic system, about a broader distribution of wealth. When you ask, you begin to question the capitalistic economy. And I'm simply saying that more and more we have got to begin to ask questions about the whole society.

We are called upon to help the discouraged beggars in life's market place. But one day we must come to see that an edifice which produces beggars needs restructuring. It means that questions must be raised. You see, my friends, when you deal with this, you begin to ask the question, '*Who owns the oil?*' You begin to ask the question, '*Who owns the iron ore?*' You begin to ask the question, '*Why is it people have to pay water bills in a world that is two-thirds water?*' These are questions that must be asked...

What I'm saying to you this morning is that communism forgets that life is individual. Capitalism forgets that life is social; and the kingdom of brotherhood is found neither in the thesis of communism, nor the anti-thesis of capitalism— but in a higher synthesis. It is found in a higher synthesis that combines the truths of both. Now, when I say question the whole society, it means ultimately coming to see that the problem of racism, the problem of economic exploitation, and the problem of war are all tied together. These are the triple evils that are interrelated.

Indeed they are. This was the gist of Dr. King's address on that historic day in 1967. As a Muslim I sincerely believe that the "higher synthesis" that Dr. King was calling for, can be found in the Noble Qur'an, and in the system of life and living that the Qur'an mandates (called Islam). This is what is meant when committed Muslims refer to Islam as more than just "religion," as the term religion is commonly understood. It's more than that; it's a way of life.

And again, I implore you not to get caught up on the less than steller examples that you have before you today—especially in the form of these predominantly Muslim populated countries that are administered by *corrupt* and *oppressive* systems of governance, often *in the name of Islam*. As a Muslim, I am the first to admit that these countries bring shame upon the Ummah!

What is important today is that we—human beings on this planet called earth—find a way out of this mess that we have collectively gotten ourselves into. We must find the wherewithal to go deep within whatever faith tradition to which we belong, and ASK QUESTIONS...and never, ever forget the common thread that binds us together as one. We must do this for the sake of future generations (God willing), and for the sake of our own souls. May God help us.

# A Few Closing Thoughts
## on the 2nd Edition

Writing in *The Washington Post* on March 25, 2007, former National Security Advisor Zbigniew Brezinski had some interesting things to say about the "War on Terror."

"The war on terror has created a culture of fear in America. The Bush administration's elevation of theses three words into a national mantra since the horrific events of 9/11 has had a pernicious impact on American democracy, on America's psyche and on U.S. standing in the world... The damage these three words have done–a classic self-inflicted wound–is infinitely greater than any wild dreams entertained by the fanatical perpetrators of the 9/11 attacks...

"But the little secret here may be that the vagueness of the phrase was deliberately (or instinctively calculated by its sponsors. Constant reference to a 'war on terror' did accomplish one major objective: it stimulated the emergence of a culture of fear. Fear obscures reason, intensifies emotions and makes it easier for demagogic politicians [or bureaucrats] to mobilize the public on behalf of the policies they want to pursue...

"We are now divided, uncertain and potentially very susceptible to panic in the event of another terrorist attack in the United States itself. That is the result of five years of almost continuous national brainwashing on the subject of terror, quite unlike the more muted reactions of several other nations (Britain, Spain, Italy, Germany, Japan, to mention just a few) that have also suffered painful terrorist acts.

"Such fear mongering, reinforced by security entrepreneurs, the mass media and the entertainment industry, generates its own momentum.

The terror entrepreneurs, usually described as experts on terrorism, are necessarily engaged in competition to justify their existence. Hence, their task is to convince the public that it faces new threats. That puts a premium on the presentation of credible scenarios of ever more horrifying acts of violence, sometimes even with blueprints for their implementation.

"A recent study reported that in 2003, Congress identified 160 sites as potentially important national targets for would be terrorists. With lobbyists weighing in, by the end of that year the list had grown to 1,849; by the end of 2004, to 28,360; by 2005, to 77,769. The national data base of possible targets now has some 300,000 items in it."

Something to think about. Truth be told, however, the war on terror has contributed to another dubious achievement for the United States of America. It has made the "land of the free, and home of the brave," the leading jailor of the global community's citizenry—resulting in unprecedented levels of fear and rage being directed at this country from all corners of the world.

Acquiescence, or silence, is no longer an option for those who truly love America. If we are to safeguard the better of the "two Americas," the time has come for good people to STAND UP! Failure to do so will certainly cause the lamentation of [Founding Father] Thomas Jefferson to become self-fulfilling prophecy:

*"I tremble for my country when I reflect, God is just; His justice cannot sleep forever."*

Yours in the struggle for peace thru justice,

Mauri' Saalakhan

# RECOMMENDED READING LIST

(A few titles related to the subject matter of this book)

- The Noble Qur'an

- An-Nawawi's 40 Hadith
  (Translated by Ezzeddin Ibrahim and Denys Johnson-Davies)

- The Life of Muhammad, by Abdul Hameed Siddiqui

- A Testament of Hope: The Essential Writings And Speeches of
  Martin Luther King Jr., edited by James M. Washington

- Islam Denounces Terrorism, by Harun Yahya

- Body of Secrets, by James Bamford

- The War On Islam, by Enver Masud

- Enemy Combatant, by Moazzam Begg

- For God And Country, by James Yee

- Enemy Aliens, by David Cole

- Terrorism And The Constitution,
  by David Cole and James X. Dempsey

- The Exception To The Rulers, by Amy Goodman

- Good Muslim, Bad Muslim, by Mahmood Mamdani

- Iraq Confidential, by Scott Ritter

- Moses Maimonides And His Time, edited by Eric L. Ormsby

- My Life As A Radical Lawyer, by William Kunstler

- The Politics of Truth, by Joseph Wilson

- The Arrogance of Power, by J. William Fulbright

- The Price of Empire, by J. William Fulbright

- Veil: The Secret Wars of the CIA 1981-1987, by Bob Woodward

- Christian Faith and the Truth Behind 9/11, by David Ray Griffin

- 9/11 and American Empire: Intellectuals Speak Out,
  edited by David Ray Griffin and Peter Dale Scott

- No Greater Threat: America After September 11,
  And The Rise Of A National Security State,
  by C. William Michaels

These are just a few titles that would serve any sincere seeker of truth well.

We also recommend an 8 CD series titled *Looking Back to Look Ahead: Contemporary Studies in Classical Islamic Political Theory* by Imam Zaid Shakir. The series is published by Zaytuna Institute in Hayward, CA. Tel: (510) 582-1979. www.zaytuna.org

# INDEX

# NOTES

# NOTES

# NOTES

# NOTES